STATESMEN OF THE WAR

STATESMEN
OF THE WAR

In Retrospect
1918–1928

By
WILLIAM MARTIN

Essay Index Reprint Series

BOOKS FOR LIBRARIES PRESS
FREEPORT, NEW YORK

First Published 1928
Reprinted 1970

STANDARD BOOK NUMBER:
8369-1675-1

LIBRARY OF CONGRESS CATALOG CARD NUMBER:
75-105029

PRINTED IN THE UNITED STATES OF AMERICA

PREFACE

THIS BOOK DOES NOT PRETEND TO BE A HISTORY OF THE WAR. It recalls many facts that are known, but some that have been ignored. It does not contain a complete and systematic account of what happened in the world from 1914 to 1918: the author goes on the assumption that most of the events of this period remain still in the memories of his contemporaries.

Nor is this book a collection of biographies, pure and simple. That field has been covered. In order to understand the sequence of events one does not always needs to know the facts of a statesman's private life. But particulars of this kind are sometimes relevant and help us to understand men's characters and historical occurrences.

Finally, our purpose has not been to lay down the law or to pronounce final judgments on the men who during those eventful years had in their hands the leadership of nations. Final judgments are for God. The time has not yet come, perhaps the time will never come, for us weak mortals to be able to declare: this man did right, that man did wrong.

But statesmen have motives, always, for their actions—motives within themselves or outside themselves. To form any kind of judgment of their actions, we must understand something about these motives. We shall try, therefore, in each instance to discover what can have been the impulses of these statesmen in acting as they did.

This inquiry will often lead us into the very heart of events which we have lived through, and it will be possible for us sometimes to base our appreciation upon personal memories and upon anecdotes which we have had at first hand. Although we have not known personally all the men of whom we shall speak here, our duties have brought us into touch with most of them, and many of them have honored us with their friendship.

It is a mistake to imagine that statesmen control the course of events; more often, it is the course of events that controls them. Not even the autocrats—nay, the autocrats least of all —are free. Their wills are fettered by their environment, by their own nation, by their allies, by their adversaries, and, above all, by circumstances. It is a rare thing for a sovereign or for a minister to have the feeling that he is doing as he likes —and a rare thing for such a feeling to be well-founded. It is a rarer thing, still, for a king or a statesman, when he does do as he likes, to modify the course of events.

Efforts have been made to apportion the responsibility of individuals in regard to the origins of the War. In vain. The individuals who at the tragic hour held our destinies in their hands did not consciously desire war—none of them. If they were responsible for its suddenly coming about, this was be-cause they were the slaves of a political and economic system which was stronger than themselves—slaves of their own earlier decisions, and of their own prejudices and the preju-dices of other nations. Far from our mind be any notion of pointing, in the network of unconscious responsibilities, of un-acknowledged motives, of mistakes, of distrust and *arrières-pensées*, to individual faults.

But if the leaders of the nations were not the controllers of events, they were the instruments. Their names are in-separable from the events, and the human mind cannot con-ceive of history apart from the personalities mixed up with it.

PREFACE

It may happen, moreover, that statesmen, without actually controlling, may influence events, and the knowledge of their lives, their character, their motives, may be not without value for the understanding of history.

Inversely, they themselves are influenced by the circumstances in which they have lived, and the knowledge of history is a requisite element in their psychology. Our purpose in presenting here a series of political portraits is the seeking out of these repercussions. We have felt that in studying the characters of the men, we might be able to explain their actions, the parts they played, the influence they exerted upon the minds of the people and upon the sequence of events. On the other hand, events sometimes enable us to understand the attitude of certain men at decisive moments of history. To explain events by the character of those who took part in them and the character of statesmen by the events in which they were involved is perhaps in the nature of a mental recreation, but it is a recreation not lacking in its use and its interest for history and for psychology.

The personalities included are of great diversity. Their choice is arbitrary. We have not tried to draw up a list of the twenty-five most important men of our epoch or of those most endowed with genius. Many others, assuredly, in certain respects, would have deserved to figure in such a list. It was necessary for us to restrict our list, and we believe that it includes no one who does not deserve to have a place in it by reason of the position he has held in the eyes of his contemporaries.

Among them are men whose celebrity has been the outcome of circumstances. What should we know, but for the War, of a Cardinal Mercier, or of a Colonel House, or of a Gustave Ador, or of a Masaryk, or of a Bénès? Others are great by reason of the influence they have exerted. What would have become of us without a Lloyd George or a Clémenceau? But this is not the stamp of true greatness. What marks great men, like great mountains, is the circumstance that a distant view increases their height. There were leaders whom the War wiped out. What will history recall of Tisza, of Czernin, of Bethmann, of Sonnino? They took part in the events but the events did not add to their stature. There were others, on the contrary, in the front rank of whom we place President Wilson, who dominated events to the point of standing out as their living symbol.

Ten years have passed since the Armistice. The perspective to-day is sufficient to allow of our attempting to distinguish, in the matters under consideration, what was lasting from what was ephemeral. This attempt at discrimination will show us that among these men those who will retain a name in history are those who understood their own time and its needs. Those who, like Clémenceau, only made war, great men though they may be, will leave behind them but a transient fame. The memory of them will fade. Only those men will live on who knew how to make peace by getting inspiration in justice and in the needs of peoples.

To make war at this moment in history was something; to be victorious in the name of justice and of democracy was much more. But the true statesmen were those who, looking beyond the immediate present and the apparent interests of their own country, devoted their efforts to preventing the return of such catastrophes in the future. To these, and to these alone, will belong the glory of having understood their time and of having exerted a profound influence on the destinies of mankind.

True it is that from the life and actions of each of these

figures we may draw forth an example or at least a lesson and a political moral. It is in this way that our book may be not without its utility. For of what would the wisdom of men consist if it did not find sustenance in the examples set them by their forerunners?

CONTENTS

Preface   v

The Three Emperors

    WILLIAM II   3
    FRANCIS-JOSEPH   18
    NICHOLAS II   28

The Origins of the War

    PACHITCH   45
    VON BETHMANN-HOLLWEG   57
    COUNT TISZA   67
    POINCARÉ   79
    LORD GREY   95

The Agony of Belgium

    CARDINAL MERCIER   109

The New Allies

    BARON SONNINO   125
    VENIZELOS   139
    JON BRATIANO   151

CONTENTS

The Interminable War

ASQUITH   167
BRIAND   179

Vigorous Charity

HOOVER   195
GUSTAVE ADOR   207

American Intervention

PRESIDENT WILSON   217
COLONEL HOUSE   234

Peace on the Way

COUNT CZERNIN   251

The Liberation of Peoples

PRESIDENT MASARYK AND DR. BÉNÈS   267
PILSUDSKI AND PADEREWSKI   282

The Supreme Effort

LLOYD GEORGE   297
CLÉMENCEAU   312

ILLUSTRATIONS

WILLIAM II	16
FRANCIS-JOSEPH	32
NICHOLAS II	32
NICOLAS PACHITCH	54
THEOBALD VON BETHMANN-HOLLWEG	54
RAYMOND POINCARÉ	92
LORD GREY OF FALLODON	92
CARDINAL MERCIER	112
BARON SONNINO	128
JON BRATIANO	128
ELEUTHEROS VENIZELOS	148
LORD OXFORD AND ASQUITH	168
ARISTIDE BRIAND	188
HERBERT CLARK HOOVER	208
GUSTAVE ADOR	208
WOODROW WILSON	224
EDWARD M. HOUSE	244
THOMAS GARRIGUE MASARYK	272
EDWARD BÉNÈS	272
MARSHAL PILSUDSKI	288
IGNACE JAN PADEREWSKI	288
DAVID LLOYD GEORGE	304
GEORGES CLÉMENCEAU	320

THE THREE EMPERORS

WILLIAM II

FRANCIS-JOSEPH

NICHOLAS II

WILLIAM II

I SAW HIM LAST AS HE STOOD ON THE BALCONY OF THE palace at Berlin, silhouetted darkly against the brilliant light from the room behind him. In the eyes of the immense crowd which was cheering him he was the Fatherland. It was the eve of the War then and there were many heavy hearts and anxious minds. To-day, to while away the long hours of his exile on the Isle of Doorn, William II saws, as he would in a prison yard.

What will be the verdict of history on this man who entered life to the sound of bells and a people's cheering, and who is ending his days bent in sorrow under the low gray sky of Holland?

Before one can judge, one must understand, and that is no easy task. "How," as a clever woman has said, "can we put ourselves in the place of a man whose cradle and baby shoes are museum exhibits?" Kings from the moment of their birth are set apart from the people. Everything conspires to isolate them, their education, their interests, their ideas, their feelings, their scale of values, and to judge them by the usual standards would be unfair.

William II was no exception to this rule—quite the contrary. His childhood was hard, destitute of all real affection. His mother did not love him, his tutors did not understand him. Deformed from birth, he had to learn after much physical and moral suffering to disguise his infirmity. Had he been a private citizen he would have been exempted from military

3

service: instead, he was to become the foremost soldier of his empire. Emil Ludwig, who has painted a masterly portrait of the Emperor, attributes all his love of pomp and display and popular applause to the fact that his education was directed wholly to things external. We enjoy only what we win by an effort, and all his life William II sought the limelight in order to conceal his suffering. It was always his desire to appear other than he was and to convince the world that he was other than it saw him.

Popular applause more than any other thing perverts the minds of royal children. It is said that on the day when he took the oath the young King Michael of Roumania was frightened when he saw the Deputies—grave, serious old gentlemen— shouting hurrah. His Majesty burst out sobbing and took refuge behind his mother's skirts.

William II, however, had no fear of popular applause. On the contrary, all his life he has sought it, and it has turned his head.

For a proper appreciation of the character of William II we must turn to the pages which Treitschke, the historian of the great German empire, devotes to Frederick William IV, King of Prussia, against whom the revolution of 1848 broke out. The picture he gives there reveals curious points of resemblance between the great-uncle and the nephew. Neurotics both of them, unstable, impulsive, superficially clever, workers but lacking in application, possessed of a lively curiosity, catholic tastes, versatile talents, natural eloquence, but lacking in good sense and with a strong leaning to superstition, these two men might have been brothers. The mystical orations of William II, his imperative need to have friends and unbosom himself to them, then cast them off, his romantic love of his people and his mediæval conception of royalty—all this

4

recalls the monarch who in a flash of intuition would put his trust in Bismarck, but who was perpetually vacillating between his ministers and his friends, pitting the one against the other.

If through many years no one in Germany dared to point this out, it was because Frederick William died insane . . .

No one who has not seen William II in the zenith of his splendor can appreciate what the fever of excitability can really mean. His car would dash along the streets preceded by a trumpet blast of the opening notes of "Die Meistersinger." He was seen everywhere. He changed his dress ten times a day. There was no ceremony he did not attend. Not a year passed but William II spent two hundred days of it in traveling, and in seventeen years he delivered five hundred and seventy-seven public speeches, that is, one every eleven days. To hold forth, to hear himself speak, and to see the multitude hanging on his words, was his ruling passion. He was a painter, he was a sculptor, he composed operas and staged them. He could always find people to praise him, although he was notoriously lacking in talent. Besides, his taste was bad. I remember seeing him one day when he was visiting an exhibition of paintings. As soon as His Majesty was announced all the other visitors flattened themselves against the wall and effaced themselves. William II swept through the rooms at full speed. He did not stop even at the pictures that took his fancy—he only indicated them by an abrupt gesture, which was the signal for one of his suite to rush forward and stick on a label bearing the words "Bought by His Majesty the Emperor." When he had left and the ordinary visitor could venture to walk round again, I saw that he had bought all the worst daubs in the exhibition.

His intelligence was superior to his taste. As a rule, those who met him for the first time were surprised at the knowledge he showed of their own particular sphere. Having made a point of finding out beforehand what the special interest of his visitor was, he primed himself specially so that they might be struck dumb with amazement. He almost always succeeded. His arm was too short, his voice guttural, and his eye steely, but when he wished he could be amiable and even charming— and he generally did wish it when he met people whom he knew to be prejudiced against him, particularly the French, and he won over a considerable number of people in that way.

William II had a clear conception of what a modern state should be. His efforts to assist the industrial development of his country, his wish to found a colonial empire and a powerful fleet gave evidence of a practical mind. Although he cannot claim all the credit for the extraordinary economic advance which Germany made in his reign, it must be conceded that he did nothing to hinder it, and even assisted it to some extent.

Material prosperity diverted the mind of the German people from political interests. When a country begins to develop, when it sees its industries, its foreign trade, its power and its prestige increase hour by hour, it does not bother to call its government to account. Bismarck had created the empire on the basis of universal suffrage, but, by reason of her industrial development, Germany had between 1870 and 1914 become changed out of all recognition. Under William II the empire had become a dictatorial and almost autocratic monarchy in which popular control had no part and the Emperor was all that counted.

Unfortunately, William II was not equal to the task which he had set himself. Although on every possible occasion he affirmed his omnipotence and the divine nature of his power, his will was vacillating and weak. He was impulsive and wayward. At the very moment when he assumed the supreme power he let it slip from his hands into those of his irresponsible nominees.

From this there followed two very serious consequences which appear to be paradoxical and yet count among the causes of the War: one was the instability of the government and the other the subordination of the civil power.

Stability and continuity of power are the great theoretical advantages which can be cited in favor of a monarchy. They are assured from one generation to another by family traditions and, in the course of any single reign, by the personality of the sovereign. Unfortunately these two forms of political continuity were both lacking in the Germany of William II.

Misunderstanding and jealousy between father and son were traditional in the house of Hohenzollern—witness the quarrels between Frederick the Great and his father. William II was no exception to this rule, either in his relations with his father or with his son.

Granted that he suffered injustice at the hands of his parents, it is nevertheless true that on the death of the Emperor Frederick after long suffering from a cruel malady, William II displayed indecent haste in his anxiety to fill the rôle of Emperor and to throw overboard all his father's ideas.

A bad son will never make a good father. Years afterwards, the Crown Prince was to show him that. Many a time in pre-war Berlin he became the center of the opposition. He had to be sent away in disgrace to a garrison in North Germany, and it is said that once at Headquarters during the War, while the Emperor was expressing ideas that were distasteful to his son, the latter turned to his neighbor at table and remarked in almost audible tones, "The old man's getting more gaga than ever!"

Just as Germany did not know what it was to have a monarchy that continued from generation to generation, so, during the reign of William II, she did not know what it was to have continuity of government. He had no sooner ascended the throne than his most urgent thought was to dismiss the Iron Chancellor (now an old man), the founder of the empire, and faithful friend of William I—Bismarck. He seemed determined to prove the truth of Bismarck's deadly remark to Bratiano at the Congress of Berlin: "Remember, Bratiano, that all the Hohenzollerns are fools, coxcombs, and ingrates!"

It must be admitted that on the question over which they parted the Emperor was in the right, for he could grasp the new political realities better than the old Chancellor. At the beginning of his reign he was bent on being the Emperor of the oppressed and the disinherited, Emperor of the Catholics and the Socialists whom Bismarck persecuted—Emperor of the workers. But that whim passed. Variable as he always was, William II tired of a rôle which did not bring quickly enough the popularity for which he thirsted. Once Bismarck was gone he had to be replaced. That was the first misguided step which led the Emperor and his empire on the fatal path to ruin.

William II was lacking in the quality which had enabled his ancestors to create Prussia and enlarge it, namely, the ability to choose wise counsellors, to trust them and keep them. The whole greatness of William I lay in his fidelity to Bismarck. William II could never remain faithful. He loved to have some one to confide in—and change that some one often. In the course of his reign he had seven different chancellors and at least four different ministers per year.

WILLIAM II

Fickleness was perhaps not the worst of it. He surrounded himself with second-rate personalities. He loved to shine, and could not bear to be put in the shade by his advisers. When his ministers had audience with him it was he alone who spoke, and he had no friendly eye for those who tried to explain things to him. This is shown by the story of his treatment of Pozadowsky, Minister for Home Affairs. This minister had the lamentable habit of explaining the business of his department to the Emperor, and the latter used to amuse himself by sending his favorite dog to and fro between the minister's legs to distract and confuse him.

These caprices, which were smiled upon for a time, were destined to have tragic consequences for the empire and the world.

Bismarck had fashioned the constitution of the German empire according to his own ideas. He had instituted between the civil and the military power an unstable equilibrium which depended for its maintenance on two conditions, namely, a strong personality in the post of chancellor and a man of well-balanced judgment and good sense on the throne. The Emperor was to hold the balance between his counsellors.

These conditions obtained during the lifetime of William I, Bismarck, and the aged Moltke. But under William II the whole edifice tumbled to the ground. The civil power fell into weak hands—an inexperienced general, a weak-willed aristocrat, an unscrupulous diplomat, and a hide-bound bureaucrat. The ministers, at the mercy of court cabals, the intrigues of their colleagues, and the caprices of the Emperor, had not even the security of parliamentary ministers who depend on public opinion. Never was there a government so divided against itself, a government in which, though strong to outward seeming, the ministers spied on each other, were

9

envious of each other, and were often not even on speaking terms.

Between a weak and disunited civil power, and a military power that was upheld by all the traditions of the monarchy and the state, William II was not content to play the rôle assigned him by the constitution. He did not know how to play it, and instead of being the arbiter between the rival powers he supplanted them both.

In a book of memoirs, one of the sailors of the imperial yacht tells that William II always wished to sail the boat himself and to take the tiller, but as he was incompetent and there was cause to fear a mishap, a false tiller was made that he could handle as he liked, while the boat was really sailed, secretly, by the pilot.

It is the same picture in the German monarchy, where William II seemed to be everything, though the state was managed, under his name, by anonymous figures.

In the domain of home affairs William II was acutely intuitive, but in diplomacy he was impulsive and romantic. He never had any broad and reasoned views on the European situation, nor had he sufficient sense to listen to his advisers.

William II—and it is a right royal eccentricity—regarded Europe as a garden plot and politics as a family affair, with the result that in dealing with his cousins on the thrones of England, Russia, Austria, Hungary and Italy, he completely lost sight of the peoples they represented and whose fate was in the balance. He never had any conception of the actual forces which were clashing with each other. He was carrying out, even in this twentieth century, a purely dynastic policy. The solidarity of thrones and the rivalry between kingdoms constituted his whole political creed. His distrust of England, which was the ruling idea of his reign, dated from certain slights received in his childhood at Buckingham Palace or Osborne. The fear of seeming inferior to his grandmother and of being baited by his uncle drove out all other ideas from his mind. On the eve of war, he thought he was the savior of the world when he telegraphed to Petrograd, and when the answer of "Nicky" came in somewhat unexpected terms he took it as a personal insult. Never before has megalomania made such deadly ravages in a human mind.

The idea of a Germany hemmed in by wicked cousins, and the necessity of breaking through some day, began to implant itself in his mind between 1906 and 1909, and, as often happens, fiction began to usurp the place of truth. But it was not until 1913 that peace was threatened by it. A double celebration was due to fall that year: the centenary of the deliverance of Germany from the yoke of Napoleon, and the twenty-fifth anniversary of the Emperor's accession. Besides, there was the marriage of the Emperor's only daughter. Throughout the year festivities, ceremonies, speeches and functions came one after another. In the spring M. Jules Cambon, the French Ambassador, a man who had time and opportunity to size up William II and who knew him well, said prophetically: "You will see that by the end of the year the Emperor will believe that it was he who won the battle of Leipzig!"

That in fact is what happened: all this incense of adulation went to his head. All intelligent observers have stated that the Emperor, whose ambitions had hitherto been peaceful, changed fundamentally at this time. He conceived a taste for martial glory and began to accustom himself to the idea of war. His resistance to the militarists and the industrialists who wanted him to take the risk of war began to weaken. It might be said that about the New Year of 1914 the fate of Europe and of millions of young men was determined.

Things were at this stage when there came the crisis of July, 1914. At first William II does not appear to have realized the full gravity of the situation. He goes off cheerfully for a holiday and complains in his memoirs of not having been kept apprised of what was going on. It was because he was distrusted at Berlin. The army and the civil heads and all his advisers felt they were on holiday when he was away. The one section hoped that his absence would make a settlement possible and the others thought he might be more easily persuaded that he was being attacked if he was not present at the negotiations. Both were agreed that he must be kept quiet and advised him to remain where he was. To return to Berlin in spite of them required an effort on the part of the Emperor.

On his return to Potsdam, Europe was already in a hopeless situation. But it is by no means certain that the decisions which it fell to William II to make would appear as harsh to him then as subsequent events have shown them to be. What was it that he had to do? He was to prevent France, England and Russia from drawing a diplomatic and economic net round Germany. To do this one threatening gesture was enough. The history of 1908 and 1911 would repeat itself, order would be restored at once and the whole world would see how great the power of Germany was. Russia would hasten to renew her commercial treaty: France would cease to increase her army, and England her fleet. The Triple Entente would be broken and the balance of power reversed. Without firing a single shot the German army would have secured the economic and diplomatic domination of Europe.

Such was the program on which William II was to rely —at least if he had one at all. War was a risk that had to be faced, but it would not occur. It was in that sense that the Emperor could go on repeating during the War, "I never wished it"; but "it" was the deadly consequence of what he *had* wished.

The German emperor entered into the War "with a light heart," as Emile Ollivier would have said. The whole efforts of his staff during the last eight days of July, 1914, were to persuade him that he was being attacked by Russia and he must go to war in the defense of his country and his honor. All the tissue of faked evidence, the story of the Russian mobilization, the Nuremberg aeroplanes, the violation of frontiers —these were thought to be aimed at the deception of the German people and the world at large. What a mistake! It was William II whom they were meant to deceive, and they succeeded.

Then there came the War. Henceforward the rôle of William II was ended. The Emperor was the first to go under in the whirlpool which resulted. At the very hour when the autocracy of which he had dreamed was to become a reality all his will evaporated. It was Germany's tragedy when the monarchy was constitutional to have an autocrat, and to be without one when autocracy was needed. Constitutionally, he was commander-in-chief of the army and the fleet—the "War Lord" of his speeches and of the German communiqués. The great fear of the German militarists had always been that he would take his rôle seriously and interfere in operations. He was known to be without ability and it was thought that he might embarrass the Staff. That was not the case. William II on this occasion showed more sense than at any other time in his career. He completely effaced himself, and all the more honor to him when we think of the incapacity of Moltke, the moral worthlessness of Falkenhayn and the noisy popularity of Hindenburg, which totally eclipsed that of the "War Lord."

The life that William II led was a life made up of railway journeys between Potsdam and the army Headquarters. At Potsdam he felt himself removed from everything, for policy was determined at Headquarters. In the palace the atmosphere was oppressive.

The life of William II had always been void of any feminine affection. His mother neglected him. His wife, whom he had married for political reasons, was too much his intellectual inferior to be able to wield the least influence over him. He never knew either the delights of clandestine adventures or the comfort of a home. The War had accentuated the pietist tendencies of the Empress and she had purged the court of all its youthful elements. William II was surrounded by solemn old men, whose company soon became unbearable to one so full of life.

Only his daughter-in-law, the Crown Princess, was able to amuse him, all the more so because they were linked by an equal contempt for the Crown Prince!

What could one do at Potsdam? Everything William II cared for—travel, hunting, ceremony, receptions—was forthwith prohibited. After some time the Emperor could stand it no longer, and he went off to Headquarters. There he was made to feel himself superfluous because he was never consulted on anything. "The Emperor," he wrote, "was ignored by all." He was only a nuisance with his pomp and his ceremonial, his white and gold train and his copper bath. When he went to the front it was to hold reviews and distribute decorations—parades which only wearied the army. Wherever

14

he was William II was *de trop* and was sensible of the general impatience which his presence roused. This soon became too much of a trial for his nerves. In 1916, when, instead of the glorious ending he had counted on, he saw the long drawn out agony ahead, he had a fit of nervous depression, and alternated between moods of exaltation and fits of weeping. After Verdun and the Somme, which proved the Allies' power of resistance, his morale gave way suddenly. He was smitten with a veritable passion for peace. This desire became at moments so intense that it was in danger of imperilling the army. The Emperor gave all sorts of mistaken commands. One day Ludendorf had to call in the Crown Prince in order to get William II to listen to reason.

The Emperor had always been superstitious and readily susceptible to fortune tellers' predictions. He often admitted it to his friends. Now there was a prophecy that his dynasty would perish tragically in the course of his reign, and when events began to go badly with the German armies the Emperor was thinking all the time of this old prophecy.

From December, 1916, his neurasthenia became acute. When, in 1917, Headquarters were changed to Kreuznach, the Emperor went for a cure at Homburg. While there, he wept practically all the time. He had to be given continual assurances of victory. He was taken to the front to be present at small local gains to see the prisoners, for it was only the sight of prisoners which could rouse him from his torpor. It was the sight of thousands of Italians taken by the Germans on the Isonzo which gave him heart and set him on his feet again.

His suite, fearful of a renewed collapse, systematically hid the truth from him. And so, lulled into false hope by optimistic news, William II did not see the disaster that was approaching.

The Staff at the beginning of 1918 had played its last card on the battlefields of France, and lost. From the end of July Ludendorf knew that there was no hope. That conviction spread from the Staff to Berlin. William II made up his mind then to appeal to what he had always denied his own people—a democratic government—and the new Chancellor, Max von Baden, got into touch with President Wilson. Peace negotiations were begun, and suddenly revealed to the German people the truth of the disaster which had been kept from them.

What was to become of the Emperor in this extremity? That did not seem to worry the General Staff. Once more there was only one idea—keep him away. The Emperor, however, whom the Chancellor no longer consulted, was getting impatient at Potsdam and suddenly decided to go to Spa. That was his last active move. From that moment his rôle was over. He was to be the sport of fate.

On all sides came demands for his abdication. William II, who had not seen the débâcle coming and who was not prepared for it, talked about it, resisted it and wrangled over it. He did not understand that there was no time to lose. He was the obstacle to peace—and did not know it. But the decisions that he could not take for himself were taken for him by others. At Berlin his abdication was published before he had signed it. At Spa he was put into a car bound for an unknown destination. The proud monarch, whose words and deeds had kept Europe busy for thirty years, was now a nameless thing without a will. On November 1st, 1918, he crossed the Dutch frontier in the gray light of the early morning.

WILLIAM II

WILLIAM II

His people have never forgiven him. The war and the defeat were misfortunes, but the flight was dishonor. There was no use saying that William II had not wanted that, just as he had not wanted the rest. It was no use saying that he had wished to spare his people the horrors of invasion and civil war. He will live in history as the man who could not bear to face the unspeakable disaster he had brought upon his people, and fled his responsibilities.

The Allies wanted to bring him to judgment. What a mistake! All they could have done by condemning him would have been to make him great. William II in the seeming quiet of his refuge in Holland is suffering the most terrible punishment that can be meted out to a man—the punishment of living through his own downfall and death.

FRANCIS-JOSEPH

FRANCIS-JOSEPH, EMPEROR OF AUSTRIA, APOSTOLIC KING of Hungary, King of Bohemia, of Dalmatia, of Croatia, of Slavonia, of Illyria and of Galicia, King of Jerusalem, etc., was called upon to bear the heaviest burden that can ever fall to the lot of a king: to live too long, to reign too long.

History records few kings who lived to grow old and yet left pleasant memories to their people. After all his years of glory Louis XIV lived to see the reverse of the Spanish Succession and to mourn the loss of friend after friend. Louis XV could arouse only contempt in the hearts of his people at the end of his reign, the brilliant beginning of which had earned for him the title of "Bien-Aimé." This is true even of Queen Victoria, for to-day her memory is dimmed by the reproach of having dominated too many generations and of having kept the throne too long from Edward VII.

Francis-Joseph is no exception. If he had died only three years earlier he would have gone down to posterity as a benevolent peace-loving prince high in the esteem of his subjects. Only some sour historian could then have ventured to criticize his greatness, whereas at present it is generally recognized that his longevity, far from being a blessing, brought countless disasters on his house, on his people, and on Europe.

The thought of so interminable a life makes the brain reel. Francis-Joseph was born in 1830. He rode on his grandfather's knee, the Emperor Francis who had been the host

18

of all Europe at the Congress of Vienna. He played at the skirts of his aunt, Marie-Louise, the wife of Napoleon. He trembled before Metternich, who was still all-powerful. He knew Europe before the coming of the railway, he was the most important ruler of a Germany still to be united and of an Italy not yet free, and was able before he died to hear the far-off thunder of the guns at Verdun. His life more or less symbolizes the history of a century.

Francis-Joseph was not destined for the throne; the revolution of 1848 and two abdications, those of his uncle and his father, were needed to place him there unexpectedly at the age of eighteen. But it is doubtful whether his youth and lack of experience are sufficient excuse for the first official acts of his reign. The first was to revoke the constitution solemnly granted by his uncle—that is, he broke faith with his people. The second was to call to his aid the autocrat of all the Russias, the Czar Nicholas I, against the Hungarians, who had revolted. These were the methods by which Francis-Joseph established his power, relying upon perjury and foreign bayonets. And the third was to abandon Russia in 1856 when she needed his help and "to astonish the world by his ingratitude." Such was the beginning of a reign that was to last for sixty-eight years.

Faith in dynasties was still very strong in Austria in the middle of the nineteenth century. It is sufficient to note the prestige still enjoyed by Francis-Joseph on the eve of the Great War and the veneration he inspired in his subjects, even though alien, to understand what his power must have been half a century earlier. If, by resolutely following a new policy, Francis-Joseph had tried to build up the glory of his house upon the satisfaction of his people he could have made of his country the strongest federation in all Europe.

He did exactly the contrary. Magenta, Solferino and Sadowa, two unfortunate wars, the loss of the dominant position held by Austria in Germany, the unity of Italy and the expulsion of the Austrians from Milan and Venice, where they had been welcomed as saviors in 1814, were necessary to force Francis-Joseph to make a compromise with his people. It was this that gave Ferdinand, who had been dethroned in 1848, the opportunity to ask the question "Why was I dethroned? I should have been quite as capable of losing battles and provinces as my nephew."

Although the concessions that Francis-Joseph had then been obliged to make still rankled in his mind and though he more than once prevented their application, the half-century that followed 1867 was the most peaceful and harmonious period of his reign.

Francis-Joseph was a short man, but all who knew him bear testimony to his imperial dignity, his simplicity of manner and to the conscientious way in which he fulfilled every duty. A believer in pomp, convinced that ceremony is necessary to the brilliance of a throne, he liked official functions, but not in excess. A great hunter, he rarely indulged in any other amusement. His journal, like that of Louis XVI and of most rulers, records nothing more important than the number of animals killed in a day. Very succinct in his correspondence, he did not hesitate to write many pages to his friend Prince Albert of Saxony, telling him all the details of a hunt at Ischl.

As time went on Francis-Joseph learned the rules of his profession. An indefatigable worker, he insisted on seeing everything himself, knowing everything, noting everything. He never, until a most advanced age, gave up the practice of giving collective audiences to those of his subjects who had any personal request to make, and he saw to it that his decisions in such cases were carried out.

Francis-Joseph was the greatest bureaucrat in his empire, the most assiduous, the most accurate, the most scrupulous. He was the very incarnation of a monarchy that had always been characteristically bureaucratic and inquisitorial. Thus he was able to inculcate methods of orderliness and accuracy into the administration of his country that had considerable influence on its development and prosperity during his reign.

But orderliness, application and hard work are not necessarily royal virtues. Francis-Joseph lacked the breadth of vision, the imagination and courage that are essential in a true head of a state. It is undoubtedly because of this that he was doubly unfortunate, in his family and in his diplomacy.

Francis-Joseph seems never to have known a *grande passion*. If he did so in his youth, history does not record it. Married to a woman, dreamy, romantic and nervous, with whom he had nothing in common, he found a sister soul in Madame Schratt, an actress at the Burg Theatre. Until his extreme old age he either went to see her or sent her a note every day—whence his affectionate nickname of "Herr Schratt" among the Viennese. But this liaison, though tolerated by every one, including the Empress, had little real influence on him in his private life and still less on his political opinions.

Francis-Joseph put his duties as head of the house of Hapsburg before those as head of the State. But his family was a source of endless trouble to him. Although faith in dynasties was still alive among the people it barely existed among the Hapsburgs themselves. This family, which a lucky chance had brought from its Swiss castle in the thirteenth century, had reigned too long. The reason why dynasties have declined or rather the evidence of their decline is that their own members have lost faith in them. Privileges are justified only by the obligations they bring with them, but modern princes shrink from the obligations while retaining the privileges. Few archdukes or archduchesses shared the Emperor's spirit of sacrifice to their name and to their blood, and he suffered greatly in his dignity and his most deeply rooted prejudices on account of numerous mésalliances, renunciations and scandals. Besides these injuries to his pride he was the victim of tragedy and bereavement. His brother Maximilian, Emperor of Mexico, was shot and Maximilian's widow lost her reason; the Archduke Rudolph, the only son of Francis-Joseph, committed suicide for love under mysterious circumstances; the Empress was assassinated in Geneva; her sister perished in a fire in Paris; and, finally, his nephew and heir-presumptive, Francis-Ferdinand, was assassinated at Serajevo on June 28th, 1914.

For a long time his stoicism was admired. These blows were powerless to shake him. He seemed to have a soul of iron; his fortitude was compared to that of the heroes of antiquity. But the world wearies of admiring. When he buried his nephew, after having buried his son and his wife, without shedding a tear, without flinching and without a trace of regret, a doubt arose as to whether this wonderful fortitude was after all merely egoism, hardness of heart and indifference.

No one who is indifferent to his own family can care for the needs of his people. What was lacking in Francis-Joseph throughout his long career was warmth, sympathy, feeling, the instinct of understanding for the sufferings of others. It was probably this trait in his character that prevented him from understanding his time and his country.

Francis-Joseph was no fool. He knew how to deal with people and he managed skillfully to "divide in order to reign." For a long time he was able to set the various nationalities against each other, arousing opposition in each and giving his support first to one and then to another, in short, as they say in Austria, to *fortwursteln*—to "wangle" his way.

But such methods are unworthy of a great ruler, and they finally brought Francis-Joseph to unprecedented disaster.

Our epoch has been dominated by the struggle of the peoples towards democracy. This is no fortuitous or arbitrary phenomenon. Democracy is the daughter of compulsory public education, itself a result of the progress of machinery. Industry has forced men to live in towns, where they have demanded better education and a greater degree of comfort. Being educated they are no longer willing to be governed without being consulted. Such inevitable and powerful tendencies should have been recognized by the head of a state.

Nationalism is the direct outcome of democracy. If men do not wish to be governed without their consent they will tolerate still less being governed by people who are of a different nationality and do not speak their language.

Austria-Hungary was a mosaic of different nations bound together only by chance events in history, having no other unity than the person of their ruler, no continuity other than the dynasty. If the Emperor had realized in time the direction in which the present epoch was to evolve he could easily have found a new and more powerful principle of unity in federalism. The loyalty of his people would not have suffered, quite the reverse, and perhaps far from being

troubled with disruptive tendencies, monarchy might have
been able to attract and assimilate certain neighboring nations.

This is what Francis-Joseph would not see. He aimed at
the material development of his country and he brought it
to a high level of order and prosperity, but without seeing
that the corollary to these advantages was the increasing participation of the people in the government. He completely
forgot and ignored the fine motto shining in golden letters
on his palace in Vienna: "Justitia fundamentum regnorum."
He substituted for it this other archaic motto: "Voluntas
regis lex reipublicæ." The loyalty of his people to him personally deceived him as to the solidarity of the state. He
devoted all his energies to retaining his royal prerogatives.
He even saw the actual symbol of his prestige and power
in such questions of secondary importance as the language
in which commands were given in the army. He made no
effort to induce the Hungarian government to adopt a just
and moderate policy with regard to the non-Magyar nations.
In short, he thought that his own person, the army and the
police, could constitute a lasting bond of union between his
people. An error indeed!

Francis-Joseph's foreign policy was based upon similar
and equally mistaken theories. He could not gauge the power
of the monarchy either at home or abroad. He forced a foreign
policy beyond its capacity upon a state already undermined
internally. After the defeat at Sadowa, followed by the defeat
of France at Sedan, the Emperor sacrificed his anger and
almost his dignity by making an alliance with his conqueror,
Bismarck. It seemed to him that this alliance would make
peace assured. And so it did, for about twenty years. But the
day came when Austria-Hungary found herself involved

in the policy of prestige and megalomania pursued by William II as he grew older. Under the shelter of the alliance, Austria-Hungary forgot her own weakness. She was deceived by internal peace resulting from the compromise of 1867. She indulged in great hopes. The annexation of Bosnia in 1908 seemed to Francis-Joseph only to compensate for the loss of Italy forty years before. All kings dream of leaving their countries as great as when they came into power. D'Aerenthal and the German alliance allowed Francis-Joseph to dream this dream.

A fleeting and dangerous triumph! Francis-Joseph did not realize that the annexation of Bosnia brought with it bitterness and irredentism, particularly the irredentism of the Serbs. From that moment the aged and peace-loving monarch became an object of hatred and attack. From that moment the government of Austria-Hungary lost its freedom of action and alliance. Bismarck is reputed to have said: "In every alliance there is one man and one horse"—that is to say, the one rides the other. Until then, Germany, surrounded by enemies, had been the horse, but from that moment the rôles were reversed.

But by one of the tricks of fate that befall declining monarchies, Francis-Joseph was left at that moment with no other adviser than Count Berchtold, an elegant aristocrat, inconsistent and weak-willed. It is said of him that it was far from the intention to the will and from the will to the decision, and still further from the decision to the action. Confronted by Tschirschky, the imperious ambassador of William II, by the heads of the army, the head of the Hungarian government, Count Tisza, and the head of his Cabinet, Count Forgasch, all of whom wanted war, this man positively ceased to exist.

It is characteristic of an improvident government to allow matters to become so acute that a peaceful settlement is no longer possible: "There are a number of questions in the world," says a certain philosopher on politics, "that can never be settled. At first attempts are made to decide them by diplomatic measures; these fail, and war is the next resource; then upon the realization that war decides nothing, there is a return to diplomacy." This thought might well be the epigraph on the reign of Francis-Joseph.

The assassination of the Archduke Francis-Ferdinand left Francis-Joseph completely cold. He did not care for his nephew. He was afraid of the complications in the dynasty that would arise upon the accession of a man whose wife and children had no right to reign. He hated the ideas of the Archduke, who supported a policy in favor of the Slav nationalists. The death of the heir came as a relief to Francis-Joseph and his court, who thought that the time had at last come to crush this nationalist movement already too long encouraged by Francis-Ferdinand. It was not to avenge Francis-Ferdinand that Austria made war; it was to kill for the second time his projects and his ideas. In order to stamp out the propaganda in favor of the Serbs, the reality and importance of which no one can to-day appreciate, these foolish advisers were going to set fire to Europe, ruin their country, and realize the wildest hopes of the unassimilated races. Truly a fine piece of work!

Austria believed that she took the initiative in this affair. She did not see that she was maneuvered. Francis-Joseph saw it less than any one. Already enfeebled by age, he meekly signed all papers put before him, with no regard for their importance. This was how he signed the first declaration of war that was to involve the whole of Europe. Without a word he took upon himself the most appalling responsibility that has ever rested upon a human conscience—that of the death of ten million men.

Francis-Joseph lived for two years longer—completely forgotten by the world. He lived long enough to witness the sufferings of his people, but not long enough to see their anger. And when on November 21st, 1916, he closed his eyes in the palace of Schönbrunn, where he had spent his whole life, he could have felt the first tremors of the shock that was shortly afterwards to bring the empire about the ears of his successor.

NICHOLAS II

THERE IS A CURSE ON OMNIPOTENCE. THE HUMAN MIND, in the average man at least, offers no resistance to the consciousness of being above control. That consciousness acts as a solvent on those souls which do not rise to exceptional moral heights. How many colonial administrators who, lost in the bush among a native population, have furnished no end of scandals for the newspapers, would have been peaceable citizens in their own land? And in time of war, when passions are unleashed and impunity assured, how many otherwise peaceable citizens have abandoned themselves to atrocities and pillage? Omnipotence is a deadly poison.

Nicholas II, paragon of all the bourgeois virtues, conscientious, scrupulous, good husband and good father, would have been the best of his own subjects. He would have lived in the respect of his friends and died in the peace of the Lord. He might even—who knows?—have made a very good constitutional monarch of the type of his cousin, George V, to whom he was further linked by an extraordinary physical resemblance. His misfortune lay in the fact that he was the autocrat of All the Russias, feeble heir to a mighty empire, the holder of colossal power, and in exceptionally difficult circumstances. It was that power and those circumstances, for neither of which he was fitted, which overwhelmed him and brought him to his terrible and undeserved end in the dark cellar at Ekaterinenburg.

Supreme power, always a test for man, becomes in reality

28

the most terrible of calamities when it is associated with weakness of character. It was so with Nicholas II; he was an autocrat by law, but he was weak-willed and changeable, and he was the head of a state whose internal weakness sprang from ancient and deep-rooted causes.

The tragedy of the Russian people has been that it has seen its natural evolution violently arrested by Peter the Great and his successors. Asiatic by origin, memories, tradition and legend, Russia has suddenly been turned with her face towards the West. From it she has had to take her morality and certain institutions, without being able to borrow with these the spirit which alone inspires morality and makes institutions live. The Russian people have never recovered from that drama of history; the soul of Russia, wrenched from its axis, has remained bewildered and disturbed. Hence her mystery, her pessimism, her leaning towards anarchy, her dreaming, her lack of the power to will and do—all the defects and all the qualities which, in the eyes of the West, go to make her charm.

This sudden break with tradition has fallen more heavily on the house of Romanoff than on any other Russian family. For the carrying out of the Western policy as conceived by Peter the Great the Tsars were unable to find in Russia the necessary personnel fitted for functions so foreign to the real nature of the Russian soul. They had of necessity to import that personnel—mostly from Germany, but from other nationalities as well. At the Congress of Vienna, Alexander I had about him two Germans (Nesselrode and Stein), a Corsican (Pozzo di Borgo), a Greek (Capo d'Istria), a Pole (Czartoryski), and a Swiss (La Harpe). In his immediate entourage there was not a single Russian. And so it was up to the very end with the Fredericks, the Benckendorffs, and the Sturmers of Nicholas II. "There are only ten Germans in Russia," it was said during the War. "But they are all around the Tsar."

There is nothing so dangerous for a nation as a division between the aristocracy and the people. From generation to generation the Tsars have been losing touch more and more with their subjects, separated from them as they were by an all-powerful administration. This bureaucracy, excellent in its beginnings and modeled on the German hierarchy, set up by the Tsars to inculcate into the people the methods and civilization of the West, lived only by its creators. The autocracy of the Tsar was at once the pledge and the basis of its power. So it was that the administration strove to concentrate all possible power in the hands of the Tsar, that is, in its own. Russia, so vast, so heterogeneous that her peoples called for a government that was localized and adapted to their individual needs—this Russia became the most centralized state in the world. And all these powers were concentrated in a single man, the Tsar, who neither knew this great unwieldy country nor ever guessed at its hidden reactions.

This régime, which might have been proper in the eighteenth century, became less and less suited to the social and moral condition of the people. The advance of industry, the concentration of population in the towns, the spread of education and comfort, created a class of intellectual bourgeoisie who suffered uneasily a rule in which they had no share. And yet, as often happens, the autocracy was to fall not by the evil that it did but by the good.

In 1861 Alexander II, the grandfather of Nicholas II, decreed the emancipation of the serfs. He saw perfectly clearly that the result of this initial reform must be the introduction of a certain amount of popular control in political institutions. But Alexander II was assassinated in 1881, without having lived to see the realization of his project, and his death marked the beginning of a period of autocratic reaction. While the social condition of Russia was approaching nearer and nearer to that of Europe, her political condition was drawing further and further away; Alexander III, inspired by Pobiedonostzev, gave to the word "autocrat" a meaning that it did not originally have. For, as M. Sazonov recalled, the word "autocrat" had in the first instance been a synonym in the history of Russia for "sovereign" and "independent"— as regards foreign control.

It was during the reign of Alexander III that the misunderstanding between the Tsar and his people was aggravated, and that misunderstanding Nicholas II inherited at his accession. The young Tsar had no sooner ascended the throne than he received delegations from the nobles and the "zemetvos" (councils elected from the provinces and towns) who had come to offer their congratulations. He was, he says in his diary, "in the grip of a terrible emotion." That did not prevent him from reading them a short speech which had been prepared for him by the late Tsar's adviser, Pobiedonostzev, and in which he said that any hope of the people having a voice in the direction of public affairs was a "foolish dream." It was on that day, the 17th of January, 1895, that Nicholas II signed his own death warrant.

There are virtues which are more fatal in a ruler than vices. None of the three emperors reigning in Europe at the beginning of the War was a man of dissolute morals, and it might be said of all three that it was a great pity. There was no feminine influence surrounding William II or Francis-

Joseph, but it was to Nicholas II, the most virtuous of the three, that his virtue proved most fatal.

The character of Nicholas II was distinguished by three main traits—submission to his father, submission to his wife, submission to God.

Nicholas II was above all a good son. His relations with his mother were very intimate and he wrote her the most affectionate letters. When his father died, leaving to the young man the burden of power, he (Nicholas) saw only an occasion for mourning and grief in the event that was to make him an all-powerful emperor.

He was a man of one idea, that God, in giving him the heritage of his father, had commanded him to hand it on intact to his son! Nicholas II never had any conception of his duty to his country, or to the people whose well-being he was to promote. Even to his ministers he was absolutely cold and never showed the least evidence of gratitude. He looked upon them as slaves. When Stolypine, the greatest of his servants, had been assassinated for him and before his eyes, his successor was about to say some words of condolence to the Tsar. The Tsar stopped him with a gesture—"He is dead!"

The only duty that Nicholas II acknowledged was to his family, to his father and to his son. His conception of supreme power could be summed up in the one word "heritage."

So narrow a view of political realities could not but lead him to his ruin. The world evolves, circumstances change every moment. To conserve what you have you must know what to give up and what to hold firmly. Immobility is only apparently conservative. Nicholas II, alone immovable in a world full of movement, could not fail to be outstripped in the race, and lose what he had tried to keep intact. He was like the unfaithful servant in the Parable of the Talents.

NICHOLAS II

FRANCIS-JOSEPH

Nicholas II, unlike William II, never had the idea of giving up the ways of his father and ridding himself of his advisers. He kept Pobiedonostzev beside him, the old man who had been his tutor and had inculcated in him the principles of unlimited absolutism. Up to the death of Pobiedonostzev he followed his advice in everything, as if it had come from his father himself. Alexander III reigned on twenty years after his own death. In a sense Nicholas II deserved great praise for taking such a stand, for by temperament he was the reverse of autocratic: he had no will power and it cost him an effort to make any decision. He was intelligent, his judgment was sure and quick, he looked at all the questions submitted to him from every point of view, weighed the pros and cons, and never came to any conclusion. All the letters which his wife wrote to him when he was at the front or traveling are full of this advice: "Be strong! Be determined! Never forget that you are an autocrat!"

Nicholas II applied himself to his task as a good pupil applies himself to a disagreeable exercise. But he never liked it; M. Paléologue, the French Ambassador at Petrograd, writes: "Nicholas II does not love the exercise of his power. If he jealously defends his absolute prerogatives it is purely on mystical grounds. He never forgets that his power comes from God and he is constantly thinking of the account he will have to give of it in the valley of Jehosaphat."

Nicholas II never ceased to suffer from the decisions that he had to make, and, moreover, he was under no illusions as to the reality of his power. "You have more power than I have," he said one day to M. Albert Thomas, French Minister of Munitions. "When you give an order, it is carried out!"

This model son was an excellent husband, a touchingly affectionate parent. Not only had he made a love-match with the Princess Alix of Hesse, but on the throne he constantly showed his affection. "Every day," he wrote, "I bless the Lord and thank Him from the bottom of my soul for the happiness which He has granted me. No one could wish for greater happiness on this earth." And his wife on her side writes: "Never did I believe there could be such happiness in this world, such a feeling of unity between two mortal beings."

These mutual feelings lasted throughout their married life. The correspondence of the Empress to the Emperor during the War has been published and is full of loving outpourings: "My dear, my treasure, my well-beloved, my very dear love, my little bird," such are the names which she constantly gives him. "I cannot get accustomed to not having you here at home, even for a little while, although I have my five treasures with me . . . my heart and my soul are always near you, with the most tender and passionate love. I shall miss you cruelly, my precious love. Sleep well, my darling. Oh, how empty my bed will be!"

These few examples, which could be multiplied, will serve to show what a love united these two beings on the most exalted throne in the world. Sir George Buchanan, a former English Ambassador to Petrograd, in speaking of the tragedy which cut off Nicholas II and his wife, wrote, "The only ray of light in the dark picture is the fact that, united as they had been in their lives, they remained so till the end, and that in death they were not divided."

Nevertheless, all those who had access to the Empress noticed the sad expression of her face and the tragic look in her eyes. The reason was not only that she detested public life and the pomp of ceremonial display, that she was never happy except in the warmth of her own apartments with her husband and children; it lay above all in the fact that her innermost life was tortured by a double anxiety: for the life of her husband, constantly threatened by assassins, and for the life of her son, threatened by an inexorable disease. It was these anxieties, all born of love, which poisoned the life of Nicholas II and finally brought him to his end. Tragic outcome of a noble emotion! The Empress, who was neurotic, and probably hysterical, found her health ruined by the emotional strain. The Tsar, fearing above all things to provoke one of the nervous crises to which she was subject, now deferred to her wishes in everything, more from fear than from love. Thus the Tsarina found herself possessed of a power quite out of proportion to her intelligence, her political acumen, and her knowledge of the country whose sovereign she was.

By an extraordinary mischance this woman, Protestant by birth, German by education, and English in feeling, acquired from the Russian character the most unlikely trait to appeal to the Western mind, its superstitious mysticism, its love of miracle and magic. All through the reign, the court of Russia was filled with "staretz," men of God who were more or less charlatans and generally quite uneducated. There was first the monk Iliodore, then an illiterate deaf-mute whose grunts were interpreted as the decrees of God, then the butcher's boy, Philippe of Lyons, then the Montenegrin Mordary, and many others even before the notorious Rasputin.

No breath of suspicion can be attached to the relations between the Tsarina and Rasputin. But this dissolute charlatan made use of his influence over the Empress, her daughters and Mme. Viroubova, who was very intimate with them, and through these women over Nicholas II, to serve his spites, his prejudices, and his interests. In the darkest hours of the War his influence was all-powerful. It was he who had Sazonov dismissed, who appointed Sturmer, protected Soukhomlinov and maintained Protopopov in favor—the vultures of Russia.

The power of Rasputin lay in the fact that the Empress saw in him the one intercessor with God, the miraculous protector of the health of her son, the dispenser of divine counsel. "The Empress," wrote M. Paléologue, the French Ambassador, on June 28th, 1916, "is going through a bad phase. Too many prayers, too many fasts, too much asceticism—excitement and insomnia. She is beside herself, and her mind is set more and more on the idea that she has a mission to save Holy Orthodox Russia and that the knowledge, favor, and protection of Rasputin are indispensable to her success. At every turn she asks the Staretz for his advice, his encouragements, and his blessing."

When Rasputin was dead—assassinated by a prince and a grand duke, the Empress wrote with her own hand this note which she herself placed on his breast as he lay in the coffin: "My beloved martyr, give me your blessing that it may follow me on the sorrowful way I have to travel here below, and remember us in Heaven, in your holy prayers!"

Unfortunately, the death of Rasputin did not serve the royal family so well as its authors had hoped. First of all he was quickly replaced, and by a man even more worthless than he—Protopopov, the Minister of the Interior. He used to crawl under tables on all fours, imitating the cries of animals, and he made use of mediums to call up the spirit of Rasputin before the imperial family. Secondly, and this proved fatal, the assassination of the man in whom Their Majesties saw their protector and their hope, confirmed the Tsar and his whole entourage in the conviction that God had forsaken them.

This conviction was of long standing. "At the court,"

a high official once said to M. Paléologue, "people have noticed for a long time how unlucky the Emperor is. It is well known that he fails in all that he undertakes, that fate is always against him; in short, that he is obviously doomed to disaster. Besides, it seems that the lines of his hand are terrifying."

At the coronation festivities in Moscow over two thousand moujiks were trampled in a crowd. A few weeks later the Emperor saw a boat laden with three hundred passengers sink in the Dnieper before his eyes. His favorite minister, Prince Lebanoff, died suddenly in his train, in his very presence; he ardently wished for a son, and four daughters were born before his wife presented him with an heir, who was smitten with an incurable hereditary disease—hæmophilia. After he had longed for peace on earth, and called the Hague Conference of 1899, he let himself be embroiled in a war with Japan in which he lost all his armies and his whole fleet. Thereupon a revolution broke out, riots and massacres followed in quick succession. The people were shot down in the public square of the Winter Palace. His uncle, the Grand Duke Sergius, the Governor of Moscow, was assassinated, then his minister Stolypine, he who seemed to be destined to be the savior of Russia, fell in his presence under the bullets of an assassin in the pay of the police. Then there was the War.

On closer scrutiny this tragic succession of events is less due to chance and ill-luck than to mistakes in government, incapable administration, and police corruption. But how could Nicholas II with his mystical temperament fail to see in all this the hand of God? "I am firmly convinced," he said to M. Isvolsky one day when the cannonade of the fleet against the revolutionaries could be heard in the distance, "that the fate of Russia, of myself, and my family is in the hands of God, who has set me where I am." And after he had decided, in 1915, to take over the command of the army himself, he said, "It may be that Russia can only be saved by an atoning sacrifice. I shall be that sacrifice. May God's will be done!"

In that respect Nicholas II was a true son of his country. Was it not one of his ministers who said one day to the French Ambassador, "When things do not go well, I am resigned. When they go badly, I despair"? And when he noticed a gesture of surprise from the Ambassador, he added, "You forget that I am a Russian."

Nicholas II had received two fundamental political ideas from his father. The one was domestic—Autocracy; the other, foreign—the French alliance. It was these two ideas combined which finally brought on the catastrophe to which he succumbed.

As we have seen, the misunderstanding which separated him from his people dated back to the first days of his reign. It was aggravated in a terrible way in 1905; the police shot down the crowd that had come before the Emperor carrying ikons. When the people had dispersed the snow was strewn with hundreds of corpses. It was an unforgettable sight. It might be said without paradox that Nicholas II was at heart gentle, humane, honorable. But how are you to make people believe this, when they see only that prisons are full, that Siberia is peopled with exiles, and that promises are violated? Kingship is subject to these contradictions.

In 1905, Nicholas II yielded to the entreaties of his counsellors and granted a constitution. But far from being proud of it, far from seeing in it the most glorious act of his reign, he never ceased to reproach himself for such treason to his father's memory. His wife, who knew his weakness, exhorted him to be strong. Consumed by remorse, Nicholas dismissed Count Witte, who had forced the constitution upon him. He appointed other ministers and allowed them to violate the promises he had made to the people. The Duma was dissolved, the constitutional safeguards abolished. The people learned that they could not trust the word of their Emperor.

There is only one justification for autocracy—that it is beneficent and efficient. This one was not. The administration was deplorable and corrupt. Far from stimulating the development of the country it opposed all individual initiative for fear of the people. Not only did the state make no roads, but it forbade landowners to make them on their own land. And two great wars revealed the fact that Tsarism was no more efficient in time of war than in time of peace.

Nicholas II had dreamed a very noble dream of universal peace. When in 1899 he summoned the Hague Conference he took the most forward step of any statesman before the War. But he was incapable of carrying out his own will. In 1904 he allowed himself to be drawn into a fruitless war with Japan and in 1914 with William II, the only man of Modern Europe in whom he could see a support for autocracy.

Nicholas II certainly did not want the War. He came into it reluctantly and he deserves great credit if he remained to the end a faithful ally of the western powers. For his entourage was German in origin, education and sympathies, and he could not fail to see the dangers in which such a conflict placed his throne. If he had been victorious (which he doubtless never for one moment believed) it would have meant the victory of western democracy, the end of all the ideas that were dear to him. If he lost, it meant revolution, which even then all the world saw coming.

One day the King of Spain asked M. Jules Cambon if he would advise him to institute compulsory military service in his country. The French diplomat, one of the cleverest men of our time, made this remarkable reply, "Sire, look to your throne!"

M. Jules Cambon was right. A professional army is a support to a throne, but universal service is a threat to it. This was peculiarly the case in Russia. Never had such an enormous mass of moujiks been brought together. They were transported far from their homes, they saw something of their country, they were better fed than usual, they were decently clothed, their horizon was enlarged, their needs were increased, and, after all that, they were given rifles without ammunition—and were sent to their death without a chance of defending themselves.

For these troops officers were needed. In a country where there is not a large middle class almost all the intellectuals have to be taken. Many of these had advanced ideas, and the army of the Tsar become a hotbed of revolutionary propaganda.

While at the front the inefficiency of the civil and military administration was obvious to all, by faults of strategy. and insufficient commissariat, a sly rumor went about that there was treason at court. But there was no treason properly speaking; there was an extraordinary accumulation of mistakes in policy. The greatest was the dismissal of Sazonov and the retraction of the promises which the Grand Duke Nicholas had made to Poland in the name of the Tsar. It was the history of the 1905 constitution repeating itself.

While the Emperor was at Headquarters, Rasputin and then Protopopov ruled in the name of the Empress; at such a spectacle the most patriotic Russians became revolutionaries in order to save their country. At last the upper classes joined with the people—but too late. M. Paléologue notes that in 1916 and 1917 Nicholas II was spoken of in court circles in the same way as was Paul I, who died at the assassin's hand. But things were to take a different course, even more sanguinary. Only the Tsarina, blinded by her love, did not see what was coming.

The revolution gave to this model family the only hours of real happiness that it had ever known. Nicholas II had ceased to be emperor: the cares of state no longer weighed on his faltering shoulders. He was no longer tortured by having to make decisions. His insomnia had gone. Prisoners together, first at Tsarskoe Selo, then at Tabolsk, the Tsar, his wife, and his children never separated, and they enjoyed their re-found happiness to the full.

Alas, that joy was not to be of long duration. Kerensky, to whom Nicholas said one day in an expansive moment, "Ah, Monsieur Kerensky, if I had known you earlier what a government we would have made between us!"—Kerensky was replaced by the Bolsheviks.

The calvary of the imperial family had begun. It was by the nobility of her attitude then that the Empress redeemed twenty years of mistaken policy. Her refusal to leave the Emperor was so categorical that even the Bolsheviks did not dare to separate them. It was by her wish that they all walked together to their death,—to that horrible massacre in the cellar at Ekaterinenburg which dishonored forever the Bolshevik régime.

Alas, Nicholas II was perhaps right. There is a fate that hangs over peoples, families and individuals. This is what the great Russian writer Merejkowski wrote in 1905:

"In the house of Romanoff as in that of Atreus, a mysterious curse passes from generation to generation. Murder follows adultery and bloodshed, the fifth act of a tragedy is played out in a brothel, Peter I kills his son, Alexander I kills his father, Catherine II kills her husband, and among these great and famous victims there are the little ones, the unknowns, the unhappy abortions of autocracy like Ivan Antonovitch, strangled like mice in dark corners, in the dungeons of Schlüsselburg. The block, the rope, the poison phial—these are the true emblems of the Russian autocracy. The divine unction on the head of the Tsar is transformed into the brand and curse of Cain."

THE ORIGINS OF THE WAR

PACHITCH

VON BETHMANN-HOLLWEG

COUNT TISZA

POINCARÉ

LORD GREY

PACHITCH

DOES THE NAME "PACHITCH" MEAN "SON OF A PASHA"? The admirers of Nicolas Pachitch will not admit this; according to them, he is descended from an old Serbian family in which there is no trace of Turkish blood. Such an origin, or at least, this surname that was given to one of his ancestors, would however explain Nicolas Pachitch's despotic and imperious nature and the way in which, for twenty years, he ruled his little nation with a rod of iron.

Pachitch, as is frequently the case with statesmen, entered politics through a revolution. When he was a student at the École Polytechnique in Zürich he became friends with the famous Russian anarchist Bakunine, but his manner of thinking was not that of an anarchist. Pachitch was of peasant stock, that is to say, he had an instinctive leaning towards democracy and social conservatism. It was the Swiss institutions that made the deeper impression upon him at a time when his political ideas were forming.

Upon his return to Serbia, at the age of thirty, he found the country under the sway of a corrupt and autocratic régime. King Milan was a tyrant to his subjects and a servant to the Hapsburgs. He was in the pay of Austria against Russia and sacrificed, without regret, his country's independence in order to be able to reign as he pleased.

Pachitch passionately opposed this régime. In the first place he hated the autocrat, for it is always home questions that excite the greatest interest. But he saw that King Milan's

45

power depended entirely upon support from the court in Vienna and he set about finding his weak spot in the sphere of foreign policy. The nation's patriotism was his weapon against a king in foreign pay.

Pachitch felt, with a sure political instinct, that Serbia, poor and defenseless as she was, had much to fear from Austria-Hungary, by whom she was geographically surrounded and who controlled her economically. Austria had only to close her frontiers to Serbian pigs in order to ruin the Serbian peasants; she had only to stop the transit of Serbian goods by means of prohibitive tariffs in order to cut Serbia off from the sea. If Serbia wished to live in freedom she must seek protection outside Austria-Hungary. Where should she find it if not in the great Slavonic power, Russia?

The game of politics is not always played according to rules of logic. Russia, whose mere name, at that time, was almost synonymous with autocracy and imperialism, came, by the force of circumstances, to represent in Serbia the hope of patriots and democrats. In his hatred of autocracy Pachitch appealed to the autocratic Tsar to help him against King Milan.

King Milan stood for a policy of servility with regard to Austria and, at the same time, for a policy of despotism with regard to his subjects. In 1880, Pachitch founded the Serbian Radical Party against him; in 1881, he started a paper, the Samouprava; and in 1883, he resorted to rebellion.

He was defeated and forced to flee, but upon King Milan's abdication in 1889 was able to return. He was elected deputy in Belgrade and quickly became the head of the government, in which capacity he accompanied the new King, Alexander, to St. Petersburg. He returned to the Russian capital during the following year as ambassador. The dealings he had with the Russian political leaders at this time and the friends he made stood him in good stead throughout his entire career and had a far-reaching effect upon European politics.

From the beginning of his reign in 1894, the young King, who was then eighteen years of age, behaved foolishly. He declared himself to be of age, caused his ministers to be arrested, suspended the constitution and recalled his father. Pachitch once more joined the opposition, and in 1899 he was involved in an attack upon King Milan. He was sentenced to death and owed his life to an imperious intervention on the part of Russia, insuring him first freedom and then amnesty.

On the night of June 11th, 1903, King Alexander was secretly assassinated in his palace by some officers who could no longer tolerate his absolutist caprices. Neither Pachitch nor Peter Karageorgevitch was in any way concerned in this plot, but both were to profit by it.

King Peter had passed his years of exile in Geneva; there he had taken a keen interest in public affairs and had learned to appreciate the value of democratic institutions. A wave of nationalist reaction against his predecessor's too pro-Austrian policy had brought him to the throne; there was more than one reason why he should find himself in sympathy with the democratic and pro-Russian Pachitch. From 1904, the latter became the moving spirit in Serbian policy and controlled it, as President of the Council, upon four different occasions. Until the end of his life the King gave his unreserved support to the Radical Party and identified himself with its leaders' policy.

With regard to home affairs, Pachitch instituted a régime of rural democracy, admirably suited to the country's social position, Serbia being a land of small estates. But it was despotic and military in its democracy. It was despotic in accordance with Pachitch's own nature. Controlling the elections, and controlling the King's mind, he systematically kept his opponents out of power and refused, even during the War, to allow them any share of responsibility. He was a partisan in the fullest meaning of the term, and his first care, even in the midst of his country's misfortunes, was to place or save his friends.

Pachitch's régime was also a military régime. This was on account of its origin; the revolution that had placed King Peter on the throne had been a *coup d'État*, carried out by some officers; the army was the only organized force in the country and Pachitch tended to be influenced by it and to pursue a nationalist policy abroad.

The period of ten years between King Peter's accession and the assassination of Archduke Francis-Ferdinand was marked in Serbia by increasingly strained relations with Austria-Hungary. The idea of relying upon Russia, a far-off and disinterested power, in order to free herself from subjection to Austria-Hungary, both close at hand and threatening, was, as has been observed, perfectly sound from the Serbian national point of view. But there was an element of danger in such a policy since it must of necessity disturb Austria-Hungary.

In the first place it was alarming from a diplomatic and military point of view. Austria met Russia on her northern frontier; if this should also be the case, through Serbia, on her southern frontier, there was the danger that one day she might find herself caught in a vice. Austria's determination to destroy this trap before it could close upon her was perhaps the main cause of the European war.

The government of Austria-Hungary also found Serbia's pro-Russian policy alarming from the point of view of the

PACHITCH

internal cohesion of the monarchy. Upon seeing Serbia follow an independent policy, the Jugo-Slav nations in the Dual Monarchy began to turn their attention to her. A certain degree of uneasiness was felt in Vienna on account of this sympathy with an enemy of the state, and the Serbian government was held responsible. There was a growing feeling at Vienna that Serbia's ambition was to play the rôle of Piedmont in the Balkans.

Austria-Hungary's displeasure increased in 1912, when Serbia threw herself into the Balkan war without permission from the government in Vienna. The great Serbian victories, first over Turkey, then over Bulgaria, and the immense increase in territory thus gained, aroused enthusiasm among the Jugo-Slav parties in the monarchy and alarm in Vienna. In all probability the decision of the Ballplatz to destroy Serbia dates from this moment.

It would be unjust to assert that the responsibility for the European war lies upon Pachitch and his country. The accusations leveled against them in this connection by Austria-Hungary have never been supported by a shred of evidence. The suggestion that the Serbian government was concerned in the outrage at Serajevo is entirely unfounded. The extreme moderation of its reply to the Austro-Hungarian ultimatum is a matter of common knowledge. Pachitch did all that lay in his power to avoid war; it was forced upon him by Austria's blindness.

However, his people justly regard him as the author of his country's present greatness, for his name must always be remembered in connection with the Balkan alliance of 1912 and the pro-Russian trend of Serbian policy. It was he who, supported by the King and the army, advocated military preparation. It was he again who, in 1914, had the courage to

49

say no to Austria. In all probability, but for his energy, the Kingdom of the Serbs, Croats and Slovenes would not exist to-day.

History is a strange thing. What numbers of statesmen have failed to achieve their aim, and how many others have achieved aims they did not seek! Pachitch is to be found among the latter, for whereas as a patriot he most ardently desired to create a Great Serbia, it was against his will that he lent his name to the creation of a state that did not represent his ideal—the Kingdom of the Serbs, Croats and Slovenes.

One day, during the exile of the Serbian government and army, the French minister in Athens called upon Peter, the aged King of Serbia, at Chalkis. He found a poor old man, shrunken and shriveled, whose eyes alone were youthful, full of fire and life. He was living on the first floor in a second-rate villa with a marvelous view. When the diplomat entered his presence, the King fell upon his neck, saying, "In you I embrace your generous and wonderful France." Then after a silence, almost in tears, he added, "For Serbia, all is over."

"How can you say that, Sire?" replied the minister. "Serbia is at the beginning, her future lies before her. The number of your subjects is increasing. . . ."

The King sharply interrupted him, his eyes blazing, "No! What are they, those people? They are slaves! The free men, the Serbs are dead!"

Pachitch thought the same. His patriotism was exclusively Serbian. His dream had been to unite all the Serbs in a single nation. He did not wish to unite with the Croats, who were Roman Catholics, with the Slovenes, who spoke a foreign language, he did not wish to unite with people who had not made any sacrifice for the defence of their common country, who had fought against the Serbs, who were not used to independence and to whom liberty was strange.

Nevertheless, he did unite with these people, although against his will. He was forced to do so on account of the terrible reverses of the Serbian army, when what remained of it was obliged to retreat through a country devoid of roads or supplies. This was one of the most difficult retreats in history.

These two great old men, King Peter and Nicolas Pachitch, both undaunted in spirit though one was broken in health, were called upon to suffer greatly at this time. At Corfu, where the Serbian government had taken refuge, in a country that was morally hostile, dissension had broken out among the refugees. A terrible conspiracy had been formed in the army, against the leader of the government and the Crown Prince. It had to be suppressed. It was Pachitch himself who gave the order to execute the ringleader, a very popular colonel. He made an attempt to carry on parliament but was defeated. The opposition held him responsible for all the nation's misfortunes. Being unable to form another government, he had to keep in power without any legal right to do so.

It will easily be understood that in such conditions, dependent upon the powers for the safety of her army, for her supplies, for her finances and for her hopes in the future, the Serbian government could not refuse the proposals put forward by the Allied cabinets. It was then that the Czecho-Slovak Legion was formed in France; after having hesitated for a long time, the Allies had finally decided to break up Austria-Hungary. They intended to use the different nationalities as an explosive to destroy the empire of the Hapsburgs and to overthrow the central empires coalition. Willing or unwilling, Pachitch was obliged to carry out his part in the affair.

This is what made him conclude the Corfu Agreement with the Croat and Slovene emigrants in 1917, take part in the Conference of Oppressed Nationalities in Rome in 1918 and sign the Charter of the Constitution of the Kingdom of the Serbs, Croats and Slovenes, drawn up in Geneva in October, 1918.

But Nicolas Pachitch could not put his heart into the affair. His vocabulary did not contain the word "Jugo-Slav" and the shrewd observer suspected that at the back of his mind lay the idea of turning the new state into a Greater Serbia. It was not a case of a true union of peoples upon the basis of equality, but of certain peoples being freed, almost conquered by certain others.

Pachitch was the president of his country's delegation at the Peace Conference. He was not a great diplomat. With his height and flowing white beard, that were so impressive at the great assemblies of Serbian peasants, he was out of his element in the Paris salons. Speaking no other language than his own, he found it difficult to get into touch with the statesmen from other countries, and rather than controlling events was carried along by them.

Circumstances are often stronger than human desires. It was fated that this man, whose instinct was for secret diplomacy and for old-fashioned methods, who brought into international politics his peasant's habits and his Oriental political attitude, should by the force of circumstances play the part of a great man ardently supporting the rights of peoples.

He was doubly fortunate at this moment. In the first place, he had a very able diplomat to help him, Vesnitch, whose wife was American and knew Mrs. Wilson intimately. This fact gave Serbia a direct means of conveying her desires to the President.

But he was still more fortunate in that he found himself in sympathy with the Wilsonian principles. His was not intellectual sympathy, for Pachitch, who always remained an Oriental at heart, certainly had no very clear understanding of the peoples' right of self-determination. But he was in sympathy with Wilson with regard to facts, the President's principles being providentially favorable to Serbian interests.

Serbia alone, of all the Allies, had not signed any secret treaty during the course of the War. She had been too weak, just as the United States had been too strong. She had treated with none, had concluded no private agreement, had negotiated with none and had refused to consider any suggestions made to her. She had no text to quote, indeed texts were quoted against her. By the Treaty of London, Italy was to receive Dalmatia, the population of which was Croat, with the exception of the middle classes in some of the towns; Rumania was to have the Banat, the population of which was Serbian. These were the claims that Pachitch had to oppose.

These treaties had never been officially submitted to Serbia, and in order to reassure her she had always been told that they did not bind her. Serbia was, therefore, in the same position with regard to these treaties as America; it was in order to explain this to President Wilson that Vesnitch specially went to Washington before the Peace Conference. Fortunately, his mission was successful.

President Wilson realized that the Adriatic question would be the touchstone for his principles. He had already given up a great deal; he felt that if he were to yield once more it would be fatal to his authority. He could not recognize the Treaty of London without being obliged to recognize a whole series of other treaties; he could not accept Italy's strategic arguments without endangering peace upon a series of other frontiers.

Fortunately for the Jugo-Slavs the Italians made two serious mistakes at that time. The first was to sink the *Viribus Unitis*, the best ship in the Austro-Hungarian fleet (it happened to be in Serbia's hands), the day after the Armistice was declared. This was a deliberate act of war among allies. The second was not to know upon what to base their claims of territory and to rely first upon treaties and then upon economic and strategic arguments, so that they could always be refuted upon one question by statements they had made with regard to another.

Moreover, it was not a case of argument. President Wilson had already been convinced, less by the Serbians themselves than by his own experts. Once his mind was made up there was nothing to do but to allow him to act and to wait. The Italians became impatient; the Jugo-Slavs were able to keep calm. Pachitch's great quality throughout his whole life was patience. "His life," writes Alfred Mousset, "is an example of perseverance, the expression of unshaken purpose backed by unfailing health. He suffered reverses, was imprisoned, exiled and sentenced to death, took part in the retreat through Albania, but never knew one moment's doubt."

The Jugo-Slav delegation was not entirely successful in Paris. It was unable to prevent the annexation by Italy of large areas of Slav territory or to obtain for the population the benefit of a minority régime. It was at least able to prevent Dalmatia from being attached to Italy and to delay the decision concerning the fate of Fiume. Taking the political circumstances into account, it must be admitted that Serbia

THEOBALD VON BETHMANN-HOLLWEG.

NICOLAS PACHITCH

benefited considerably by President Wilson's protection and by the application of his principles.

Upon his return home, Pachitch set about drawing up the constitution of the new state. This was to be his last great piece of political work; unfortunately, it came too late, at the end of his life. No man of seventy-five can be expected to have much political imagination or to be very adaptable. Pachitch was a Serb; he had been passionately attached to Serbia and had devoted his life to her. He knew what sacrifices his people had made and valued their good qualities; he trusted them implicitly.

He did not appreciate the other Jugo-Slav nations in the same way; he had not the same confidence in them. As a democrat, he looked upon the Austrian Slavs as people who were unaccustomed to independence, who had no experience as members of a state and had no democratic traditions. He could see only one thing, namely, that after having freed these people, Serbia still had to educate them.

But these people considered themselves superior to the Serbs, both on account of their Western culture and the quality of their administration. Under Austrian rule they had been accustomed to despise the Serbs and were not at all ready to be governed by them. One of them said later, having lost all patience in the struggle, "We have exchanged Germany for Turkey."

The natural political form for a state so constituted would have been federalism. Federalism requires two conditions: common patriotism and ethnic differences. These two conditions were to be found in the Kingdom of the Serbs, Croats and Slovenes immediately after the War. A far-seeing statesman would have been able to found a united and prosperous state upon such a basis. But Pachitch did not trust the patriotism of the Croats and the Slovenes. He thought that the unity of the country could only be assured by centralization and by concentrating all the power in Belgrade.

This was Pachitch's last mistake. The country that had grown so much larger was no longer his country. He could not realize this. He had never made a mistake in psychology with regard to the Serbs; he knew them and could read their minds. But he did not understand the Croats and allowed their first friendly feelings to degenerate into impatience and anger.

The last years of his life were marked by very violent political storms, but Pachitch no longer realized their full significance. He was still the leader in a country where men of character were rare, in a country for whose welfare he had struggled all through his life, and he lent his name to a policy the true importance of which he failed to understand. When he died on December 10th, 1926, the death of the man who had been everything to the state barely made a ripple upon the surface of the water.

VON BETHMANN-HOLLWEG

BISMARCK ONCE SAID OF HIS SUCCESSOR, GENERAL VON Caprivi, "He might be worse; wait until there is a bureaucrat at the head of the government, then Prussia's fate will be sealed." This bureaucrat was Von Bethmann-Hollweg.

Bismarck knew what the German constitution was, since he had made it to suit himself. He knew what responsibilities it laid upon the Chancellor and thought that only a man of his own calibre could carry such a burden. He knew from personal experience in 1870, how the civil authorities were hampered by the powerful military traditions of the Hohen-zollerns and how he had needed all his strength to oppose those traditions. Moreover, he had no illusions as to William II's desire for personal power, and he foresaw the misfortunes it must bring upon Germany. The bureaucrat he had in mind was the type of man who would not be strong enough to with-stand both the Emperor and his generals combined.

Events followed exactly as he had foretold. William II tried to govern alone. In 1908, after the interview by the *Daily Telegraph*, Prince von Bülow attempted to take the reins of the government into his own hands. William II deeply resented his action and at once began to look for some one to succeed him. His choice fell upon Von Bethmann-Hollweg. In his memoirs, William II explains why he chose Von Beth-mann-Hollweg as his Chancellor. In 1877, he was billeted as an officer on Herr von Bethmann, senior, at Hohenfinow: "I felt drawn," he says, "to this intimate friendly circle presided over by worthy Frau von Bethmann, a pleasant and tactful woman of Swiss origin. Both as prince and emperor, I frequently went back to stay at Hohenfinow. I was always received by the young deputy-prefect of the district and so learned to know him and more and more to appreciate his capacity for work, his brains and his character. His qualities remained unchanged throughout the whole of his career."

Von Bethmann-Hollweg remained what he was, a Prussian civil servant, until the end of his days; he rose through various stages of promotion from referendar to assessor, government counsellor, president, chief president, secretary of state, to Chancellor, and he looked at life only through administrative papers. He was elected as deputy to the Reichstag in 1890, but was obliged to resign suddenly, in order to avoid being disqualified. With the exception of the year during which he was a provincial governor, Von Bethmann-Hollweg always lived in the shadow of the imperial palaces at Potsdam and Berlin. If the decision had rested only with William II, he would have been a minister in 1901. An administrator rather than a statesman, deeply attached to the country in which he was born and that he had always governed, Von Bethmann-Hollweg's first care was the good will of his master. The career of a civil servant trains a man to obey rather than to command. This is expressed in his family motto: "Ego et domus mea serviemus domino." He was the typical servant, loyal and short-sighted.

Tired of having too gifted and too brilliant a collaborator, who threatened his own authority, William II appointed Von Bethmann-Hollweg to restore the royal prestige. There was never any misunderstanding upon this point between the Emperor and his Chancellor; the latter fully realized that he had been appointed to obey.

VON BETHMANN-HOLLWEG

Von Bethmann-Hollweg had too high an idea of his duties to be regarded as a mere figurehead, puppet or buffer. Moreover, William II was not a hard worker and left a good deal to his subordinates. Von Bethmann-Hollweg had been appointed in reaction against the system of Prince von Bülow, whose policy was that the government should obtain the support of the Reichstag. From the beginning, he put himself, both by design and by necessity, above parties, without support from anywhere unless it be from his sovereign. He was the favorite, and all his power depended upon that fact.

As much upon this account as by his natural loyalty, Von Bethmann-Hollweg found himself obliged to take the responsibility for an unstable and capricious policy with which he was often not in sympathy. To quote but a few examples, in such incidents as William II's assertion of his divine right at Königsberg, his theocratic appeal to the monks of Beuron, his threat at Strasburg against the rights of the Alsatians ("I will smash them to bits," he said), the Chancellor invariably took all the responsibility upon himself.

There was nobility in such unswerving loyalty, but it sometimes led Von Bethmann-Hollweg into awkward contradictions.

I can see him now, in the Reichstag during the discussion of the Franco-German Morocco agreement, his tall thin figure accentuated by a somewhat tight-fitting frock-coat that flapped round his calves, as swaying slightly to and fro, he made a monotonous speech devoid of rhetoric but clear and to the point. A sudden tremor went through the crowded hall. Von Bethmann-Hollweg had turned towards the Right and pointing at the Conservative leader, Von Heydebrandt, he exclaimed: "I dislike people who always carry their swords in their mouths."

This remark caused a sensation. It not only stood out against the dull background of Von Bethmann-Hollweg's speech, but it particularly contrasted with his policy of seeking the support of the Nationalists and the Agrarians.

The explanation of the incident was to be found in the New Palace where Von Bethmann-Hollweg had dined. The day before, the Conservative leader had made a fiercely nationalist speech in the Reichstag. The Crown Prince had purposely left his quarters and had ostentatiously applauded him, tapping his white gloves on the red velvet edge of the royal box. William II cared little for his son and much disliked Heydebrandt, who was known as "the uncrowned king"; he was enraged at the incident. It was he, who, while smoking after dinner, had used the expression: "carry their swords in their mouths" that Von Bethmann-Hollweg had repeated in the Reichstag in order to flatter his sovereign at the risk of compromising his parliamentary position.

I remember another sitting, this time in the pale green hall in the Prussian Diet. The Socialist leader, Herr Scheidemann, his bald head shining in the light from the window, had just said, in one of those flights of coldly calculated and previously prepared rhetoric of which he was the master: "It is a tradition among the Hohenzollerns to break one's word." Confusion followed. The deputies on the Right leapt to their feet, shouting and gesticulating, while Von Bethmann-Hollweg, white with rage, towered above them all.

The Chancellor was not the man to subdue a troublesome majority. He had neither the necessary faults nor strength. He could be eloquent, he expressed himself clearly, and what he said was sound, but he lacked warmth and brilliance. He taught his audiences and sometimes was able to convince them, but he never carried them away. He was never in touch with them, he had no magnetism or vivacity, he was impersonal and reserved and, although his logic was excellent, he had no influence on assemblies. He was shy and appeared proud; he looked uninteresting. With his taste for philosophy and his scholarly mind he was ill-equipped for the work of a leader and man of action. His career is marked by indecision and contradictions.

This is why he continually allowed difficulties to increase because he did not foresee them in time and why he was finally overwhelmed by pan-Germanism, the existence of which he had always denied.

The war found him, as always, a prey to external and conflicting forces. He controlled nothing and submitted to everything. The history of this period could be written without mentioning the name of the Chancellor of the German empire. The generals, the admirals, Tirpitz, the military cabinet, the ambassadors, Tschirschky and Pourtalés were all eager for war. Lichnowsky was against it. The Emperor became excited and sent telegrams. And what of Von Bethmann-Hollweg? Did he even know of the Austro-Hungarian ultimatum to Serbia? He said not. Was he informed of the telegrams sent to William II by the Tsar? Some are missing in the diplomatic records. When the *Lokal Anzeiger* prematurely announced general mobilization, did Von Bethmann-Hollweg know that the decision had actually been taken, the night before, and cancelled? He formally denied it. The whole world thought that this government was a model of organization, that the machine ran without a hitch—and the head was absent!

The fact is that from this moment the real power lay in the hands of the military authorities, and in the army Bethmann had only to obey.

I remember perfectly the opening of the Reichstag, in 1912, in the White Hall of the Royal Palace. There was nothing military in the ceremony; however, and this is sufficient to show the character of a régime, the Chancellor of the empire was in uniform. Von Bethmann held the rank of major. The Emperor hastily promoted him to that of general so that he might hold his own, but senior generals took precedence before him. I still see in my mind's eye, the symbolic picture of the highest civil servant in Germany standing to attention!

This scene suffices to explain what took place at the beginning and during the course of the War.

Von Bethmann-Hollweg, who was in possession of all the diplomatic documents, could not believe the story that Germany was attacked. He knew that this was not the case. The military authorities, however, were convinced that Russia and France were preparing war for 1916 or 1917. At this date the Russo-German commercial treaty was to expire and the great Russian railway programme was to be completed. M. Poincaré was reputed to have said: "I shall have my war in 1916!"

It was on such flimsy evidence that the German military authorities had decided that they must take the initiative and declare war before their enemies were ready. The task of explaining this to the German people they generously left to Von Bethmann-Hollweg.

The Chancellor could not state publicly that this was a preventive war. Bismarck had formerly said, "A preventive war would be a crime." This remark was in all the papers and in every one's mind. How could he tell the people that it was precisely such a war that they were invited to undertake? Von Bethmann-Hollweg dared not tell them. He preferred to say that Germany was attacked. From that moment he forsook the truth and was lost.

If one tells the truth one must tell the whole truth; if one lies one must lie thoroughly. Von Bethmann was incapable of either. Among all the official falsehoods he was obliged to tell it is the two occasions upon which he told the truth that will blacken his name in history.

He had tried to oppose the violation of Belgian neutrality. The military authorities did not allow him to speak. When a country goes to war it must win; nothing else counts. What business was it of his with his fears and scruples? England? She will not budge.

Von Bethmann went to the Reichstag. And after announcing that the German troops were at that moment crossing the Belgian frontier, he added with sudden sincerity, "When the war is over Germany will make amends for the wrong she is doing to Belgium." It is this admission that the majority of the German people have not forgiven him and will never forgive him.

He then retired to his room, where a few hours later he received the Ambassador of Great Britain, who had come to bring him England's declaration of war.

Confusion reigned in the Wilhelmstrasse during the last days of July, 1914. Every one was disclaiming responsibility. Officials who were normally most friendly seemed to have lost their reason; one of the most courteous attacked me as the correspondent of a French paper, declaring: "It is all your fault!"

It is easy, when one has lived through tense moments, to imagine the celebrated scene that took place in the Chancellor's room on August 4th, 1914. Sir Edward Goschen found Von Bethmann-Hollweg in a state of agitation and excitement quite unlike his usual demeanor. Upon seeing him, the German Chancellor, with a break in his voice, exclaimed, "You won't do that . . . for a scrap of paper!" This phrase will be a blot upon his name for all time and the world will always see in it the unvarnished admission of an appalling state of mind.

The fundamental cause of the war of 1914 was the gulf that had slowly opened between the moral evolution of the German people and that of the western countries. In France and England pacifist propaganda had penetrated deeply among the masses and war was to them a horrible crime. Germany however was still in the state of mind of 1814 or 1870. War had saved the country and its unity. Germany feared war, she did not hate it; it did not appall her.

This is the state of mind expressed by Von Bethmann-Hollweg when he referred to international treaties as "scraps of paper." In his eyes there could be nothing more important than the welfare of the state. He was a century behind the moral evolution of humanity.

From this moment onwards Von Bethmann-Hollweg's life became a calvary. Those who came into contact with him during the War met a stooping, gray-haired, broken man: a "knight of the rueful countenance." He seemed to have a load upon his conscience. He was caught in the machinery he had set going. He saw all the political mistakes made by the military authorities and was powerless to prevent them.

The most serious mistake was to declare unrestricted submarine warfare. Von Bethmann-Hollweg saw clearly that it would result in bringing America into the War. For two years, 1915 and 1916, he was able to use his influence with the Emperor to prevent him from supporting this policy. Von Tirpitz, who hated him, the admirals, Marshal Hindenburg and

General Ludendorf, in common with all the German Nationalists, looked upon him at that time as one who opposed victory, almost as a traitor.

At the beginning of 1917, he was forced to give way to the Emperor's military advisers and the Reichstag. But in his opinion, if the submarine campaign was to be effective, it had to be short and should quickly bring about a negotiated peace. Upon these grounds he tried, in agreement with the Reichstag, to obtain peace in July, 1917.

He made use of the two great international forces, Socialism and Catholicism. The Stockholm conference failed. Then the leader of the Catholic party, Erzberger, went to Munich, where he saw the Nuncio, and to Vienna, where he was received by the Emperor. The result was the peace resolution voted by the Reichstag.

Von Bethmann-Hollweg once more came into conflict with the Supreme Command of the army, and this time his resignation was demanded. The Crown Prince left his army and established himself in Berlin, at whose request none knew. He then summoned Hindenburg and Ludendorf, who began to negotiate and govern over the Chancellor's head. Authority went to pieces, the Emperor was entirely eclipsed, and Von Bethmann-Hollweg ceased to exist. Some one asked to whom he should apply in a certain matter. "Apply to whom you choose," was the reply. "We have no government."

It was rumored for five days among circles on the Right that the Emperor would abdicate in favor of his son. In order to retain a shadow of authority William II decided to sacrifice his most faithful adviser, that is to say, in effect, to commit suicide.

The German military authorities needed a scapegoat. They wanted some one upon whom to cast their overwhelming responsibilities. They found such a man in Von Bethmann-Hollweg, the man who had declared to the world that the violation of Belgian neutrality was a crime, who had opposed the submarine campaign, who had promised the German people universal suffrage and whose pacifism and "defeatism" stood in the way of victory.

Von Bethmann-Hollweg resigned from his office without one word of thanks either from his sovereign for whom he had sacrificed everything, or from his people. And history will lay upon him the burden of his own mistakes and of the mistakes of others.

COUNT TISZA

NOT ENOUGH IS KNOWN ABOUT THE CAREER OF COUNT TISZA, for it teaches some moral and political lessons of moment. One lesson is that you may have a great and admirable personality and yet be a bad statesman: you need more than a pure conscience to govern a country. Another is that you may carry the sentiment of duty to the point of heroism and yet bring down upon your race an infinity of ills. A third is that the instinctive convictions of Tisza's compatriots as to his responsibility for the War had more of essential truth in them than those historic documents which prove that the War came against his will.

Count Tisza belonged to a landowning family of Magyar source and Calvinistic conviction. This origin explains his character.

Hungary has been ruled from the first by a very restricted oligarchy, and is still. When one ministry resigns, they ask in Budapest: "Which Count will take office?" Tisza's title was of recent date. His father had refused it when it was offered by Francis-Joseph, and he himself inherited it from an uncle in 1897. But his family was of very ancient lineage; it had had great military traditions and in the course of time had amassed considerable wealth. It used to be said of all the Tiszas—and this was particularly true of the last of them— that they had three ruling passions: horses, politics and the Bible!

Count Tisza was a feudal aristocrat in every sense of the

67

term. He was a man of his own caste and placed confidence always in his peers. He had no love either for Count Czernin or for Count Karolyi, but to win Tisza's trust it sufficed that one or the other pledged his word. He ruled his own home and his tenantry in patriarchal fashion. He was fond of the people but never understood their actual needs; in a more democratic state, there would certainly have been no possibility of a public career for him. Even at the height of his power he was unpopular.

Count Tisza's personality was not fascinating or endearing, but it was strong and dominating. Even the most important men felt small in his presence. Behind the thick glasses which he had worn ever since an operation for cataract, his blue eyes seemed to pierce like steel. Frederic Naumann, who was one of the best known politicians in Germany towards the end of last century, stuttered and stammered the first time he was presented to Tisza, and he was trembling like a leaf after the interview was over. "Since Bismarck," one of Tisza's biographers has remarked, "nobody has made so strong a personal impression upon people."

The comparison comes naturally, for Tisza always had an unbounded admiration for Bismarck. Unless I am mistaken, the only book he wrote in the whole course of his career was the one entitled "From Sadowa to Sedan," and it was devoted to a glorification of Bismarck. One cannot say whether he consciously took the great Chancellor for his model and political inspiration, but it is certain that many episodes in his life could not be properly understood if one were unaware of his feelings in regard to Bismarck and to Prussia.

And yet, for all his German sympathies, Tisza, we must not forget, was a Magyar; he belonged to one of the most powerful races of Europe. The Hungarians like to say of themselves that they are a "Race of Rulers." There is no good cause for boasting in that, because it is the source of all their woes, but it is true. And when we see a Magyar who is at the same time a feudal noble, we may be sure that we have before us a fine specimen of the ruler type.

Now, this particular feudal Magyar was a Protestant. He belonged to that section of the Magyar race which had remained the most undiluted and which by tradition was the most uncompromising in its nationalism. The Catholics have sometimes come to terms with the Court of Vienna and thus experienced the infiltration of western blood into their veins. The Protestants, never; they would have preferred to ally themselves with the Grand Turk!

The Calvinistic element in Tisza is to be found in his principles, his sense of duty and his absolute loyalty—the quality which Francis-Joseph most appreciated in his servants and which attached him to Tisza more than to any other Hungarian statesman.

On several occasions Count Tisza displayed his lack of political vision, psychological insight, understanding of men. But no one ever questioned his upright character; his life, like his death, set a fine example. His opponents sometimes called him derisively "the Man of the Bible." Could higher praise have been accorded him?

Hard with himself, Tisza was equally hard with others. Once certain members of his party had complained that he was neglecting them. He made this profound answer: "What would become of me if I had to be amiable even to my friends?" But this stiffness of his was not from hardness of heart. His sense of duty was not without a tender side to it. While he was ill once during the War, he ceased entirely to give attention to affairs of state—except for one single matter: he made his secretary come to his bedroom every day with the applications from war widows which needed signature by the head of the government. One morning a great personage called to see him on a matter of importance. He was given this astonishing reply: "His Excellency cannot come at once as he is busy massaging his valet!"

When one has come to realize these outstanding features of the man—the Magyar, the Calvinist, the aristocrat—one is able to see how Tisza's political career outlined itself clearly and logically, without hesitation or inconsistency.

His father had been President of the Council in Hungary for fifteen consecutive years, from 1875 to 1890. This greatly facilitated his own political début and he was elected deputy in 1886 at the age of twenty-five. At first he was regarded merely as the inheritor of the name. But his father had once remarked: "You will soon see for yourselves, my son is a very different man from me." And this was the truth. For the father had been, above all, an opportunist and a sceptic, and the son was a rod of iron.

He did not, however, abandon his father's policy of loyalty to the Austrian throne and close relations with Austria. On the contrary, he pursued it with much more thoroughness and force of character. And (what was surprising and destined to have a tragic aspect to it), he did so in the full conviction that his efforts were in vain.

In his view the Dual Monarchy was necessary to Hungary as the only means of ensuring her independence and integrity. Tisza cherished no illusions regarding the sentiments of the other races of Hungary towards the Magyar domination. Therefore he saw in the King the only link which could hold together these mutually hostile peoples. On the other hand, Hungary was necessary to the monarchy, of which it was the healthiest and strongest element. Tisza had no understanding or admiration for anything but force; force was with him a dogma. Hungary needed the monarchy, and the monarchy needed Hungary, if both were to be strong. Within the monarchy, it was necessary that Hungary should dominate because she alone was strong. In other words, it was essential not to touch what Tisza regarded as the very basis of the state: the army.

Tisza saw the World War coming sooner than any other European statesman. He saw it too soon, at a moment when his foresight had in it less of vision than of imagination. "For twelve years past," he wrote in 1889, "we have been more or less threatened by a European war. This war will be no child's play; it is possible that it will decide whether the Hungarian nation shall live or die." That was the reason why he always resisted anything that could weaken or jeopardize the army.

In this fashion it came about that the ardent Magyar patriot seemed at certain moments almost a traitor in the eyes of his countrymen. While the whole Hungarian people insisted that Magyar should be the language of the army, he alone accepted the view of the King that there should be but one army language—that the army must not be divided in two. At a time when the army was unpopular in Hungary, because it was thought of as the King's army, as a means of Germanization and an asset of Austrian imperialism, he alone was in favor of its being developed and increased. In the eyes of the people, his own people whom he loved and whose welfare he had at heart in his own way, he appeared as *homo regius*, the king's man. He would not hear of universal suffrage, for the people in his view were not sufficiently educated. The Nationalists, the party of Kossuth, demanded universal suffrage so that they might be able to impose the will of the people upon the King. Tisza, on the contrary, championed the Crown unceasingly, unshakingly. During a great part of his political career, this great patriot, this statesman whose memory is now venerated, could scarcely issue forth from his house without encountering threats and jeers.

The tragic element in his attitude was that he had no real belief in it himself: "Throughout twenty bitter years," he once wrote, "I have been tortured by the thought that this monarchy was destined to ruin and, with it, the Hungarian nation!" What is one to say about a man who combined in himself heroism enough and blindness enough to pursue throughout twenty years a policy based upon a supposition which he believed false and which throughout all this time was preparing the way for a war which he ought to have known must be a catastrophe?

Force may perhaps be justified in the case of the strong. The monarchy was not strong. Tisza knew that his efforts to strengthen the army had failed; he knew that a state to which the people is not attached is weak. Yet he did not cease to act as if this state and this army were capable of defying the centuries and of moving mountains.

To Tisza's upright and thoroughgoing character mere opportunist moves were repugnant. A poor psychologist, he did not understand men or how to use them. Not being naturally eloquent, and impressing others only by reason of the infectious force of his convictions and sincerity, he disdained parliamentary tactics, for which he had no talent and which would have been a concession to democracy. Throughout his whole career he always made frontal attacks upon all his difficulties.

Against his people, to whom he was bound by every fibre

in his soul, Tisza carried on a continual warfare of *coups d'État*. In 1904, in order to overcome obstruction in Parliament, he had a new regulation carried *en bloc* by the vote of a majority devoted to him. The only effect of this was to unite all the parties of the opposition into a *bloc* which won a crushing victory over him in the election of 1905.

After this set-back, Tisza disappeared from the political scene for several years. Like Cincinnatus, he devoted himself to agriculture. But in 1912 he became President of the Chamber. Now came another *coup d'État!* In order to overcome the resistance of the Opposition he called in the police and had the Chamber cleared. A deputy then proceeded to fire at him three times with a revolver. There were several persons wounded, but Tisza was untouched: "Gentlemen," he said, "the sitting will continue."

He had put himself in the wrong, legally and politically. Legally he had violated the constitution; politically he had once more provoked his opponents and rendered all coöperation between the Hungarian parties impossible in the future. This mistake was to bear ill fruit during the War. Hungary through Tisza's action was one of the few belligerent countries in which it was impossible to bring about a truce between parties and to create a united national government.

On June 7th, 1913, Count Tisza regained power. This man whose figure dominated modern Hungary was only twice at the head of the government and only for brief periods on each occasion—on the first only for some months, on the second for three years—but the importance of events cannot be gauged by their duration. Tisza was Prime Minister of Hungary when the Archduke Francis-Ferdinand was assassinated on June 28th, 1914.

Tisza saw at once that war might ensue and he immediately expressed this view to the King. In the council held by the King on July 5th, 1914, at which the final decisions were taken, he alone, in opposition to all the other members present, set his face against war.

We must try to understand his motives. Tisza, we know, had seen the war coming. He had regarded it as inevitable. Perhaps, as a Christian, he was against it, but he did not imagine he could prevent it. He was in the same state of mind as his colleagues. They all believed the war to be inevitable and they wished to choose the right moment for it. It was precisely as to the rightness of the moment that Tisza disagreed with them.

It was said that Tisza's only objection was in respect to the date. The Hungarian people, he is supposed to have argued, cannot enter into the war until the crops have been cut and harvested. This statement of his position is not altogether accurate. He did, indeed, make the remark attributed to him and it was duly noted. It was this remark, even more than President Poincaré's visit to Petrograd, that had the effect of postponing for some days or some weeks the beginning of the dreadful butchery.

But even when he had carried this point, Count Tisza was not won over. When a state is waging a defensive war, it should choose both its moment and its pretext. The pretext in this case seemed to Tisza badly chosen; the proof of the Serbian government's complicity in the Serajevo murder was not sufficiently established. From a military standpoint, Austria-Hungary was not ready; its army was mediocre, inadequately equipped, badly organized. Diplomatically, the preparations had been no better—they could count on neither Italy nor Rumania. Finally, this war would be purposeless.

What was it intended to do about Serbia? Geographically, that country could only be united with Hungary. The Hungarians had no wish for it. They had their hands full enough with their Croats. Events were to show how completely Count Tisza was right. But he was not listened to. Count Berchtold took it on himself to refute his diplomatic objections, Marshal Conrad dealt with his military objections, and the Joint Minister of Finance, M. Bilinski, backed them up. The Emperor gave his signature.

History has its paradoxes. Count Berchtold was a man of sceptical temperament, alert and wary. Tisza was of the authoritative type, lacking in political wisdom, a devotee of force. Yet it was he who sought to prevent the war, and he who was right, not the warlike diplomat!

It was at this juncture that Tisza's moral greatness showed itself. Never during his lifetime did it become known that he was against the War. On the way back from Vienna to Budapest, after that fateful conference, he was cheered by the peasants in a village. He exclaimed to his secretary: "If only they knew how little I deserve their cheers!"

Nobody else knew the truth. He assumed complete responsibility for the terrible decision. For years he lived alone with his secret and never made a sign to exculpate himself. When things began to go from bad to worse, he felt that his unpopularity was increasing. He had but to utter a single word and he would have been the most popular man in the monarchy and in the whole world: he would have emerged as the only statesman in the central empires who had opposed the war. Imagine the moral standing he would have had today! This word remained unsaid. He trod his calvary serenely —and once again for a cause which he deemed lost.

Tisza's last official act was to place the royal crown upon the head of King Charles IV—the Hungarian title of the Emperor Charles I. This supreme honor contributed to his fall. In court circles, it was a matter for complaint against him that he, a Protestant, should have insisted on taking part in a ceremony which was of a Catholic and liturgical nature. Tisza, moreover, did not get on with the young sovereign, whom he dominated physically and who in the Prime Minister's presence must always have felt as though he were a small boy. King Charles wished to grant universal suffrage to the peoples of his monarchy, knowing that in this way he would be giving freedom to the national minorities. Count Tisza, always unshakeable in his convictions and obstinate in his errors, refused. He opposed also the Polish policy of the Emperor, who wished to get an archduke on the throne of Poland and to give him Galicia. Tisza felt that if a new Piedmont were thus created all the Slav provinces of the monarchy would go that way one after another. He no longer had enough assurance in the solidity of the state to believe in the possibility of such perilous experiments. He preferred to resign and left for the front as a Colonel of Hussars. It was there he spent the last years of his life.

Even those with whom he was not in agreement regretted him, for he represented in Hungary a force on which one could lean. His relations with Czernin were sometimes difficult. Tisza, although he foresaw the débâcle, did not see it come. He was against the peace offers because in his philosophy it was only the strong who counted—and to be strong one must not seem to be weak. But when you did win him over to an idea, he was like a rock, while his successors were irresolute puppets upon whom the Emperor could never rely.

Tisza did not return from the front until the eve of the

defeat. The empire was breaking up in every direction. Charles hurriedly appealed to him and sent him to Serajevo to calm down the leaders of the people there in revolt. This mission turned out ill. For the Bosnian leaders having already spoken to him in terms which did not please him he treated them in a lofty manner, adopting a severe, authoritative tone, as though he still occupied the position he had held of old.

And yet he knew that he occupied it no longer. On his return to Budapest, he undertook one more painful duty—his last. It was he who announced to the Chamber the news of the defeat: "We have lost the War!" He thus continued to give the impression that it was his own war, that he had willed it, and that he was *le grand vaincu*. He offered himself up as a holocaust to the rage of the people.

His days were now numbered and he knew it. Insurrection murmured in the streets and demanded his life. Tisza never left his house; he made no change in his habits. He merely burned some documents—those which proved that he had not willed the War, those which would have exculpated him. To some one who wanted to know why he did so, he replied: "You never know what may happen. I don't want my papers to be used by people to bring charges against my former colleagues when I am gone."

One day, the 31st of October, 1918, some armed soldiers forced their way into his house. They found him standing in his salon and without a word they killed him with a volley of shots. Tisza was the first victim of the Hungarian revolution, and the most illustrious; alas, he was not the only one.

Count Tisza was innocent of what he was charged with; he had not willed the War. But the War came about inevitably as the result of the political system which he represented and which he unfalteringly applied in the full measure of his strength. There was no stronger partisan than he of the Austro-German alliance; no one desired more strongly than he the domination·of the Magyars over the other nationalities. He was the opponent of federalism and of universal suffrage, of all the ideas of Francis-Ferdinand, of everything that represented any possibility of solving pacifically the internal difficulties of the monarchy. He was the irreconcilable adversary of the Croats and he helped to deepen the ditch which separated Austria from Serbia. He was the instigator of the policy of economic oppression which the Dual Monarchy pursued against Serbia, and which ended by driving that country to despair. In a word, he made war enter into all his political calculations and rendered it necessary.

In executing him, popular justice was guided by wrong information but by a sure instinct.

POINCARÉ

THE GREAT GOOD FORTUNE OF M. RAYMOND POINCARÉ HAS
been to seem in the eyes of his compatriots on three or four
historic occasions the man essential to the welfare of their
country. This was the case in 1912 and in 1919, then in 1922,
then again in 1926. Rare good luck! M. Poincaré owes it to
the fact that, thanks to certain of his abilities and to some
of his defects, he has been the most representative man of his
time and of his race.

M. Poincaré was born at Bar le Duc, in 1860, of a bourgeois family. None of these details can be overlooked if we
would understand his character: the Lorraine birthplace;
the year, 1860; the bourgeois origin.

Raymond Poincaré was ten years old when the Franco-
Prussian war broke out. He saw the enemy occupy his native
land. He saw Lorraine torn in twain, the German frontier
brought quite close; the sound of the passionate protestations
of an entire people rang in his ears. These were impressions
never to be effaced. The Lorrainers are not better Frenchmen
than the Frenchmen of other provinces, but they saw invasion and annexation from nearer at hand. They only just
missed being victims—like their brothers of Metz and their
neighbors of Strasburg. This memory throughout their lives
evokes in them the same emotion, the same anger, the same
dread.

M. Poincaré's grievances against the Germans are the
same as those of other Frenchmen, but to the end of his days,

as M. Briand has expressed it, they will be "filtrés par un esprit lorrain."

This generation of 1870 has played a special rôle in the history of modern France. It grew up under the shadows of misfortune. Young people are always disposed to scorn what was done before their time. But when the deeds of their elders have spelt defeat and the dismemberment of their country, their contempt knows no bounds. France showed her greatness at that hour by never losing heart. She did not let pessimism bow down her head. She did not lose faith in her destiny. She did not seek solace in oblivion. All her thoughts, all her energies, were directed to the work of restoration.

The young men who assumed the duties of citizens in the early Eighties had been taught to cherish a sentimental and idealized conception of the republic. The republic stood out before their eyes just as before the eyes of their fathers living under the empire. But they saw the reins of government in the hands of men grown old. "What was" did not accord with their notion of "What should be." After Boulanger's pseudo-heroic adventures, with their blend of the romantic and the ridiculous, came the explosion of the financial scandal of Panama, in which almost the entire officialdom of the Republic was involved—including even the President himself.

It was at this juncture that Raymond Poincaré and the men of his generation entered upon their political life, adopting a program of moral cleansing, recovery and revival. They were not long in making their mark. Elected a deputy at the age of twenty-seven, he himself was three times a minister before he reached his thirty-fifth year.

"Etre ministre," his mother once said to him, "ce n'est pas un métier pour un jeune homme!" (To be a minister is not a profession for a young man.) But this particular young man was to show that, while he was quite equal to other *métiers*, that of being a minister was quite sufficient for him.

M. Poincaré's family belonged to the *grande bourgeoisie*. His mother was the grand-daughter of Jean Landry Gillon, who was nine times deputy for the Meuse under the monarchy of July. His father, Antoine Poincaré, was inspector of bridges and roadways, his uncle professor of medicine at Nancy. His brother has come to be a highly placed official in the University of France; a first cousin of his is one of the most illustrious mathematicians of our time; a cousin by marriage is a famous philosopher.

It may be seen, therefore, that M. Poincaré comes of a stock of great intellectual culture. But there is more to be said than this. He comes of a stock more representative than any other of modern France. It was the bourgeoisie that directed the French Revolution. The Revolution, in return, created the millions of peasant-proprietors and *rentiers*, as we call them, now to be found in France. It was the bourgeoisie that brought about the revolution of 1830—and that dominated the monarchy of July. It brought about also the revolution of 1870 and created a republic in its own image. It has governed France for more than a century.

The bourgeoisie in France has its essential basis in landed property and in the state funds—that is to say, if we go deep enough into the matter, in *savings*. Other countries are dependent upon production and commerce and on the rapid circulation of wealth. With France it is quite different. The bourgeois class is dependent upon wealth long since acquired and it becomes richer only through economy. Therefore it is in its interest to an exceptional degree that the state should be prudently administered, that the budget should be balanced, the *rentes* kept safe, the government kept above reproach. It is this spirit of order and economy that M. Poincaré has brought to the conduct of public affairs. And that is why, in 1926, when he said to the country: "To save the franc, we must economize," he was understood by all the bourgeois of France.

The intellectual origins of the bourgeoisie go back to the eighteenth century, to Voltaire. The bourgeoisie gathered strength in the course of its struggle against the monarchy and against the church, and although both the monarchy and the church have ceased to be formidable, it still preserves the spirit of hostility against the forces of reaction. M. Raymond Poincaré in this respect has not moved away from his stock. He is by temperament anti-clerical. If he has sometimes had the support of the Parties of the Right, on the strength of his national policy, this was contrary to his own liking; and in 1924 this support cost him power, so profound is the instinctive prejudice of the French bourgeoisie against the Church. M. Poincaré was enabled then to note that his success came entirely from his fidelity to the stock to which he belonged and whose feelings he stood for.

It is from the bourgeoisie that M. Poincaré derives the fundamental traits of his character: love of work and clarity of mind.

M. Poincaré is a great worker. He is at his desk from early morning to late at night. He reads all the documents submitted to him, annotates them, drafts the replies. His assistants prepare his work for him, but he does the work himself. He insists on going into everything. An opponent of his exclaimed once while M. Poincaré was at the Élysée: "Mon Dieu! Quand donc aurons-nous un président paresseux." (For Heaven's sake let us have a lazy President.)

His range of knowledge is prodigious. Throughout the affair of the Ruhr, he had all the reports from all the French Consuls in Germany laid before him. He wished to be *au courant* with everything that was said about him, with all the criticisms called forth by his policy. And this mass of reports had not a little to do with the aggravation of his mintrustful attitude towards Germany.

There are no details too minute to escape M. Poincaré's attention. It is with pleasure that I record some illustrations of this which seem to me altogether to his credit.

While the War was on, in 1916, I had written from Paris, where I was staying, to my newspaper (as to the discretion of which I felt at ease in my mind) a letter in which I had recorded certain criticisms called forth by the military operations. This letter was read by the censorship and, without my being informed of the matter, was made the subject of discussion by the Council of Ministers. The Minister of the Interior, M. Malvy, showed much feeling over it. The President of the Republic, M. Poincaré, on the contrary, expounded with much perspicacity and good nature the character of my articles, which apparently he made a habit of reading, and it was he, by his authoritative intervention, who protected me—unknown personally to him, as I was at the time— from the troubles which this incident might have caused me.

It was at a much later date and only by chance that I heard about this. I at once asked for an interview with him so that I might express my gratitude. The President's chamber at the Élysée is at the end of a long series of rooms in which the offices of the military staff and the civilian secretaries are located. On entering each of these elaborately gilded rooms, the attendant who ushers in the visitor proclaims his name out loud.

In his chamber M. Poincaré awaited me standing up in front of his desk. I recall vividly the impression made on me by his reception, at once cordial and matter-of-fact, his trenchant voice, his precise language. But what I remember best of all was the surprise and slight disquietude aroused in me by the extent of his information. He discoursed to me on the state of the public mind in France and quoted some observations of mine on the subject which he had read: "Your impressions of the state of the public mind in France," he said, "are not very favorable. I quite understand that. The circles in which you mix are the least satisfactory in the country— namely the intellectuals, who hold forth not on their own feelings but on the feelings of others: 'Provided the people hold on!' they exclaim. For 'the people' no such doubt exists. These intellectuals live in coteries—they represent the newspaper world, the clubs, the two houses of Parliament—the sets they belong to are the most nervous groups in France. . . . "

Since then, I have seen M. Poincaré on several occasions. I have always been struck by the extent of his knowledge, the clearness of his views, and the intuitive understanding he has shown of his countrymen.

It has often been said that M. Poincaré lacks charm. This is true in a sense. There is no warmth in him. His voice is precise and a trifle sharp. Beneath the vaults of the Sainte-Chapelle, where I once heard him, his voice seemed almost to crack against the stained windows. But M. Poincaré makes up for his lack of charm by the spirit of loyalty and genuineness which characterizes him.

M. Poincaré's mind is, so to speak, essentially *scriptural*. He loves the written word. This is observable even in his elocution, for he writes out his speeches and delivers them by heart, with the help of a marvelous memory. He seldom excites his audience by his eloquence. His strength as a speaker lies in the effects of his impeccable logic. The French mind, trained as it is by a drastic philosophical discipline, excels in the analysis of a situation and in expressing it synthetically. This is the great faculty of a political advocate and it is this faculty which M. Poincaré has brought to perfection in politics.

M. Poincaré has the qualities of an advocate and some of the defects. "He pleads a case admirably," M. Briand has said of him, "but he does not know how to deliver a verdict." The passage from analysis to deduction, from theory to action is difficult. It is a mistake to think him strong-willed. On several occasions in his life his energy and determination have failed him. He did not know when to finish with his adventure of the Ruhr and he hesitated long regarding the stabilization of the franc.

His conception of law is rigid. It was M. Briand again who said of him, at the time of Ruhr occupation: "M. Poincaré does not embody Law and Justice. He embodies the School of Law and the Courts of Justice."

Others may be philosophers; he is, first and foremost, a man of law. He sees the world through legal spectacles; he has a horror of vague promises, loosely worded documents; he wants a guarantee in every case. In a dispute, he sees only what is his due.

His whole policy gives evidence of this.

M. Poincaré's career had undergone a long eclipse. Little by little, however, the former minister came back to the minds of his fellow-citizens, he reconquered their belief in him, and soon he came to appear to them once more the Indispensable Man. When did this happen? When Germany, trying to burke her old engagements, put in a claim for compensations in Africa in return for a neutrality in Morocco to which she had already committed herself. This was something which Poincaré, the jurist, would not tolerate. An act is an act, an engagement is an engagement. He came into power with a one-item program—to say no to Germany, if need be!

From that moment onward European politics were to take a new course. The French people, who had been burdened by the sense of their weakness, began to breathe afresh and to hope. They instituted their three years military service in reply to the new military laws of Germany and felt thrilled by their own audacity. Russia, who had been doubtful regarding the efficacy of her alliance with a somewhat decadent democracy, regained courage also. And England, alarmed by the German menace, rejoiced to find a supporter.

It has often been asserted, and even in France, that M. Poincaré was responsible for the War. This is untrue if it be meant that he wanted war or that he did not do all he could to prevent it. But it is perhaps true if one enquires into the subtle inter-relationship of events.

On coming to power in 1912, M. Poincaré, far from wanting war, had but one idea: to prevent it. But he was convinced that Germany was resolved to wage it. In order to prevent it one last hope remained: to show Germany that she would be stood up to. "France," he therefore declared, "is not afraid of war!"

This bold language, of a kind to which the statesmen of the third Republic had allowed Europe to grow unaccustomed, enchanted the French Nationalists. Without wishing it, M. Poincaré became, in the eyes of the world, their man, if not their tool. It was they who in 1913 brought about his election as President of the Republic. And inevitably the Germans saw in his election a menace, almost a provocation.

The true cause of the War was that every one believed it to be inevitable; the election of M. Poincaré to the Presidency of the Republic was not unconnected with this belief. The Germans imagined themselves to be encircled. They took up arms to break the circle. The French thought they were threatened; they took up arms to nullify the threat. And thus, bit by bit, we came to the threshold of the War through the most tragic of mutual misunderstandings.

In July, 1914, M. Poincaré paid his visit to St. Petersburg. He has been blamed for this journey and for everything he said in the course of it. But what was it exactly that he said? He repeated merely in every possible tone of voice what he had always said: "France is not afraid of war." To the Tsar, to the Austro-Hungarian Ambassador, to the Serbian Minister, he repeated: "France will be faithful to her alliances." That seemed to him only natural. An alliance is a contract. How could one fail to honor it? But he did not realize that certain words, uttered at certain hours, acquire a special weight. He did not imagine that the trenchant nature of his utterances on board the Russian imperial yacht could draw from the lips of two Grand Duchesses the wistful reflection: "That's how an autocrat ought to talk!"

The War approached. M. Poincaré returned to Paris. He met with a tremendous reception. At that moment he incarnated France in the eyes of his countrymen. "Never have I witnessed a sight so moving," he himself wrote afterwards. "Never have I found it so difficult to remain unmoved. The grandeur, the simplicity, the enthusiasm, the solemnity—all helped to make of this welcome something unlooked for, unimaginable, and of infinite beauty."

Alas, this apotheosis was to be without a morrow. This man upon whose shoulders were to rest the responsibilities of the War, and who at that moment seemed the incarnation of France, was to become conscious of the isolation all around him throughout the five sad years that followed.

The President had no function to perform beyond going from time to time to the front or to the munition factories, and holding reviews of troops or distributing decorations. On these occasions he showed himself lacking in cordiality and address. In his own words, he forced himself to "remain unmoved." When standing beside the bedside of the *poilus*, he did not know how to express himself. His heart was too full for speech. And his costume—his cap and gaiters, which made him look like some wealthy family's chauffeur—aroused the derision of crowds endowed with a quick eye for absurdities.

The most serious reproach against him was that he withdrew to Bordeaux when the Germans were advancing. Nothing could be more unjust. The President did not wish to go. It was the military authorities who forced him to do so, in order that the head of the government might not fall into the hands of the Germans should they win the Battle of the Marne. The move to Bordeaux was a perfectly natural move and reflected in no way on M. Poincaré's courage. But the populace did not understand it—they got it into their heads that the President had fled before the enemy and for a long time they looked askance at him on this ground.

The Presidency of the French Republic, which calls above all for qualities of parade and pomp, did not offer adequate scope to the active mind of M. Poincaré. A man for whom idleness is a burden, he found he had almost nothing to do. His compatriots were dying before his eyes and he could not help. His ministers did not consult him much, least of all M. Clémenceau, who had no love for him. On one occasion, when M. Clémenceau remarked at a meeting of the Council of Ministers: "I have spent four days in solitude," M. Poincaré replied with a tone of bitterness in his voice: "My room was not so far away."

We must not, however, underestimate the influence that M. Poincaré was able to exert on the conduct of the War. He studied the state papers, he kept himself in touch with public matters, and intervened frequently at meetings of the Council of Ministers and of the War Cabinet. His intervention was sometimes decisive, but it became less efficacious after Clémenceau became Premier and especially during the Peace Conference. What little one knows of his interventions throws much light on his character. France had been drawn into the War by force of circumstances without having been able to insist on any promises from her allies. M. Poincaré, who believed only in the written word, was disquieted to note that no ally had committed itself to any promise that Alsace-Lorraine should be returned to France. It was he who inspired all the steps taken by French diplomacy to secure engagements to this effect, especially the letter addressed by M. Aristide Briand to the British government on the Allies' War Aims in January, 1917.

In the same way, during the Peace Conference, M. Poincaré insisted that the amount to be paid by the Germans should be definitely fixed and it was in agreement with him that Marshal Foch stipulated for territorial guarantees on the left bank of the Rhine. He brought into the settlement of these international questions the mind of a lawyer entrusted with the execution of a contested will.

This explains the seemingly contradictory attitude which

the President adopted later towards the Treaty of Versailles. He never concealed his disapproval of this Treaty. Nevertheless, in his policy towards Germany, M. Poincaré has taken his stand upon the Treaty as upon the Bible and has never allowed one iota of it to be touched. Even when it had been violated already in all its articles, he would not consent to the slightest revision of it. The fact is he considered the Treaty inadequate; it represented in his eyes the minimum of what France ought to have obtained and he would not allow Germany to use this minimum as a starting-point for concessions.

M. Poincaré's term as President ended in 1920. The French Parliament recorded formally that he had "bien mérité de la patrie." But this official approbation did not satisfy him. The President did not forget certain criticisms that had been passed upon him. He has devoted all his energies ever since to refuting them.

M. Poincaré—and this is yet another of the bourgeois traits in him—is very sensitive to hostile criticism. He has never forgiven those who at an earlier period criticized his marriage. Without knowledge of this, it would be difficult to understand certain incidents in the political life of France —certain enmities, certain quarrels, certain hatreds which are not explicable by any difference of views or ideas.

In the same way, M. Poincaré has never forgotten the accusation of having provoked the War. He has devoted four large volumes to refuting the little book of a young man who had repeated this accusation. "The memory of the responsibilities which he assumed," writes this young man, M. Fabre-Luce, "has created in Poincaré a sort of obsession. He tries to provide retrospectively the best possible excuse for an imprudent policy by representing Germany as a nation of prey; as she has committed so many crimes, we must now chastize

her. . . ." But the attacks for which he has been the target
in the German press have helped in no small degree to confirm
him in his feelings.

This uncompromising attitude, based upon the Treaty and
the memories of the past, brought M. Poincaré to power in
1922.

Of all the sections of the Treaty that which concerned
reparations was the worst formulated. Badly informed regarding the economic situation in Germany, the peace negotiators
thought her less exhausted than she was. They overestimated
the period of industrial prosperity which Europe would be
traversing after a war of four years; they did not foresee
what would happen—the financial crisis. Finally they did not
realize the technical impossibility of the transference from one
country to another sums of money of the magnitude specified
in the Treaty. Only the Americans saw things clearly, and they
were not listened to.

M. Poincaré is a jurist and not an economist. These difficulties, these impossibilities, escaped him. He learned later the
importance of the question of transference—when the question arose of paying France's debts to America. But at that
time he did not trouble himself over the matter. He had in his
hands a contract; he knew of nothing but this contract. If
Germany did not pay, it was because she was unwilling to pay.
If the mark was falling, this was because the Germans so
willed it. It was necessary to make Germany pay and to send
in the bailiffs.

M. Poincaré, who is a bourgeois, knows the French bourgeois. He knows how their minds work, for his own mind
works in the same way. The "bailiffs" idea was a huge success.
The whole of France was persuaded that if Germany did not
pay, Germany was to blame. And when M. Briand endeav-

ored at Cannes, at the beginning of 1922, to bring about a rapprochement with Germany and to settle the reparations question in a friendly way, he was swept away by a great wave of feeling which carried his antagonist M. Poincaré into power.

M. Poincaré did as he said he would do. He sent his bailiffs into Germany; the Ruhr was occupied. But the result was not what he expected. France continued to go unpaid; the mark dropped more and more; terrible feelings of bitterness grew up in the hearts of men and France found herself completely isolated in Europe.

The great mistake of M. Poincaré's policy at that moment was that it was not adapted to post-war needs. "Do you really believe," he once asked M. Briand, "that the French people can take any interest in the League of Nations?"

"The President of 1914," writes M. Fabre-Luce, "petrified, as Nietzsche would say, at the declarations of war, has retained all his old qualities. . . . But these gifts, which served him well in the days of secret diplomacy, did not suffice to solve the complex problems of the post-war period. In this new era, during which political ideas escaped out of the chancelleries and entered into open discussion in the market places and sought to move and to convince, a jurist counted for less. We see better now that mere intelligence is not always enough, if it be separated from the sources whence it takes its life: sympathy, tolerance, faith in the future of mankind. . . ."

We do not know if M. Poincaré has ever understood his mistake. Sunday after Sunday for two whole years, struggling against an invisible force—the force of reason, he has gone about in the provinces explaining the felony of Germany and the right behavior of France. Every Sunday he set himself to revive the memory of the dead, rekindling the embers of

RAYMOND POINCARÉ

LORD GREY OF FALLODON

hatred, reviving the war spirit. At last the French began to tire of this monotonous speechifying and of being universally held responsible for the ruin of Europe. In 1924, M. Poincaré was overthrown. Once more, his rôle seemed at an end. In France a politician is never finished with until he is dead. Two years had not passed before M. Poincaré reappeared as the savior of the country.

It often happens that the men who fail in their home policy succeed in their foreign policy and *vice versa*. After 1924, France contributed powerfully towards the bringing about of peace in Europe, but at home she saw classes divided, confidence shaken, the franc in danger. This nation of *rentiers* felt the breath of failure passing over her. She turned at once for the third time to M. Poincaré as the only man able to save her, the only man who really understood her needs.

M. Poincaré has said of himself that he has accomplished no miracle. That is true, but he has succeeded in being a good domestic economist in reuniting the country, in stabilizing the franc, in restoring confidence to an entire people. All the French bourgeois qualities of order and economy have reappeared in him. This has been the secret of his success and of his popularity.

After 1924, M. Poincaré would have left to history only the memory of his mistake and of his failure: the War and the Ruhr. Providence has been kind to him by allowing him to show his full powers and to leave behind him the renown of the man who saved his country from ruin and Europe perhaps from revolution.

His new rise to power gave M. Poincaré the opportunity to prove, in spite of his well-known stubbornness, that he was able to adapt himself to new circumstances. Up to this time, his foreign policy had been marked by a serious weakness. He had considered each question by itself without reckoning its international reverberations.

Of late he has learned, under the softening influence of M. Briand, that some victories cost more dearly than compromise, and that sometimes it is to the best interest of a nation to sacrifice its immediate advantage. It is thus that we see a Poincaré inclined towards an understanding with Germany and sincerely upholding by his authority, which is great, the policy of international good will of his Minister of Foreign Affairs.

It is by this trait that one may distinguish the great statesman: that after having long produced a division of minds, peace at last settles round them. M. Poincaré has been the incarnation of his race; he has always wished to be a link between all his countrymen. The national union, the cult of justice, have been the aim and source of all his actions. But it is only of late that he has been allowed to see a France united at last in respecting his name.

LORD GREY

IN ANY OTHER COUNTRY EDWARD GREY WOULD NEVER HAVE been a minister. To the outward observer there was nothing to suggest such a career for him; his one great passion, an absorbing love of nature, trees, animals and fishing, led him away from politics. Edward Grey was of a gentle and kindly disposition and a born country-man. He had been brought up in the country and "could not breathe in the town"; his only literary achievement is a book on fly-fishing. He admits, in his memoirs, that politics and public affairs never interested him; he was thrown into them by chance and always regarded his public life in the light of dull and disagreeable duties. He was not an orator and was always somewhat nervous when speaking in public. Just as the diary of Louis XVI records the word "Nothing" on days when there was no hunting, Edward Grey's diary refers only to week-ends. To him the events of the week were merely an accompaniment to the song of the birds in the beeches.

He was twenty-two years old, as he says of himself, when first, and in quite a modest way, he developed a taste for general ideas. At twenty-three he was a member of the House of Commons and a minister at thirty. What is the explanation of so strange a fate? It is that Edward Grey belonged to a dynasty. His grandfather had fought with Lord Melbourne, Russell and Palmerston in their political battles; his name was connected with the electoral bill of 1832. This was sufficient reason why, in a district where all the gentry were Tory, the young lord of Fallodon should be chosen by the Liberals; for the English like to follow their aristocracy.

The same reasons for which the Berwick-on-Tweed electors had sent Edward Grey to represent them in the House of Commons, caused Lord Rosebery to make him his parliamentary under-Secretary of State when he became Minister for Foreign Affairs in 1892. Grey was entirely unprepared for the profession that lay before him and was forced to learn it from the beginning and not without considerable effort. But he was one of those persons whose innate loyalty and lack of personal ideas form the ideal qualities for an assistant.

He must certainly have made a good impression at the Foreign Office since in 1905, when the Liberals returned to power, this time for a considerable period, Sir Henry Campbell-Bannerman made Edward Grey a Secretary of State and intrusted him with the foreign policy of the greatest empire in the world. A crushing burden for such weak shoulders.

One of Lord Grey's most marked characteristics was his modesty, but his comments upon his own weaknesses must not be taken too literally. According to him, Sir Henry Campbell-Bannerman's choice was entirely unfounded and Grey's own success in carrying out his high functions inexplicable. Nevertheless, it must be admitted, his writings do not give the impression of a quick, creative or original mind.

An Englishman related how one of his ancestors had been beheaded for plotting against the king: "Since then," he added, "my family has always been Whig." Lord Grey was always surprised that ideas, plans, projects and combinations should be attributed to him. He lived for one day at a time, following only the dictates of his own conscience; he sought for the best solution of every problem as each fresh set of circumstances arose. He played the game of politics as amateurs play chess; and since he was well endowed with the two fundamental qualities of the English people, common sense and a feeling for tradition, and since, at the Foreign Office, he was surrounded by the most capable advisers, he almost invariably acted for the best.

Among the Latin and Slav races there are nations that are collectively mediocre while producing outstanding individuals; among the Germanic and Anglo-Saxon races, on the contrary, the people in the mass frequently surpass their individual leaders. Great Britain is one of history's most extraordinary productions and her statesmen, in many cases, seem out of proportion to the great issues in which they are elements. Lord Grey is a striking example of such a statesman.

Pictet de Rochemont, the minister plenipotentiary of the Republic of Geneva at the Vienna Congress, once wrote that Lord Castlereagh annoyed him: "One needs to be very powerful if one is so stupid." It would be unjust to apply this remark literally to Sir Edward Grey, but it may truly be said that any deficiencies among Great Britain's public men are covered to a large extent by her greatness. He who speaks in the name of the British Empire need not himself be a great man, he must only be honorable and know how to carry out orders. It must be acknowledged in his favor that Edward Grey performed this duty perfectly.

England produces many types of statesmen. The demagogue, such as Lloyd George, is comparatively rare; the scholarly type, such as Asquith and Balfour, occurs more frequently; the most usual of all is the country gentleman, to which class Lord Grey belongs.

A country gentleman from the north of England cannot be expected to know geography and continental history. Countless anecdotes, more or less authentic, are told of Sir

Edward Grey, as of the majority of his predecessors. At the time of the Agadir crisis, there was a conference of British ministers and generals; one of the latter, when it was pointed out that the Germans might be tempted to go through Belgium or Holland, mentioned the Rhine. Sir Edward Grey interrupted him, saying, "But the Rhine is a German river." Asquith, the scholar of the Cabinet, had to explain. "Quite so, Sir Edward," he said, "the Rhine lives in Germany, but it is born in Switzerland and dies in Holland." Upon another occasion, Sir Edward Grey called an expert on Persian affairs into consultation. After an hour of somewhat confused conversation, the latter realized that the minister was confusing the Persian Gulf with the Red Sea. When some one who knew him intimately was asked if this could be true, the reply was, "Sir Edward's enemies may say all they like about his ignorance; only his friends know how deep it really is."

In any case this is of little importance. A British Secretary of State has enough people around him to correct his mistakes in geography. The vital thing is that he should have the authority that is based upon loyalty and a sense of the general interests and traditions of the empire. Sir Edward Grey had this authority in a very high degree. He did not know the world; when he went to Paris with King George, he took a childish delight in the uniform of the escort. But he had an intimate knowledge of Fallodon and Northumberland and would never have made the least mistake with regard to the instinctive reactions of his people and his country's needs. When he came into power in 1905, Edward Grey found the policy he was to follow well marked out for him. His predecessor, Lord Lansdowne, had already undermined the pro-German policy of the nineteenth century governments and although Edward Grey denies that he was influenced, consciously or subconsciously, by Edward VII, it would have been difficult for him to have opposed the King's sympathies or to have acted against the obvious interests of his country.

It has always been a tradition with Great Britain to prevent the strongest continental power from aspiring towards naval hegemony. So long as the land and maritime power are divided there is no danger that one country may dominate the world. The day upon which these two powers were united would be fatal to the freedom of the seas and to the British Empire. From the moment that Germany began to build a powerful fleet Anglo-German competition was, as it were, fated and inevitable. Edward Grey was not responsible for this policy, he was an instrument in carrying it out.

This policy cannot be criticized; no British statesmen could have followed any other. But, in some cases, it might have been applied with more foresight and logic.

While carrying out this new policy, imposed upon him by the force of circumstances, he still clung instinctively to the ideas of his predecessors, of those who had been his masters and guides. He carried out a policy of uniting with France and intervening on the continent with the mentality of those who, in the nineteenth century, had gloried in the splendid isolation of their country. And, what is more serious, he did not see the contradiction between these two attitudes. He was inadaptable in the full meaning of the word.

During the ten years preceding the War, Sir Edward Grey had only one idea, not to bind England, not to restrict her freedom of action and decision in whatever circumstances might arise. If Germany had been wise she would have endeavored to foster and encourage this tendency. Prince Lichnowsky realized this and one day obtained a letter from Sir Edward Grey in which he declared that England was not bound to France. This letter was a palliative, but the German press could have made much of it. Instead of accepting the declaration, the German government proposed, in London, a general engagement of neutrality, that is to say, one of those "commitments" of which Sir Edward Grey would hear nothing.

"I breathed again," said the French Ambassador, Paul Cambon, relating the incident, "when the reply arrived and took the opportunity of exchanging some letters with Edward Grey myself, letters that meant nothing alone but that would enable us, at any time, to start conversation on our common interests."

Sir Edward Grey's great mistake was not to see that the freedom of action he valued so highly, was deceptive, dangerous and, what is more, non-existent. It was deceptive in that a country is not only bound by treaties; it is far more tightly bound by its own interests. It was certain that in event of war between France and Germany, whatever the cause, it would be impossible that England should remain indifferent, and still more impossible that she should side with Germany. The destruction of France and the victory of a Germany bent on being mistress of the seas as well as of the land would have meant a terrible defeat for England, with or without hostilities.

This being so, it would have been wise to have secured this interest by treaties; for in the absence of any engagement there was the risk of feeding the illusion of British neutrality in Germany and of encouraging the German government to take chances.

England was, before the War, in more or less the same position as America is to-day. It is certain that if a country were to declare war, the United States could neither assist nor remain indifferent. By refusing to bind herself in advance, she encourages, without wishing to do so, the aggressive tendencies of certain countries and endangers the peace of the world and her own peace with it.

It was a terrible misfortune for Europe that Sir Edward Grey did not realize this soon enough. However, with regard to certain points, objective necessity was stronger than his desires. He was obliged to authorize staff conversations that, though not the equivalent of an alliance, nevertheless restricted freedom of appreciation in the House of Commons to a certain extent. He was, in particular, forced to agree to give France the guarantee that in case of war the British fleet would protect her seaboard so that she might concentrate her own fleet in the Mediterranean. Such an engagement very obviously implied participation in event of war.

Was Sir Edward Grey aware of this? It is not easy to answer this question. When the world crisis came, he clearly saw that England was in honor bound to help France. On the other hand, he solemnly declared, on August 3rd, 1914, in the House of Commons, that England was under no obligation whatever. He was not the man to play on words, but how, otherwise, is this contradiction to be explained?

Sir Edward Grey plainly saw that it was both England's duty and in her interests to fight with France. But he was held back by the fear of promising France and Russia more than he felt sure he could fulfill. The Cabinet was not in agreement with public opinion; he was afraid that he would not be supported, and he preferred to be overcautious rather than not cautious enough.

One of the Conservative leaders said, at the beginning of the War, "If we had been in office, we would have declared war two days earlier, but we should have had half the country against us." This is what Sir Edward Grey thought. It was not so very certain. There are many people who think if he had engaged the government it would have supported him and once pledged to the War the country would have followed. There might have been some trouble at the beginning but the first defeats would have brought unity.

Sir Edward Grey did not dare to take such terrible responsibility; he lacked courage and foresight. He was the tool of circumstances and missed the only remaining opportunity of stopping Germany and Europe at the edge of the abyss. But no one can say that by acting differently Sir Edward Grey might have prevented the War. It is difficult enough to understand history without trying to re-write it.

However, it is easy to point out two mistakes in British diplomacy at that serious time: the first was to believe that the situation could be handled by diplomacy, the second was to misjudge the relations between Germany and Austria.

During the Balkan war, the ambassadors in London had held a congress, under the presidency of the British Secretary of State, and satisfactory results were obtained by coördinating the action of the great powers. Sir Edward Grey was so proud of this result that he tended later to exaggerate its value. He thought that by this means he could, in no matter what circumstances, save the peace of Europe as he had done before. When he saw in 1914 that a fresh crisis was approaching, his one thought was to repeat what had been so successful the year before. Germany's refusal left him stranded and with no solution to offer. One may say that he gave up his attempts at mediation after the first failure and from that moment Sir Edward Grey resigned himself to watch, in despair, events that he could no longer control.

Sir Edward, who was a true gentleman, regarded the

ambassadors of the great powers in London with esteem and even as personal friends; he wrote himself that he had complete faith in Paul Cambon and that this was mutual. Prince Lichnowsky praises Sir Edward Grey very highly in his memoirs. His mistake was to suppose that this personal regard could have any real effect upon politics. Except in a very few cases ambassadors have little influence upon their governments. Sir Edward Grey had a wrong perspective of the European situation; he saw it through his friendship for the five or six men who represented the world in his eyes, but did not control it. Thus the success of the Ambassadors' Conference in 1913, far from being a blessing to Europe, became a curse.

Sir Edward was also mistaken with regard to the relations between Austria and Germany. From the obvious premise that Germany was stronger than Austria, he falsely deduced that decisions were made in Berlin and not in Vienna. He did not realize that Germany, wedged between France and Russia, could under no circumstances forsake her only ally, and that Austria, in spite of her weakness, could always go ahead and rely upon being supported. This is what happened in 1914. Bismarck's remark that "in every alliance there is a man and a horse" may well be applied to this situation. The horse may be the stronger but the man holds the reins.

Once Belgium was attacked all his scruples vanished. From that moment, Great Britain's moral duty and her interest made war inevitable; she had signed the treaty of 1839 and it was to her interest to prevent the Flanders coast from falling into the hands of a great power. The duty and the honor of explaining to the world, on August 3rd, 1914, why his country had unsheathed the sword fell upon Sir Edward Grey.

On that same evening Great Britain's declaration of war was sent to the German embassy in London. After it had been sent, the Foreign Office was advised that another formula should be employed. A fresh text was drawn up in haste to be delivered by the son of Sir Arthur Nicolson. When he arrived at the Embassy, he was told that Prince Lichnowsky was asleep—asleep at such a time! The young English diplomat could not believe it; he insisted and was finally ushered into the ambassador's presence. The prince was in bed, and the declaration of war lay on a table by the bed. The envelope had not been opened.

Sir Edward Grey, whose faith means much to him, has often asked himself "at about four o'clock in the morning, when vitality is lowest, and the spirit is depressed and a prey to doubt and anxiety" whether he had truly done his duty in these circumstances. Walter Page, the United States Ambassador, said in his letters to President Wilson that he had often seen the British Secretary of State, "worn out by insomnia, sometimes weeping or, on the contrary, fired with indignation, seeming confident and invincible." A man's conscience can reproach him only for what he would have been capable of doing. Sir Edward Grey could not have acted other than he did.

Lord Grey finally found the peace that his spirit needed in the contemplation of nature, that had always been his great passion: ". . . and waking or asleep the war is always present inside one. But the indifference of natural things, the beauty of them unaffected by our troubles, the seasons progressing as they did before the war, give a certain assurance that there are elemental and eternal things which human catastrophes, such as this war, cannot shake."

This conviction enabled him, better than any other statesman in Europe, to understand the message brought to him by

Colonel House, from President Wilson, in the summer of
1915. The two men understood and liked each other and this
doubtless greatly influenced the course of events. At that
moment nothing could be said with regard to the offer of
mediation from the United States, and Grey and House discussed the future. It was Grey, it appears, who most insisted
upon the necessity for a League of Nations.

This is what he wrote to the Colonel on August 10th, 1915:
"My own mind revolves more and more about the point that
the refusal of a Conference was the fatal step that decided
peace or war last year, and about the moral to be drawn from
it, which is that the pearl of great price, if it can be found,
would be some League of Nations that could be relied on to
insist that disputes between any two nations must be settled
by the arbitration, mediation or conference of others. International law has hitherto had no sanction. The lesson of this
war is that the powers must bind themselves to give it a
sanction. . . ."

Had Colonel House suggested this idea to him, or had he
thought of it himself, comparing his experiences of 1913 and
1914? No one knows. But this shows, in any case, that the
idea was in the air. Great discoveries are almost always made
simultaneously in several parts of the world. The League of
Nations had become so necessary that the thought of it had
impressed itself upon the minds of all those who were thinking for the future.

Lord Grey left the ministry at the same time as Asquith.
He retired to the country among his beech trees, his flowers
and his animals. He gave up his power without a shadow of
regret and never thought that the world would benefit by his
leadership. He thus resembled in his retirement the wise men
of Antiquity.

THE AGONY OF BELGIUM

CARDINAL MERCIER

CARDINAL MERCIER

THREE MEN MAY BE SAID TO REPRESENT BELGIUM IN THE
War: the King, Cardinal Mercier, and the Burgomaster of
Brussels. These men personified the three traditional forces of
the country: the State, the Church, the City. But the King was
at the head of the army in the part of the country which was
not occupied by the enemy and he was cut off from communication with his people, and Burgomaster Max was deported
into Germany almost at once.

So it was that throughout the greater part of the
war Cardinal Mercier stood out alone in the eyes of
the Belgians as the incarnation of their country and in the
eyes of the rest of the world as the incarnation of indomitable
resistance to the foe.

Désiré-Joseph Mercier belonged to one of those families
many of which were to be found in the ranks of the Belgian
bourgeoisie during the last century and a few of which still
exist—large families each of which includes among its members several priests and several nuns. He devoted himself to
the Church quite naturally, without effort, not under pressure
from a devout home circle, but by the inclination of a mind
drawn towards the faith. A good son, a good scholar, a good
priest, the Abbé Mercier became, while still a young man,
Professor of Philosophy at the Seminary of Malines. He distinguished himself there and when, at the request of Pope Leo
XIII, who wished to bring the philosophy of Saint Thomas
Aquinas back into esteem, a chair of Thomist instruction was

created at the Catholic University of Louvain, Monseigneur Mercier was appointed to it.

This position brought him before the eyes of the public and enabled him to enter into personal relations with the Pope. When the archiepiscopal see of Malines, the most important in Belgium, and one of the most considerable in the world, became vacant, he was called to it. The following year, 1907, he was made a Cardinal.

Monseigneur Mercier found in a nature richly and variously endowed the resources necessary for a task of a kind quite new to him. Until then he had been a thinker and a director of consciences, a philosopher and a professor. He was about to become a man of action and an administrator.

Down to this point, there was, indeed, nothing exceptional in such a career. In our time the higher ranks of the clergy comprise a large number of men of great merit. The Catholic Church knows the priests to whom it confides the supreme posts in its hierarchy; its choice is made from an immense number of individuals and there is no reason for surprise if it discovers those who are best fitted to govern souls. A great bishop, good, pious, active, Cardinal Mercier did not differ in anything from so many other bishops of the Roman hierarchy, equally active, pious and good.

It is the circumstances that create the hero and the saint. How many of those great bishops of the fourth and fifth centuries whom the Church has rightly canonized, men like Augustine, like Athanasius, like Ambrose, would have been merely humble priests in our time! It was the invasion of the barbarians that made of them the protectors of their cities, the refuges of the faithful. Such was the rôle to which Cardinal Mercier rose quite naturally in face of the German invasion of Belgium, and he deserves to take his place in the canons of the Church by the side of his great predecessors.

When the War broke out Cardinal Mercier was at Malines. But it was not long before he was called to Rome, to the Conclave at which Pope Benedict XV was elected. Despite the gravity of the circumstances, he did not hesitate as to his duty. A prince of the Church, it was to the Church he owed his first allegiance. He quitted Belgium the very day the Germans entered Brussels, the 20th of August, 1914.

When he returned to his diocese less than a month later Louvain and its library had been burnt down, the whole country was strewn with ruins, a prey to devastation and death. At first Cardinal Mercier said nothing. He suffered in silence; he made the round of his diocese, he visited the parishes which had suffered most severely, comforting the priests and the faithful. He was merely the shepherd of his flock.

But on returning to that somber bishopric of his at Malines, he reflected that he was also the primate of Belgium, the spiritual guide of a whole race, and the representative of outraged rights. It was then that in prayer and silence he composed that admirable pastoral letter of his of Christmas, 1914, which was to reveal his personality to Belgium and to the world.

"Belgium is bleeding," he wrote. "Her sons are falling by thousands in our forts, on our battlefields, in defense of their rights and of the integrity of their land. . . . Thousands of Belgian soldiers have been deported into the prisons of Germany, hundreds of innocent men have been shot. . . . But God will save Belgium, my brothers, you cannot doubt it. On the day of our final victory, we shall all share the glory!"

After these words of hope and faith, Cardinal Mercier admonished his people to obey the invaders, but he added:

"The power which has invaded our soil is not a legitimate authority. In the intimacy of your own minds, you owe it neither respect nor regard, nor obedience. The sole legitimate power in Belgium is that which appertains to our King, to his government, to the representatives of the nation. That power alone has a right to the affection of our hearts and to our submission—that power alone has authority over us."

These words were absolutely in agreement at once with the teachings of the Church and with international law; there was nothing revolutionary about them, they combined counsels of patience and of obedience with a reminder of principles. There was in them nothing of a nature to disquiet the German authorities. But the invaders' rule over Belgium was of such a kind that the letter had the effect of unheard-of daring in the eyes of Belgians and Germans alike.

For months past the population had not read a newspaper nor heard an outspoken speech. They had been living in an atmosphere of war with the menace of the death-penalty hanging over them for the most innocent acts. The men of the nation, those at least of them who could take up arms or get across the frontiers, were far away in the allied countries, and their families were without news of them. The protestations which, the whole world over, were making themselves heard against the violation of Belgium's neutrality and the atrocities which accompanied it, had not reached Belgium itself. The population of the country were feeling isolated and abandoned.

It was over this moral desert that the Cardinal's words resounded. They had the effect of a liberation. The congregations wept in the churches; people accosted each other in the streets: "Have you read the pastoral letter?" they asked. At

CARDINAL MERCIER

last, their country, mute for six months, had found a voice, and it was the voice of justice!

It was precisely this that disturbed the Germans. The Cardinal's letter had been taken by hand through the parishes, in the absence of a postal service, by the seminarists who were going home to their families on Christmas Eve. It was read aloud in its entirety in all the parishes of the diocese, and on the Sunday following in all those of the whole country. At once hundreds of parish priests were arrested. The Governor General sent an officer to the Cardinal to call upon him to withdraw his letter immediately. His Eminence refused and protested against the action of the Germans in prosecuting his priests for a deed of which he alone was the author. The matter rested there. But this incident had revealed to the Cardinal himself at once what he could do and what he should do.

It revealed to him, in the first place, what he owed to his people. His pastoral letters followed each other, a succession of them each year, each of them an event in the monotonous and dismal existence of the invaded country. "The sower," he wrote in September, 1915, "must await the harvest at its proper time; it will come and will not escape us. Do not let your courage sink! . . ." His letter of October, 1916, was entitled "The Voice of God"; that of February, 1917, "Courage, My Brethren!"; that of May, 1917, "Justice and Charity". Each one of them was an act.

These letters represent only a minor part of the activities of Cardinal Mercier. He alone retained the privilege of moving about Belgium, which came to be, as it were, clogged with military regulations. Of all the terrorized inhabitants he alone retained freedom of action. Therefore he made himself ubiquitous. He preached, he presided over ceremonies, he organized good works, he visited the unfortunate. This man, who by temperament was a thinker and an ascetic, was at every one's disposal. He neglected none of the duties of his high calling. On the contrary he multiplied them. Nor was this all. He alone could address the invaders as an equal to an equal, as one power to another. He did not fail to do so. His correspondence with the Governor Generals who succeeded each other at Brussels was unceasing. We find him protesting against their barbarities, making himself the interpreter of legitimate requests, stigmatizing the injustice of deportations.

In a letter to his colleague, the Archbishop of Cologne, he proposed to Germany the institution of an impartial tribunal to inquire into the atrocities that were being perpetrated. "I affirm," he wrote, "upon my oath that I have not down to the present been able to establish the reality of a single act of barbarity committed by a Belgian against a German soldier but that I know hundreds of cruel acts transgressing all the laws of civilization committed by German soldiers against innocent Belgians. Your Eminence will understand that patriotism and justice make it our duty to protest against these acts until they have been punished, and I may add that if you knew them as I know them the probity of your conscience would oblige you to add your protestations to ours."

At the same time the Cardinal was calming impatient spirits and doing what he could to prevent collisions. He was able to render some services and thus came to be in a position to ask some in return. It was he who at the suggestion of the German authorities addressed to the Kaiser the petition of which the latter was in need in order to be able to stop the deportations of Belgian workers to Germany. Face to face with Germany, the Cardinal was a power whose basis was moral and spiritual.

CARDINAL MERCIER

Cardinal Mercier could do anything because nothing could be done against him. The Church insures to its dignitaries such prestige that the civil power and, to an even greater degree, the military power, is disarmed against them. The Germans were able to shoot Miss Cavell, to deport Burgomaster Max, to take hostages, to massacre civilians, to burn down villages. Their fury stopped at the gates of the Archbishopric of Malines. They never dared to take the slightest measure against this man, who more than any other defied their authority.

The power of Cardinal Mercier found its source in his dignity as Archbishop and Cardinal, in the justice of his protestations, and in their moderation. But it went further back still—to the Pope himself. In 1916 the Sovereign Pontiff sent his portrait to the primate of Belgium with this inscription:

"Upon our venerated brother, Cardinal Mercier, We bestow with a full heart the apostolic benediction, assuring him that We take part in all his sorrows and tribulations and that his cause is also Our cause."

Would it have been possible after that for the Germans to take sanctions against the Cardinal without striking indirectly at the Pope?

The authority of Cardinal Mercier had in truth a yet higher source. It came from the universal Church with all its moral prestige which has always imposed itself upon even the non-Catholic peoples. Ever since the times when the great Popes of the Middle Ages rose up against the Emperor, this unarmed force has been more powerful than armies. It has been weak only at those periods when, forgetting its true nature and the source of its influence, it has entered into politics and levied troops. But that period has passed and the word of the Church in our epoch of feeble faith has an authority beyond discussion.

Finally the Cardinal was strong in the support of the universal conscience of mankind. His journey to Rome in 1916 was a veritable triumph. It was not without apprehension that his people had suffered him to go. It seemed when the Cardinal was no longer in Belgium that new dangers threatened the nation. The Belgians just then were like children traversing a wood at night, they dared not let go of the hand of their father. The Cardinal at that time was truly the father of his people. As long as he was there and could lift up his voice, it was felt the invader would shrink from new measures of oppression. But with him away, what might they not fear?

The journey, however, was to bear fruit. The Cardinal was the object of ovations without end; the crowds gathered wherever he passed; the statesmen of the Allied countries, assembled in conference at Rome, laid their homage at his feet; in his person Belgium was acclaimed along the entire length of his route. And it was this that enabled him on his return to assert solemnly: "The independence of our country is no longer in doubt."

Yes, wherever he went, in Switzerland and in Italy, Belgium was acclaimed; from France, from England, from Spain, he received the most thrilling testimonies of respect, of admiration, of worship, of the moral grandeur, the nobility of soul, the calm and resolute patience of the Belgian nation.

"Suppose," he exclaimed, "suppose that on the 4th of August, 1914, the Belgian people had not known how to die, suppose the youth of our country had fled at the sight of danger! Great God, where should we be now! And if you yourselves, wives and mothers, lamenting your husbands and your sons far off, perhaps lost to you forever—if you had not known how to wait for the providential hour and had clamored for a peace which would have been a truce merely and a lure, will you not admit that you would have tarnished the honor of our fatherland!"

Thenceforward, strong in the support he felt he had won on his journey, the Cardinal became more persistent, more direct, more energetic. Preaching in 1916 in the Cathedral of Sainte-Gudule in Brussels on the 21st of July, the day of the Belgian national festival, which was then a day of public mourning, he uttered this phrase: "Crime, whether emanating from an individual or from a collective body, should be repressed. The hour of our deliverance draws nigh."

These words at such a moment, in such a place, before an audience athirst for encouragement, caused a sensation so profound that, when the sermon was over, the organist, disobeying the military regulations and braving the anger of the authorities of the Occupation, gave forth the Belgian national hymn, "La Brabançonne." And the entire congregation, rising to their feet as though electrified, took up in chorus three separate times the heart-moving refrain: "Le Roi, la Loi, la Liberté!"

The Governor addressed to Cardinal Mercier a strong remonstrance: "This demonstration, incompatible with the state of occupation, had its source in Your Eminence." The Cardinal restricted himself to the answer: "I spoke as a Bishop and I uttered only words of charity and comfort." The Germans dared to do nothing.

And yet this man of power was a solitary man. The burden of a crushing responsibility lay upon his shoulders and he could not share it with any one. Each of his utterances had extraordinary effect; he was upholding the country's hopes, but he might, had he been lacking in prudence, have called forth impatience and perhaps revolt. Above all, being himself personally out of the reach of sanctions, he knew that every time he raised his voice he brought down sufferings on others. His parish priests were punished for his pastoral letter of Christmas, 1914; each of the subsequent letters had its painful sequels—prison or exile sometimes for the printers, for the brave fellows who carried the copies about, for the priests who read them in the churches. For a sensitive mind what could be more miserable than to be oneself immune while bringing down dangers upon one's friends? This was the misery which the Cardinal had to face if he was not to be reduced to silence.

In his own heart also he had difficulties to overcome. Cardinal Mercier, if he had no distaste for the pomps of the Church, was in himself a man simple and modest. The necessity now to be in the center of the stage, to take his place in the forefront, in the eyes of his own people and of the whole world, must have been a heavy burden to him.

He had to do violence to his feelings in yet another way. It was the force of circumstances that made him into a fighter; he was by nature a man of peace. All through his career his bent had been to soften differences, to tone down antagonisms. A Walloon Bishop of a Flemish diocese, both before and after the War, he was a promoter of national union in Belgium. He was, moreover, the inspirer of those Malines Conversations which have worked for a rapprochement between the Churches. And even during the War, what gave to his words so much force and authority was that they were truly Christian and had no bellicose ring about them.

Mr. Brand Whitlock, who was United States Minister at Brussels during the invasion and who has written the best book of memoirs covering this period, thus describes a visit paid to him by the Cardinal:

"He entered, advanced, tall and strong and spare, in the long black soutane with the red piping and the sash, not with the stately, measured pace that one associates with the red hat, but with long quick strides, kicking out with impatience the skirt of his soutane before him as he walked, as though it impeded his movements. He was impressive in his great height and he bent slightly forward with an effect of swooping on, like an avenging justice. But his hand was outheld, and in his mobile countenance and kindly eyes there was a smile, as of sweetness and light, that illumined the long lean visage. . . .

"His hands were large and powerful and of the weathered aspect of his face. It was a countenance full of serene light, with little of the typically ecclesiastical about it: a high brow, a long nose, lean cheeks, strong jaw, and a large mobile mouth, humorous and sensitive—the mouth of the orator, with thin lips that could close in impenetrable silence. The eyes were blue, and they twinkled with a lively intelligence and kindly humor. Perhaps I could do no better, in the effort to give some impression of him, than to say that had it not been for those touches of red in his black garb he would have recalled some tall, gaunt, simple, affectionate Irish priest, whose life was passed in obscure toil among the poor, in humble homes, amid lowly lives whose every care and preoccupation he knew and sympathized with, going about at night alone in all weathers, unsparing of himself, visiting the sick and the imprisoned, forgetting to eat, accustomed to long, weary vigils, and of an independence that needed none of the reliances or approvals of this earth.

"There was something primal, original about him, a man out of the people, yet above them—one of those rare and lofty personalities who give the common man hope because they are like him and yet better, greater than he, who create in him new aspirations and higher hopes because they demonstrate in their sufficient selves what a common man may become if only he have the will by devotion, by abnegation, by sacrifice, and by love. In his mere presence one felt all little things shrivel up, and wondered why small annoyances should fret and irritate; and when he had gone, the impalpable influences of his lofty spirit hung for hours about one in the air. He was the incarnation of the principle that is the antithesis of that upon which the nation that had overrun his country is founded, and because of this, all its armies and all its guns and bayonets and Kommandanturs were powerless; its minions, who had not hesitated to destroy whole cities and communities, did not dare even so much as to touch a hair of his head. Ultimate history, written at that hour when mankind shall have emerged out of the darkness and savagery of these times into the light of those better days that must come if there is any meaning of order in the universe, will celebrate the astonishing coincidence that, in the little nation which the most ruthless power of all times chose as the first and most tragic of its many victims, there was a man whose personality, alone and of itself, proved the superiority of moral over physical force."

The Pope said to Cardinal Mercier: "You have saved the Church!" Nothing could be truer. For the universal Church, torn between enemy peoples, remained strangely silent throughout these years. The Pope could take no part without shocking a great portion of his faithful and tearing the Church in twain. He was paralyzed by the extent of his responsibilities. But it is fortunate for the moral authority of the Church that one of its highest dignitaries was to be found ready to protest against injustice and to speak in the name of Right. It was Cardinal Mercier who in that time of sorrow made the Catholic Churches an asylum for the harassed people.

In thus saving the Church, the Cardinal proved faithful to his mission—his mission of personifying his country. Without him Belgium would have remained mute in the War. The world would not have known its feelings and might have misinterpreted them—might have doubted whether the souls of the people had risen to the height of the circumstances. Without such a leader, indeed, the people might have wavered. Their protestations might at the start have been unanimous, but lassitude and discouragement might have gained ground. Belgium might never have become in the eyes of the world such a symbol of fidelity and heroism.

The Germans themselves saw this and it was to the Cardinal that in October, 1918, the Governor General conveyed the first official notification of the impending retreat of the army: "In our eyes you are the incarnation of occupied Belgium, of which you are the venerated pastor, to whom all your compatriots listen." Could one imagine a tribute more unlooked for, more honorable and more amply deserved?

In saving his people, the Cardinal did more. He laid the foundation for the New City which must be built upon patriotism, justice and faith. A man of war from love of peace, Cardinal Mercier at a cruel hour stood out as the incarnation of his country, of invincible justice and of faith in God.

THE NEW ALLIES

BARON SONNINO

VENIZELOS

JON BRATIANO

BARON SONNINO

BARON SONNINO WAS AN EXTRAORDINARILY COMPLEX PER-
sonality—Italian on his father's side, English on his mother's,
a Protestant by religion, yet somewhat of a Jew by blood.
His loyalty, his intellectual integrity, his culture, his personal
disinterestedness were never called in question. All that was
wanted to make him a real statesman was a touch of political
insight.

But Baron Sonnino was no politician; he set no store on
popularity—in fact he despised it. He set no store on power.
For twenty years Giolitti governed Italy as Bratiano governed
Rumania. When he grew tired of it, he could call upon one of
his opponents, a Luzzatti, a Sonnino, a Salandra, to take his
place for the moment. After a few months he would then overthrow that government and take up the reins of power again.
It was by such precarious tenure that Baron Sonnino twice
governed Italy for ninety days, but he never had the chance
of putting his ideas into practice and showing the stuff he was
made of.

He was a liberal in politics and an aristocrat by nature.
He hated the crowd. He was a fine scholar, an ardent student
of Dante, and he was happiest in his library, round which
there ran this proud motto, the keystone of his life's philosophy: "Quod aliis licet, non tibi!" ("What others may do,
you must not!")

Baron Sonnino was not in Rome when the Great War
broke out, but he returned at once, and his friends met him at

the station with the words "Italy has declared her neutrality." Sonnino threw up his hands in despair—"We are dishonored," he exclaimed. That was the sort of man he was. Not, as was alleged, a Germanophile or a zealot for the Triple Alliance—that has been completely disproved by subsequent events—but a man who honored all treaties and written pledges with a loyalty so scrupulous that it sometimes became shortsighted. It dictated his actions during the early days of August, 1914, and later, at the Peace Conference, was the basis of his advocacy of the application of the Treaty of London.

Seldom has a statesman been put in so difficult a position as Signor Salandra, the Italian President of the Council, when the War broke out. He was at the mercy of the Parliamentary majority which Signor Giolitti commanded, the army was totally unprepared, Austria and Germany both accused the Italian government of treachery, and Signor Salandra, who appreciated how necessary it was for Italy to come in on the side of the Allies, found ranged against him a large section of the people, comprising the Catholics, the Socialists and the Freemasons.

When Signor San-Giuliano, the Foreign Minister, died in October, 1914, Signor Salandra was faced with the difficult problem of finding a successor. Most of the men who were qualified for the office were committed to Signor Giolitti and were sworn partisans of neutrality. Signor Salandra could appeal to none of these for help in bringing his country into the War. He had to have a man gifted with political acumen in whom he could put his whole trust, and who would inspire an equal trust in the country.

In these circumstances Signor Salandra turned to Baron

Sonnino, who was an old friend and held political views similar to his own.

The only difficulty was that, at the time, Sonnino was opposed to his foreign policy. Hostile to neutrality, he was still more hostile to the War. His aim was by diplomacy to obtain from Austria the realization of Italy's national aspirations, and especially the unconditional cession of the Trentino. Signor Salandra gave him his confidence, trusting in his loyalty, and knowing that if eventually he did not come round to his point of view he would go.

The upshot was that Baron Sonnino found himself intrusted with the historic negotiations which were to end either in bringing Italy into the War or keeping her definitely out of it. It is well known that Germany sent Prince von Bülow specially to Rome to be intermediary between Italy and Austria. He failed. "Silence is not the outstanding characteristic of this nation," he said, "but it was my misfortune to strike the one Italian who did not talk."

Baron Sonnino was indeed no talker. His compatriots nicknamed him "the Taciturn." During the negotiations he listened to his visitor, and when he felt that no useful purpose could be served by the conversation he simply did not answer, and the interview degenerated into a monologue.

Baron Sonnino saw very soon that there was nothing to be expected from Austria. That country had no desire to pay for the neutrality of Italy and reward what she looked upon as treachery. Nor had she any desire voluntarily to dismember herself and encroach upon the very territorial integrity that she was at the moment defending by force of arms. But the frontier adjustment that she did offer, the *parecchio*, the small concessions that Signor Giolitti was prepared to accept, were to enable Baron Sonnino to obtain large concessions from the Allies. For if the Central Powers would give Italy something to remain neutral, what would the Allies not give her to enter the War on their side?

It was thought at the time that the intervention of Italy would end the War, and no price was too high for such a result. Besides, Italy's price was the annexation of enemy territory, and why should the Allies be niggardly over that?

What Baron Sonnino did not see, and never even suspected, was that this war was not the same as other wars and that it was above all a conflict of moral values. Perhaps at that time his colleagues, the Allied foreign ministers, did not see it any more than he did, in spite of all their protestations. Devoid of imagination, one and all, they could not believe that the future would be different from the past. In all the previous wars—even the Balkan war of 1912—countries had found themselves in difficulties because they had not sufficiently specified their claims in advance. Baron Sonnino took this lesson so literally that he was too specific in his claims.

Imbued with the spirit of the old diplomacy he felt that he would be failing in his duty to his country if he did not obtain for her every possible aggrandizement. In his eyes the War was nothing more than a question of the balance of power, and he thought that when the other allies were enlarging their territories Italy, to preserve her relative position, should expand as much or even more.

Then Baron Sonnino made the great mistake of his career. He was lacking in that spirit of moderation which is the first essential in a statesman. In the name of the right of nationality Italy claimed the Trentino and Trieste. That was clear and logical, and if Baron Sonnino had stopped there he would have had the moral support of all the Allies and of a great part of the people of Austria-Hungary, and the power of the

JON BRATIANO   BARON SONNINO

Italian Army would have been increased tenfold. But Baron Sonnino then embroiled himself in questions of military safeguards and balance of naval power, questions which were incompatible with the principles for which the Allies were fighting. That was how he got promises regarding the Tyrol and Dalmatia, which were territories whose population was German or Slav, and which recoiled with horror from the idea of annexation by Italy. All this strengthened the morale of the Austrian army against which his own soldiers had to fight.

This error of judgment had serious consequences for Italy. Her policy, instead of being clear, definite and logical, became involved in a series of paralyzing inconsistencies. The Treaty of London might be justified if the new Europe was to be like the pre-war Europe; Austria-Hungary, although beaten to the point of accepting the harshest conditions, was not to be allowed to break up; Russia was not to be so victorious that she could take Serbia under her wing or get a footing in the Adriatic; Germany, although beaten, was to remain a counterbalance to the power of France; Serbia, although victorious, was not to claim Austro-Hungarian territory; Greece was to keep out of the War and not to seek aggrandizement in Asia Minor. In a word, things were to remain exactly in the position most favorable to Italy; or rather, to put it a better way, the easy working of the Treaty of London postulated that Italy would have to emerge the only victor from the War! It is really surprising that a man of such penetration as Baron Sonnino should not have seen how precarious and artificial his position was.

Or rather he *did* see it, and that is what explains his war policy. First of all, his fear of publicity. He knew that his treaty would not bear any public discussion which proceeded on the principles in the name of which the Allies boasted they had taken up arms. So he resolutely maintained that the Treaty of London must remain secret, and he would not have it officially communicated to the Serbs. It was the Bolsheviks who were good enough to publish it for him. He would not even take part in diplomatic conversations on the Treaty, for to his mind it was inviolate and beyond all discussion.

With much more reason he set himself against all *pourparlers* with the Emperor Charles, who was in such straits that he was prepared to give the fullest satisfaction to Italy's national aspirations. But it was obvious to Rome that if a separate peace were concluded with Austria she could not be asked to cede German or Slav territory. It was not for the districts inhabited by Italians, the Trentino and Trieste, that Italy fought so long, it was for the Brenner and Dalmatia. This explains the vehemence with which the Italian delegation pushed their claims at the Peace Conference.

But although Baron Sonnino set his face against a separate peace with Austria, he was equally opposed to the nationalist movements which were working for her disruption, for he knew that if these movements succeeded the Italian claims to Slav territory would come up against insurmountable opposition. This was why he was opposed to the Congress of Rome which Signor Orlando favored against the wishes of his Foreign Minister, and this was why, by analogous reasoning, he opposed the claims of Poland.

In law the position of the Italian government was unimpeachable. As the inducement for Italian intervention in the War, the Allies had made Italy certain promises, and these promises should now be redeemed. But in equity her attitude was less justifiable, and from a political point of view indefensible. This territorial greed not only deprived Italy of almost all the moral credit she might have drawn from a war waged for the rights of nationalities, but also gave rise to grave misunderstandings between the Allies.

Baron Sonnino was in power throughout the War. He seemed to his compatriots to be the right man in the right place. It was to him personally that the Allies had pledged themselves, and he alone had the authority to see that they fulfilled their pledges. One might well believe that if Sonnino fell his treaty would fall with him. It was thus imperative that Baron Sonnino should be the Italian plenipotentiary at the Peace Conference. That is why Signor Orlando did not dare to dissociate himself from his policy, although he disagreed with it. The onus that would rest on the man who overthrew Sonnino would be staggering, for he would have to carry on his shoulders the sole responsibility for the Peace.

Baron Sonnino arrived at Paris with a threefold handicap —his conscience, his delegation and his Treaty.

First of all his conscience. He had taken upon himself the most terrifying personal and national responsibilities, and several times he reminded the Conference of it:

"You others," he said to his colleagues, "who have been attacked or provoked, you have had no choice but to go to war. No one can reproach you with it, but I am in a different case. Impelled by no such necessity, I have involved my countrymen in a ghastly war by making them specific promises. I have on my conscience six hundred thousand Italian lives, and what shall I say to my people if I fail to keep these promises?" And then he added, with a shudder, "I am a criminal!"

These words, spoken in all sincerity, undoubtedly made a great impression on President Wilson, and probably secured the Brenner Pass for Italy, but they also prevented Signor Sonnino from being an agile and adroit negotiator, an artificer of the New Europe.

He was further handicapped by the divergence of views that showed itself within the Italian delegation and also in the country. His idea was to hold fast to the Treaty of London and demand its application pure and simple. To gain that point he was naturally foreclosed from any other claim. Now, Signor Orlando, President of the Council, had neither eyes nor thoughts for anything save Fiume.

The Treaty of London was based on the assumption that Austria-Hungary would remain a power; no one had dared to take away Hungary's only maritime outlet. To ask for Fiume was thus to go beyond the scope of the Treaty, to recognize that circumstances had changed, and thus to preclude any possible claim to Dalmatia. Baron Sonnino was well aware that Signor Orlando was damning his policy by introducing this inconsistency into it. But he succeeded neither in converting Signor Orlando, who was more interested in Fiume than in Dalmatia, nor Signor Tittoni, who wanted neither the one nor the other. That is partly the reason for the creation of the Council of Four. Signor Orlando wished to be rid of Baron Sonnino and found ready support in President Wilson, who was embarrassed by Mr. Lansing, and in M. Clémenceau, who found M. Pichon troublesome. From that moment Italy was represented by Signor Orlando alone.

Signor Orlando was clever, but he was variable, weak and sentimental, and given to weeping. With tears in his voice he would make touching speeches to his colleagues on the "Italianity" of Fiume, only to succeed in irritating them and supplying them with arguments against the Treaty of London.

The Italian delegation to the Peace Conference gradually slipped into the rôle of Oliver Twist. Italy had entered the War freely and voluntarily, for the realization of a national ideal which was in perfect accord with those of the Allies;

she had rendered them great service and had fought heroically. In the peace as in the War, she could have held an outstanding position. This, however, was not to be, because instead of taking her stand on the rights of nationality, instead of invoking President Wilson's Fourteen Points, instead of collaborating wholeheartedly in the establishment of a just and lasting peace, the Italian delegation concentrated its efforts upon the strict execution of a Treaty which practically the whole world recognized as fundamentally unjust.

Was the Treaty still valid and did it morally bind the Allies? That was the first question which the Conference had to answer. The Italians contended that as they had carried out their engagements they were entitled to look for the promised rewards. But President Wilson was not a signatory to the Treaty of London, which was indeed in conflict with his principles. Moreover, Italy had obtained the Treaty on the grounds that she must have strong frontiers against Austria-Hungary, and protection against the dangers of Russia establishing naval bases on the eastern coast of the Adriatic. But now Austria and Russia had ceased to exist as great powers.

It must be admitted that Italy had a case. She had turned down the Austrian overtures in 1915. She had lost six hundred thousand men, she had seen two of her fairest provinces laid waste, and now after four years of sacrifice she was almost brought back by virtue of the principle of nationality to the *parecchio* which she could have got by remaining neutral.

A story was told at that time of a father whose son, an Italian aviator, had been killed in an air combat during the last days of the War. After the Armistice he visited the scene of the combat and there found his son's victorious adversary, an Austrian officer who now sported the Jugo-Slav colors in his button-hole and held out his hand with the words "We are allies now!"

That story illustrates how the Italians felt towards the Jugo-Slavs. In the Lombardy country the old people who remember the Austrian régime still call their former oppressors "Croats". It was hard to have to regard as friends the enemies they had fought so fiercely for four years from trench to trench.

But if it was natural for the people to have such feelings, the duty of the government surely was to educate them past these sentimental considerations to conceptions of higher policy.

That is just what the government did not do. The Italian delegates refused to recognize the Jugo-Slavs as Allies. They refused to sit with them in committee, and would not even shake hands with them. On the eve of the Armistice Baron Sonnino had arrested on Italian soil the Jugo-Slav representatives who had come to hand over the Austrian fleet: and its finest unit, the *Viribus Unitis*, was sunk by the Italians while still in Jugo-Slav hands. It was in truth an act of war.

From the very beginning of the Conference, therefore, the Italian delegates found themselves in open conflict with the Serbs, and, what was more serious, with the Americans. They were thus driven to countenance and support all those who at the Conference were claiming more than their due. They pushed France to the Rhine, Poland to Danzig, Rumania to the Banat, in order to create precedents which they could invoke later, and in order to render services which they could be sure of turning to account. When the Council of Four was considering problems that affected Signor Orlando and Baron Sonnino, the two Italians almost invariably pressed for a solution which was most inimical to peace. They could all do whatever they liked, provided always that they did what Italy wanted!

It has been said that at Paris Baron Sonnino carried out simultaneously the policies of Metternich and Machiavelli. That is too sweeping—he contented himself with Metternich. He had law and logic on his side, but the logic was cast-iron. He was a jurist of the same type as M. Poincaré. All his law was written law and the law of contractual obligations. Once beyond these and he was out of his depth. Baron Sonnino was out for the Treaty and for nothing else.

The question has often been asked, why did Italy get no share of the German colonies along with the great powers? The answer is simple. Baron Sonnino was afraid that if he accepted the slightest thing outside the Treaty of London, that would give the Allies an excuse to demand a *quid pro quo* and reopen discussion on the Treaty. From that standpoint he never moved an inch. He asked for nothing more than had been promised him in 1915, and it was not of him, but of Signor Boselli, that M. Briand could say during the Inter-Allied Conference—"If this goes on, I'll get away with nothing but the seat of my pants!"

And it was not he, but Signor Orlando, who at the Peace Conference laid claim to Fiume on the one hand by invoking Wilsonian principles, and to Dalmatia on the other by taking his stand on the text of the Treaty of London.

This was what in April, 1919, precipitated the fateful crisis of the Peace Conference.

President Wilson had gone to Rome to try to convince the Italian people over the heads of their delegates. He had failed and had come back very displeased. Various incidents had combined to upset him still more when on April 22nd he suddenly learned that the Italian government was getting ready to proclaim the annexation of Fiume. There was no time to lose, and he published his famous declaration at once. Signor Orlando made an impassioned reply and decided to return to Rome, partly for reasons of domestic politics and partly to exert pressure on President Wilson. Rome gave him an enthusiastic welcome and the U. S. Embassy had to be put under military protection.

Signor Orlando's idea was that the departure of his delegation from Paris would prevent the Allies from concluding peace with Germany. Baron Sonnino never approved of this policy, which he characterized as that of "the servant who trundles her trunks into the hall." But he yielded eventually to Signor Orlando's urgent representations and the delegation left Paris.

This move did not have the intended result. The Allies were exasperated with the Italian delegates. After one of the meetings where the British, American and French had been present, Mr. Seton-Watson, who was reputed to be implacably hostile to the Italian policy, said with astonishment, "I was the only one to say a good word for Italy!"

The Supreme Council—in Signor Orlando's absence the Council of Three—came to the conclusion that as the Italians had taken part in the drafting of the Treaty, their absence need not postpone its being communicated to the Germans. It was in vain that Baron Sonnino tried to make out that this was a breach of the agreement between the Allies that they would make no separate peace, and the Italian government, appreciating the fact that the absent are always in the wrong, decided to send back the delegation in haste to Paris.

Naturally this episode did nothing to increase the prestige of Signor Orlando or Baron Sonnino. For, although the latter had had nothing to do with the decision to return to Rome, public opinion, which is incapable of drawing fine distinctions, held the Foreign Minister responsible. The result was that, as often happens, Baron Sonnino, who had made so many mistakes, found himself blamed for one which was not his.

"We have the whole Chamber with us," said a member of the Italian government, "but in a week we shall be out of office." His prophecy came true. Immediately after the Peace Treaty was signed Signor Orlando was disowned by a Chamber which would not even listen to him. Baron Sonnino fell with him.

True to his character, Baron Sonnino maintained his attitude of silence throughout his retirement and to the moment of his death. He put forward no attempt at personal vindication, he gave no explanation of his conduct, he offered no *pro domo* defense. He despised the abuse of the mob just as he had despised its plaudits.

Two lessons, both of them melancholy, may be learned from this story. The first is that it takes more than an upright conscience to make a great statesman. Baron Sonnino on his death-bed could say with truth that he had served his country wherever his conscience would let him. His patriotism and his honesty were above suspicion. More than once, for love of country, he had submitted to opinions which he did not share, and the tragedy was that a man with a will and a definite policy could carry into effect neither the one nor the other.

But when all is said and done, it must be admitted that Baron Sonnino has probably done his country more harm than good. For he failed to understand the spirit of his age, and, in the name of Italy, and in the days of President Wilson, he tried to carry out the Bismarckian policy which brought Germany to her ruin.

The second lesson which is to be learned from all this is

that nations do not always understand the causes of the fortune and misfortune which is their lot. For the Italians, instead of blaming Baron Sonnino for his reliance on force, his contempt for principles, and his fetish of the balance of power, have reproached him with too much weakness and moderation. From his failure they have not learned the lesson that they should adopt a policy different from his, but believe that they must follow the same policy, only with greater force and better results.

And that perhaps shows that Baron Sonnino was the sport of fate, and that what he did he could not have done otherwise.

VENIZELOS

SOME YEARS BEFORE THE WAR AN ENGLISH DIPLOMAT AT
Constantinople asked a friend to name the greatest statesman
of the day. His friend mentioned several well-known names—
Poincaré, Grey—but it was none of these. At last, the Englishman confided: "It's a young man. He lives in Crete. But I
can't remember his name!"

At that time M. Venizelos was a member of the revolutionary government of his native island, which had revolted
against the domination of the Sultan. It was in that capacity
that he came into touch with the consuls of the great powers
at Canea, and addressed notes to them which they in turn
transmitted to their respective governments. In this way the
word was passed round the various chancellories that somewhere in the South there was an outstanding man with the
political sense of a Pericles and the eloquence of a
Demosthenes.

He was known in Athens too. Greece at that time was a
country of barely two million inhabitants, with its government in the hands of a few powerful but rival families. How
could this country on which the Turks had just inflicted a
crushing defeat, take the helping hand stretched out to it by
the island rebels? How could it dream of retaliating when its
government, preoccupied with domestic squabbles, gave in to
the powers, and cringed to Turkey?

But in the universities and the army, among the youth of
the land, there was being born a new hope and a new discon-

tent. Their love for freedom and the traditions of their country made them suffer acutely under defeat. It was the call to nationalism. One day in 1909, the Military League was formed. At the mere sight of it the government fell, the League took control, and chose as its head Eleutheros Venizelos, come post haste from Crete.

This man, who in one day was called upon to take charge of another nation's destiny, had three fundamental characteristics: he was honest, he was an optimist, and he was a liberal.

His honesty could be read in his eyes, clear as a child's. In the course of his career he has proved it many a time. During the War it was his honesty that rebelled when his government refused to come to the aid of Serbia under the pretext that the alliance only held good in connection with Balkan affairs. Venizelos knew that this was not true, for he had been the author of the treaty, and he refused to lend his name to what he considered an "infamy." At the elections of 1915 he declared that his policy would be towards immediate intervention on the side of the Allies, and when some one remarked to him that it might have been politic to leave that point vague, Venizelos answered hotly, "I would never want any Greek to be able to confront me and say that I had deceived him or won his vote on false pretences."

Later still, when he was rebuked for his bad choice of friends—a failing which was eventually to lead him to his fall—his reply was: "They have left everything and risked everything to follow me to Salonika. I could not desert them now."

Besides being a faithful friend, he was an optimist. His optimism has been the cause of all his big achievements and of not a few of his mistakes. When he was still in Crete, an unknown, powerless subject of Turkey, he astonished those who met him by the assurance with which he spoke of the union of Crete with Greece. It was the vision he already had of the expansion of Greece which enabled him to make it a reality. Nothing great can be done in this world without optimism.

From the beginning of the World War he never for a moment wavered in his belief in the victory of the Allies. "We must make up our minds to intervene at once," he said to the Cabinet in 1914, "for in three weeks the Allies will be in Berlin." He maintained that confident attitude in spite of all reverses, and it more than once led him into an error of judgment. For, convinced as he was that Allied victory was imminent, M. Venizelos lived in perpetual fear that Greece would come in too late and that the Allies would be victorious without her.

His optimism was again evident at the Peace Conference. No task seemed to be beyond the resources of his country. Without the flicker of an eyelid he took the risk of the Asia Minor gamble from which all competent observers tried to dissuade him. He would have tackled Constantinople itself, if the powers had asked him!

Finally, besides being an optimist, he was also a liberal. The term is somewhat surprising when one remembers that M. Venizelos has been responsible for seven revolutions in his lifetime. The figure is his and should be correct.

In Crete he headed several revolutions against Turkey. He arrives in Greece and straightway finds himself at the head of a Military League which overthrows the constitution. The war breaks out, and on his dismissal by King Constantine, he organizes a revolutionary government at Salonika. Still another revolution was needed in Athens before he could reenter the capital. The elections drove him out again and he was recalled as a result of a new *coup d'État*.

But it is not by temperament that M. Venizelos has been a revolutionary during his whole career; it is rather by the force of circumstances and the turn of events. In his heart he has always been for law and order. In the autumn of 1915, when he was rudely dismissed by the King, a foreign diplomat hastened to his house and found him there with some of his supporters, dejected and forlorn. "This is rank treachery," he exclaimed. "Your place is in the Chamber. You must defend yourself."

But Venizelos refused, with the remark, "It is not power that I hold to—I despise it. All I hold to are my convictions."

When, on the day after the Peace Conference, a fanatic shot at him in the Gare de Lyon at Paris, Venizelos was holding in his hand a little book entitled "Small History of English Liberalism." It was his breviary.

After the War he was an all-powerful dictator. He could do what he wanted in Greece, and the continuance of that power seemed to rest entirely with him. But he had had no respite in which to prepare for the elections and put his power on a constitutional basis. Blinded by his optimism, he could not see that these elections would prove disastrous to him. By very reason of his revolutionary career Venizelos had to exert himself more than any other to prove to the people that he was not merely destructive, but that he was a statesman.

A statesman he has always been. When he arrived in Greece that first time, carried on a wave of national feeling, he exercised moderation in his dealings with Turkey, reassured the powers, and himself advised the deputies elected from Crete (which did not yet belong to Greece) not to take their places in the Chamber, in order to avoid raising international

VENIZELOS

issues for which Greece was not yet prepared. In that way he gave himself time to organize the army and set on its feet the Balkan League, which was to give the signal for war by driving the Turks from nearly all their European possessions. When the Balkan allies began to quarrel among themselves over the partition of the conquered territory, he worked more than any other man to establish the Greco-Serb alliance and crush the Bulgarians.

When the World War broke out, the reaction in Greece was unanimous. That country, maritime and open to easy attack, was wholly at the mercy of England. Even before the Battle of the Marne, the Greek government had made an official offer of coöperation to the Allies. The Allies thanked them but refused their aid. Turkey and Bulgaria were neutral; every one believed that the war would be over quickly, and Greece could not bring any additional help to the Allied cause —quite the contrary.

When Turkey entered the War, however, the situation was changed; the help of Greece had now become valuable, and it was asked for several times. But from that moment a fundamental difference of opinion between M. Venizelos and the King began to show itself.

King Constantine believed in the victory of Germany, in the word of William II, and in the divine right of kings. He wanted to be the Kaiser of Greece. He had defeated the Bulgarians because they were exhausted, but he believed that another war with them was inevitable, and he wished to keep his army fresh for the struggle.

Actuated by the same motives, Venizelos bestirred himself in quite the opposite direction. "Greece," he said to me later in a conversation I had with him in Paris, "entered the war to escape the dishonor of having violated her treaty. She entered it at the worst possible moment, yet I do not regret it. Better that Greece should be beaten along with the Allies—which I cannot for one moment believe—than that she should remain neutral and be beaten alone in a few years by a greater Bulgaria. Besides, it is unthinkable to me that an autocracy, however perfect, should win a lasting victory over democracy."

Venizelos was anxious for the victory of democracy, because his liberalism urged him to make autocratic government impossible for Constantine. Moreover, he believed that England would win. To some one who predicted a German victory he answered: "Germany will win when England has lost her last ship." He understood, too, that France and England, even if beaten, could not be kept out of the Mediterranean, and that they would continue to have Greece at their mercy. For the Greeks, therefore, it was better to be beaten with the Allies than to conquer with the Germans.

To appreciate the full extent of the clash of policy between the King and his minister, one must bear in mind the fact that in modern as in ancient Greece politics are neither domestic nor foreign; they are purely personal. Now, the King and Venizelos both possessed, although in different degrees, the power of personal fascination. Both had emerged with glory from the Balkan wars, the one as a statesman, the other as a military chief, and both had a following.

At all public functions the King and his ministers were followed by their partisans in two processions, and it was patent to every one that M. Venizelos had the larger following. Yet his excessive optimism so blinded him that he could not see how precarious such popularity was.

The new Greeks were afire to deliver the millions of their brothers left in Turkey. By instinct they welcomed the War as a new crusade. But the old Greeks, tired out by two wars, felt that after its recent rapid development what their country needed was peace.

Venizelos naturally turned to the newcomers. He had against him all the traditional forces of the nation ranged round the King and his vassals. His friends were in Macedonia and the islands, but it was his enemies who were at Athens in the Cabinet and at the court.

This difficulty might have been resolved by patience. If Venizelos had waited Greece might have voted unanimously for intervention when America entered the War. But he could not wait—that was his greatest mistake. M. Bratiano failed through excess of caution, Venizelos through excessive zeal. He lived for three years in the fear that the Allies would win the War without him!

It would have been a simple matter for Venizelos and the King, if they had joined forces, to bring their country into the War on the side of the Allies. But from the moment of their disagreement it became a superhuman task for either of them, particularly for Venizelos. The King, after all, stood for constitutional continuity. In separating himself from him Venizelos once more had the appearance of putting himself in conflict with the constitution. Many of his friends hesitated to follow him. No one knew how things would turn out, and was it not safer to remain faithful to the constitution? Those who did follow him were not the best, with the result that Venizelos was often obliged to say, "I am no Venizelist!"

Last but not least, Venizelos in his struggle with the King got no support from the Allies. They were continuously favorable to Constantine—Russia for dynastic reasons and to keep the Greeks away from Constantinople, Italy to keep them out of her way in Asia Minor, and England out of opposition to the eastern campaign. France alone upheld Venizelos, but unenergetically and of no set purpose. The Allies made one mistake after another. As the price of his joining them the King asked only one thing, the guarantee of the integrity of his territory—a guarantee which William II had already given. The Allies, in deference to the susceptibilities of the Bulgarians, refused, and even went so far as to offer the latter Kavala—unknown to the Greek government. They gave no reply to certain of the King's proposals, and on occasion even broke their word to him.

Their biggest mistake was the blockade which, although intended to punish the King and his entourage, only succeeded in making the people suffer. Venizelos, who was supposed to have influence with the Allies, was held responsible. It was then that he said: "Not only have I had to defend myself against my enemies abroad and at home, but even against my friends, and that is the most difficult task of all." After he had explained this situation to the Inter-Allied Council at Versailles, Lloyd George said, "I am ashamed of the way in which we have treated our friend M. Venizelos."

How bitter was the hatred of the Greek people against Venizelos was shown in the revival from ancient times of the terrible ceremony of the curse. The words of the curse were pronounced by the same Bishop of Patras who was later to congratulate him on his return to power. Then forty-five thousand people, among whom were many society women, came in procession, each bringing a stone as a sign of the evil they wished to heap upon Venizelos.

During that time the object of their hatred was at Salonika trying to improvize an army from a people who did not wish to fight, from a state without money, and from a government without men. He was equal to every task, with an activity, an energy, and a perseverance that were wholly admirable. But these years undermined his health, and to-day his premature old age bears witness to them. When at last he could return to Athens after Constantine had been deposed by the Allies, it was under foreign patronage and with half the nation against him. Yet if his return did not contribute anything to his personal popularity in Greece, at least it allowed his country to figure among the conquerors at the Peace Conference.

It was then that M. Venizelos showed his mettle and appeared as a statesman of the first rank. His country, whose efforts during the War had been tardy and restricted, could not claim great authority at the Conference, but he, as the man who had rendered great services to the Allies and risked his popularity for them, could. His cleverness lay in the skill with which he turned this authority to the benefit of Greece.

M. Venizelos had brought his country into the War without haggling about conditions. Unlike Italy and Rumania, therefore, she did not have the advantage of a secret treaty. This was her chance. For M. Venizelos had to appeal not to memoranda but to principles, not to pledges but to rights. He put himself firmly on the side of moral forces, and that is what enabled him to win a complete victory.

"If you tell me," he declared, "that President Wilson refuses Thrace to us because he does not believe the population is Greek, I undertake to demonstrate that he is mistaken. If you tell me he refuses it to us for any other reason, I will undertake to prove that that is not consistent with his Fourteen Points."

So apt a student was he of the Wilsonian phraseology that when the Conference was nominating the provisional members of the Council of the League of Nations, Greece was an obvious appointment.

But even this success could not postpone his fall. When,

in the name of the rights of nationalism, he had asked and won for Greece Smyrna and its hinterland, he believed that the United States would accept the mandate of Armenia and that Turkey would thus be kept at bay. As things turned out, however, the nationalist element in Turkey started the War again, Europe washed her hands of the whole business, and it became clear that the occupation of Smyrna would be a difficult and costly affair. At a time when every other state was demobilizing, Greece alone was compelled to remobilize her army.

All this naturally renewed Venizelos' unpopularity. That he had saved his country from defeat and its dire consequences, was forgotten in a moment. Forgotten too was the fact that he had twice doubled her territory. The people saw no further than the burdens which a new and probably protracted war would place upon them. For twenty-two months Venizelos, though continually on the move, had practically never set foot in Greece. His opponents on the other hand had been there all the time, and they had spared neither his own mistakes nor those of his colleagues.

It was at that particularly unfavorable moment that Venizelos, carried away once more by his optimism, and his desire to be constitutional, decided to appeal to the people. The elections which he had counted on to strengthen his hand, turned out in fact to be a crushing defeat for him and a vote of confidence in his enemy, King Constantine. Venizelos had to go into exile. One of his old friends, an Englishman, W. R. Miller, who saw him then at Rome, said he was a broken man. Shortly afterwards he was afflicted by congestion of the lungs.

His sole satisfaction was that he could watch the blunders of his successors, but it hurt him to see the unhappiness of his fellow-countrymen.

ELEUTHEROS VENIZELOS

VENIZELOS

The elections had been won on the cry "Down with the Asia Minor campaign," but when Constantine came back he had to look round for some means of gaining prestige and success. He increased the army from 60,000 to 300,000 men. He sent them right into the heart of Asia Minor to meet the Turks, who inflicted a crushing defeat. The Allies, on their side, were engaged in reprisals of every kind against Constantine; they cut off his credits, supplied his enemies with munitions, and broke his blockade. The Greek army was pushed down to the sea and with it the whole Greek population of Turkey. Millions of them poured into Greece in utter destitution. It was an unprecedented disaster, and the Lausanne Conference completed the ruin of the diplomatic policy of Venizelos.

He did not even have the satisfaction of healing his country's wounds. He came back twice to Athens, but only for very short periods. He could not take office again because of his health, but at least Greece was willing to take advantage of his great diplomatic reputation; she sent him to Geneva. But he had greatly changed. The man who had so admirably understood President Wilson's ideas at Paris, was now defying the Council and mocking the League of Nations. His defeat was lamentable, and I can see him still after the meeting sitting alone in a corner, his black skull-cap on his head, deserted by all.

The saddest thing of all is that Venizelos has lost his genius for power, but not his taste for it.

Several times he has taken the road to exile, and each time he has returned; he has promised never again to take power and has broken his word; he has put lieutenants in his place and then overthrown them; after having fought the republic against his friends, he has come to save it when it was no longer menaced; after having preached stability of government and the reconstruction of his country, he has interrupted the work of stabilization and reconstruction of his successors. Finally, he—the great liberal—has put the crowning touch on his career by elections that have made him a dictator. Unfathomable contradictions of ambition!

The great misfortune of this man who loved his country as no other has, will be to leave behind him a greater Greece but one which is, through his mistakes, more divided than ever before. As one of his biographers has said with verity and severity, "His name is still a symbol of glory to some, of hatred to others, and a source of discord to all."

JON BRATIANO

THERE ARE TWO DYNASTIES IN RUMANIA, ONE NATIONAL
dynasty, that of the Bratianos, and one German dynasty, that
of the Hohenzollerns, the national one being, naturally, the
stronger.

A dynasty is a family that has gained ascendancy over the
others; in Rumania no one noble family has been able to overcome the others. For centuries the great Rumanian aristocratic
families had fought amongst each other. One of the last
princes, Georges Bibesco, who had for a time united the country, was overthrown by a coalition of his brothers and cousins.
Bratiano realized that it was useless to count upon a self-
seeking aristocracy and that another house, a foreign dynasty,
must be found to rule in Rumania.

Jon Bratiano, senior, was one of the revolutionaries of
1848 and had fought on the barricades in Paris. Upon his
return to Rumania, he became the savior of his country,
founded its national unity and placed the King on the throne.

In the nineteenth century it was thought that kings could
be transplanted like shrubs. Experience has proved that in the
present epoch of nationalism, such imported dynasties do not
easily become acclimatized and that they find it difficult to
gain the hearts of their subjects. This may be seen in Greece
and Bulgaria. In Rumania, King Charles remained a German
until the end of his life in spite of his high ideal of royal duty
and the great services he rendered his adopted country.

Unfortunately, the principle of heredity broke down upon

two occasions. King Charles did not have a son, and in order to insure the succession it was necessary to bring his nephew, Prince Ferdinand, who was then twenty years of age, from Germany. At this age a man is already formed, and although Ferdinand, a German prince and a Catholic, became loyally and completely King of Rumania, it was at the cost of a daily effort of will and not without spiritual suffering. A devout Catholic, he was obliged to baptize his six children into a religion that is excommunicated by the Church of Rome. A German, he had to make war upon his own country, a war that brought him great affliction, from the betrayal of his Russian allies to the separate peace.

The comfort he needed was not to be found in his family. His last grief was to see the heir to the throne, the first of the princes born in Rumania, desert his post in the army in the midst of the War, retire behind the enemies' lines to get married, become successively a Fascist and a Bolshevist and, rebelling openly against his parents, find himself obliged to renounce the crown. The King died without any assurance for the future, for he left the crown to a child of five.

What, one wonders, would have become of the country if it had not had a native dynasty of statesmen besides these foreign princes?

When he came to Rumania, Prince Charles had wisely realized that his position in the country had no foundation and that his name alone was not sufficient to inspire loyalty to the monarchy in a people who did not know him. He needed a support of some kind and found it in the person of Jon Bratiano, who had called him to the throne. He understood that this little man was a great man and for twenty years based his popularity and authority upon him.

Bratiano, senior, was the first to die, but he left the King a son, two sons in fact. Jon, the elder, had inherited his gifts as a statesman and all his ideas. He became the King's advisor and the leader of the party, while his brother, Vintila, became the Minister of Finance.

Until the War, the Liberals and Conservatives in turn were in power in Rumania. But the Conservatives were disunited and the Liberals always had the advantage of superior organization. It was they who set the pace, taking power or letting it go, as it served their purpose. It was this that enabled Bratiano to be the moving spirit of Rumanian policy, from 1907 to 1927, whether he was on the stage or in the wings.

Elections are what one makes them in a country where eighty per cent of the population are illiterate and the man is all-powerful who can control the country through the banks and the court through the women. Bratiano's régime was a dictatorship thinly masked by constitutional forms.

Jon Bratiano's work is marked by two outstanding facts that to some extent changed the history of his country: Rumania's entry into the War and the agrarian reform.

Before the War, the King of Rumania was bound to the Triple Alliance by a secret treaty that, however, not having been submitted to Parliament, had no legal validity. It was renewable every ten years and the King arranged that the Minister of Foreign Affairs at that time should be a man upon whom he could rely. Therefore, only a few of the King's ministers, two or three at the most, knew that such a treaty existed. A royal council was called in haste, at the end of July, 1914. One of the statesmen present, the former Minister of Foreign Affairs Lahovary, asked the King whether his allies had consulted him before declaring war. The King was obliged to admit that they had not done so. "We do not allow our King to be treated as a vassal!" was Lahovary's reply. Neutrality was proclaimed and King Charles never recovered from the blow. He died shortly afterwards.

Jon Bratiano thought, from the beginning, that the Allies would be victorious. He saw Rumania must enter the War on their side if she was to realize her national aspirations. The mass of the people had no expression of opinion and the only persons who had any influence upon the attitude of the public were the Transylvanian intellectuals, who hated Hungary. The politicians, such as Take Jonesco, the idealists and the enthusiasts, such as Filipesco, all men who might have harmed Bratiano, were in favor of war. He understood very early that Rumania must intervene.

But it was not easy to make the decision. Cut off from all direct contact with the West, it was difficult for Rumania to follow what was happening on the various fronts and to estimate which side might be expected to win. The King pinned all his faith upon the Prussian infantry, to which he had belonged. Bukovina, in which Rumania was directly interested, changed hands four times in two years. And the belligerents were doing their best to bespatter each other with mud, overwhelm the enemy with propaganda, obscure the issues and confuse men's minds, affirm lies and give the lie to truth. This was the maze through which the Rumanian government had to find its way.

Suspicion was the fundamental trait in Bratiano's character: in connection with Russia it became a frenzy. Bratiano was the son of the man whom Gortschakof had played false in 1878; he was the minister of King Charles who was accustomed to say, "All Russia's belongings, her treasury, her cannons, her guns, her munitions, everything is to be found in one place, in Monte Carlo."

Bratiano saw Bessarabia losing her nationality more

quickly than Transylvania. He saw Russia becoming stronger and Austria-Hungary declining. In his opinion, Rumania should first increase her territory at the expense of Russia.

These were the grounds upon which he pursued at the same time, despite their apparent contradiction, a policy of neutrality and a policy for the extension of Rumanian frontiers. He endeavored to put as high a price as possible upon his intervention by showing himself to be resolutely neutral. By making exaggerated claims for territory he was able to reserve the possibility of remaining neutral as long as he wished. He used his neutrality as a weapon and his claims for territory as a shield.

He had decided to enter the War, but in his opinion, the question of date was of first importance. He knew that the Rumanian army was very weak and, lest his country might run undue risks, he did not wish to intervene until the last minute. He intended to do so, however, early enough to share the spoil. "We will only keep," he said, "the country that we occupy." This saying was utterly false, as events subsequently proved. At the end of the War, the Rumanians, completely beaten, occupied nothing and they received in all more than they had been promised. But Bratiano, who was free to intervene or to remain neutral, firmly made up his mind only to enter the War when he should think fit.

Thus for two years, he allowed every opportunity to slip. He allowed Serbia to be overwhelmed; he allowed Italy to intervene alone, Bulgaria to join the Central Empires, and the Russians to advance to the borders of Hungary. It was never the moment, the Rumanian army was never ready, the strategic position of the Allies was never sufficiently favorable. In the end, he declared war upon the central empires at the least favorable moment and under the worst military conditions, when Russia's approaching ruin was obvious to all and when the destruction of Serbia freed a large number of German divisions.

Excessive suspicion is profoundly naïve. Bratiano wished to be so clever that he finally became entangled in his own subtleties. The day when the Allies, weary of his evasions, suddenly agreed to all his demands, he could no longer retreat. The surest way to fall into an abyss is to look into it. Bratiano was so completely hypnotized by the Russian abyss that he became giddy.

The history of this decision has not been written. It is said that Sturmer, the Tsar's first minister, had urged that Rumania should enter the War immediately, and that he had made this suggestion to the German Staff, with which he was in touch. This may be true, but there is no proof. What, however, is certain, is that the French Minister was given orders to deliver to Bratiano a common ultimatum from the Allies, agreeing to all Rumania's territorial claims and saying, "Now or never!" There were tears in the eyes of the English military attaché as he came from this audience. "We have committed a great crime!" he said.

He knew the state of the Rumanian army. It had no supplies, no munitions, no barbed wire. The policy of neutrality had prevented Rumania from buying arms; such an action would have appeared suspicious. Moreover, Rumania could obtain nothing through Russia, who was not able to supply her own needs. "Rumania," it has been said, "was thirsty beside a sponge."

Having no supplies, had the Rumanian army, at least, experience? It had none. Bratiano had not dared to send any military missions to the belligerents. The Rumanian army was worse than inexperienced; it was an army of recruits. The soldiers did not know how to dig a trench or put up barbed wire. "One might have thought," wrote a French officer, "that the Rumanian officers had never read *L'Illustration.*"

Rumania even had no allies. Bratiano, fearing to tie his hands, had refused to enter beforehand into any negotiations with Russia concerning possible military agreements. Then, when the force of the contingent to be sent by Russia to help the Rumanian army had been fixed, Russia and Rumania had agreed upon the lowest possible figure; Rumania, because she was afraid that if the Russians once came into the country they would never leave it; Russia, because she was in the state of mind, with regard to Bulgaria, of "the gentleman who thinks that some one is in love with him." Russia imagined that she had only to show herself in order that Bulgaria should throw herself into her arms.

The worst was, however, that, faithful to the principle that he must occupy the territory that he claimed, Bratiano refused to send troops against Bulgaria, from whom he demanded nothing and to advance to the aid of the Macedonian army. He threw his entire army into Transylvania, where it was confronted by the combined forces of Germany and Hungary.

In short, the whole affair was a pitiful adventure that soon became a disaster. The Rumanian army was completely overcome and the Germans occupied the country. To crown all, the Russian Revolution broke out behind Rumania's back and spread to the Russian troops stationed in the country. Every Russian regiment became a hot-bed of mutiny and agitation. The effect upon the Rumanian army was less serious than it might have been on account of the fact that the Rumanian peasant despises everything Russian. In Rumanian, the word "moujik" means "base," "abject," "despicable."

The Rumanian government, fleeing before the invaders, retreated to Jassy. The town was occupied by the Russians, whose one idea was to dethrone the King. The people blamed Bratiano, holding him responsible for all their misfortunes. He went in terror of his life and fell a victim to neurasthenia; at night his house was lighted by six arc lamps for fear of any sudden attack. Exanthematic typhus was raging in the town. Cut off as it was from the rest of the world, seething with intrigue and political passion, Jassy was both morally and mentally unhealthy. "At Jassy," it was said, "they are all at daggers drawn; it is a wonder they don't knife each other." Only one man was contented and had any authority, the French Minister, De Sainte-Aulaire, who said, "It is the best year of my life."

When Russia had concluded the peace of Brest-Litovsk, it must be admitted in Bratiano's favor that he clearly understood the situation. In opposition to his Conservative colleagues, who were in favor of resisting to the bitter end and of the retreat of the court and the army through Russia in the throes of revolution, he himself advised the King to appoint a minister with German sympathies and to conclude a separate peace.

The mistake made by the central empires gave Bratiano his opportunity. If the peace had been moderate or even tolerable he would have been held responsible for the disaster and would have had to face a long period of unpopularity. But from this peace, whereby they even lost the territory promised them by Bratiano, the Rumanian peasants drew the paradoxical conclusion that the War had been justified. Both before and after the declaration of war there had been a certain amount of opposition to Rumania's intervention; after the peace there was none. There was a change of feeling in favor of the King and his minister, and when in their turn the central powers collapsed, it was Bratiano who was called upon to negotiate for peace.

The internal situation in Rumania was extremely difficult immediately after the War. "We live on ukases and dry bread," wrote a Rumanian at that time. "There is a new decree every day but there is no wood for heat. Nor is there any longer a parliament; only the government flourishes. It is the same with cancer, it thrives, the patient becomes pale and thin." In these circumstances, Bratiano fell back upon the traditional resource of a government in difficulties, that of a counter-irritant. He thought that the only way to extricate himself was to present his people with Bessarabia, Bukovina and half Hungary upon a silver salver. He wished to demand the utmost for the nation; none should go further than he.

Bratiano managed to persuade his compatriots that he was the only man for whom the Allies would fulfil the promises made to Rumania through M. Bratiano himself, by the treaty of 1916. In order to regain his popularity he promised Rumania the impossible and left for Paris with the very definite mandate to obtain the execution of the treaty to the letter. His mistake lay in accepting such a mandate; having to comply with it was his ruin.

For the 1916 treaty no longer existed, either legally or morally. It pre-supposed the existence of Austria-Hungary and excluded the separate peace. But Austria-Hungary had disappeared and Rumania had concluded a separate peace. She had even received Bessarabia for her trouble, a colossal tip that she intended to keep.

It would have been logical, under these conditions, to have

allowed the 1916 treaty to lapse. It was obsolete, it had been made before President Wilson's messages by people who knew nothing of the mystic meaning of the War. It would have been wise simply to have pleaded the people's right of self-determination. Bratiano's failure to realize this was the most serious mistake in his career. He still belonged to the old school of diplomacy; "I come of a race of peasants," he himself said during the Peace Conference, "and I never think the harvest is assured until I have the money for it in my pocket."

Too much cannot be said of the evil effects upon certain countries of such false realism on the part of statesmen who consider themselves shrewd. President Wilson could not recognize the secret treaty between the Allies and Rumania, for in that case he would have been obliged to give Dalmatia to Italy and Shantung to Japan. These treaties were against his principles and he had not signed them. If the 1916 treaty, giving Hungary to Rumania as far as the Theiss, had been carried out integrally, war would long ago have broken out again in Europe.

Bratiano, otherwise so able, did not realize this. The frontiers he demanded would have entailed a permanent state of war for his country, both at home and abroad. For weeks he fought for the Banat, against the Serbs, his allies in the past and his natural allies in the future. It was President Wilson who had to protect Rumania's true interests and her permanent welfare from Bratiano!

At the Peace Conference there were two groups of statesmen. Those who had gauged the true strength of their country, such as Bénès, took up their stand with President Wilson. The others—the Bratianos, the Dmowskis, the Sonninos—

underestimated Anglo-Saxon influence and came into opposition with President Wilson.

Thus Bratiano found himself involved in the Italian policy; he stood by it without reserves and fell with it. He followed the Italian delegation in its retreat. He preferred to go away rather than to sign a treaty that made his country three times as large as it had been and that was subsequently to surround his own name with a halo of glory!

Upon his return to Rumania he made a fresh attempt to retain his power. He freed Europe of Hungarian Bolshevism; the Rumanian armies were in Budapest in no time. Curiously enough, instead of bringing him the congratulations of the Allies, this earned him their dislike. At the Peace Conference Marshal Foch had been asked for a plan of invasion of Hungary. He replied that it would demand considerable resources such as were not available. Bratiano proved that Foch was mistaken and instead of thanks he met with reproaches!

However, Fortune is stronger than human error. In spite of serious defects of character and judgment, Jon Bratiano was and will remain in the eyes of posterity, the instrument of his country's greatness.

Bratiano soon returned to power. Upon him fell the burden of settling the difficulties arising from the War and the increase of territory. The greatest of these were economic and, more particularly, agrarian.

Bratiano had had the idea of the radical reform of the land policy since 1907, the year of the great peasant revolutions. After the Russian Revolution he realized that an immediate and fundamental agrarian reform was the only means of protecting the Rumanians, almost exclusively peasants, from the spread of Bolshevism. When Bessarabia and Transylvania were united and Rumania found herself wedged between Russian and Hungarian Bolshevism the reform was finally carried out.

It would be a mistake, however, to think that the agrarian reform was forced upon Bratiano solely by external and fortuitous circumstances. It corresponded to a plan upon which he had been meditating for some considerable time.

Jon Bratiano's idea, from the beginning of his career, had been to establish his power upon the middle classes in the towns. A strange and daring scheme, because thirty years ago this class barely existed in Rumania. But it was a brilliant idea because this class was in the process of formation and owing everything to the Liberal party, supported it unreservedly in return. The Liberal policy was nationalist and protectionist and in a purely agricultural country favored the introduction and development of industry. Consequently, Bratiano was able to help himself with both hands to the funds of the banks for election purposes and to impose upon his country an unrestricted political and economic dictatorship.

These facts must be realized in order to appreciate the extent of the three-fold agrarian reform carried out by Bratiano. It was his idea, certainly, that the land should be given to the peasants who demanded it. But, above all, it should be taken from those who were in possession, the economic power of the landed proprietors, that is to say, of the Conservatives, should be broken and a middle class should be formed in the towns.

Bratiano achieved a great deal, but he was not wholly successful. A Rumanian lady who has a deep knowledge of politics combined with considerable literary talent, Princess Bibesco, once said, "Nations are like trees. They always bear the same fruit." This is profoundly true; Russia produces terrorism, Turkey produces despotism, China produces anarchy, Italy produces dictatorship, etc. As for Rumania, she produces great estates. The middle class, having become wealthy through the Liberal economic policy, hastened to become landed proprietors, Bratiano first of any, in his beautiful property Florica, with the whole Wallachian plain spread out before it.

Bratiano went a step further. The object of his policy and of that of his father was to break down the supremacy of the old feudal families. By his marriage he entered into one of them. He did with regard to the Stirbeys exactly as they had done, two centuries before, with regard to the Brancovans. This man from the middle class, who was jealous of all aristocrats, became a great landed proprietor, the husband of a princess and the brother-in-law of a prince.

It should be observed that Prince Stirbey, Bratiano's brother-in-law, had considerable influence upon the King and Queen. He had persuaded them that he was their only true friend and that the day upon which he disappeared, they would disappear with him. He had identified himself with the dynasty and his wealth proved that he was disinterested. "If I am attacked," he said, "you are lost."

Only one man dared to oppose Stirbey and Bratiano, Prince Carol, the heir to the throne. He was broken for it. Everything had been forgiven, and Heaven knows there was much to forgive. This alone was unpardonable. Bratiano forced him to leave the country, deprived him of the throne and instituted a regency under his own control in order to prevent the prince from returning.

Bratiano was too clever to imagine that a regency with three heads could last. Perhaps the worry it caused him hastened his end. In any case, if he had lived, he would certainly have taken further steps in this connection. It is said that he had thoughts of a republic, a dictatorial republic with himself, naturally, in control. Thus, imperceptibly, perhaps unconsciously, he approached the throne set up by his father and in actual fact tended to replace these foreigners by a national dynasty.

He was unable to complete his task. There are times when Fate seems particularly hard upon a country. In the space of a few months, Rumania lost, first the heir to the throne, under conditions, for her, worse than death, then the King, then the man who for twenty years had represented the stability of the country and the continuity of her policy. Her two dynasties have died out together and she is left bewildered seeking to steady herself once more.

THE INTERMINABLE WAR

ASQUITH

BRIAND

ASQUITH

WE DO NOT KNOW WHETHER HISTORY WILL RANK LORD
Oxford as a great statesman, but it will rank him certainly
as a great character. Mr. Asquith united in himself some of
the finest masculine qualities, and all that was lacking to him
for political greatness was—defects.

To understand Mr. Asquith, it is necessary to remember
that he was English. He was not only English by birth, race
and education; he was in every sense of the term a typical
Englishman. He was, to begin with, English in his physique
and appearance. Princess Bibesco—not his daughter, but the
cousin of his son-in-law—in an admirable article which she
wrote about him at the time of his death told how a painter
of her acquaintance, meeting her in Mr. Asquith's company,
alluded to him afterwards as that "magnificent old pink and
white Englishman." "Everything about him," Princess Bibesco
proceeded to say, "substance, form, tone, tastes, ancestry, came
from England." He was an English "thoroughbred." She liked
to think of him, she declared, alternately wearing the crown of
the Saxon Kings or the sober headgear of Cromwell's Ironsides.

Morally, too, Mr. Asquith was a true-born Englishman.
Everything about him was racy of the English soil—his
abilities, his loyalty, his sensibility, his reserve, his silence,
his distinction, and certain of his faults, in particular that
slowness of conception and decision with which he was so
often reproached.

But there are several kinds of Englishmen. Lord Oxford

was an Englishman of the cultivated type. There are extraordinary intellectual resources in this English race which is credited with being devoted to sports and beefsteaks. Few of the races of the world can boast of a culture so ancient, so refined, and so deep. And if the sporting Englishmen are in the majority, when one does meet an educated Englishman one usually marvels at his knowledge.

It was remarked of Mr. Asquith: "He knows how to read." That is high praise for a man, but in his case it was inadequate. For reading was his chief passion down to the last days of his life. Once every year he re-read the works of Dickens and those of Sir Walter Scott. The Greek tragedians, the Latin poets, the philosophers of antiquity, were familiar to him. When he wanted to condemn the Kaiser, it was a line from Horace that came naturally to his lips: *Delirante reges, plectuntur Achivi.* . . .

Colonel House, speaking of Lord Balfour, declared: "I should be disposed to place him intellectually on the same level as our President and Mr. Asquith—that is to say, at the summit."

No classical culture was foreign to Mr. Asquith. He traveled widely and he remembered everything. He knew the history of the Italian republics of the Middle Ages as well as that of antiquity and of his own country. And he possessed the kind of mind that is produced only by deep culture and an old tradition. Many illustrations are given of this. After the close of the War and his great electoral defeat, Mr. Asquith went to Spain to find a diversion for his thoughts. He was received there by the King. It was a dark hour for monarchies, and Alfonso XIII confided to the English ex-Premier something of his apprehensions: "Thirty-five Kings have been dethroned," he said. "Who will be the thirty-sixth?"

LORD OXFORD AND ASQUITH

Mr. Asquith replied with feeling: "Sire, do not think of that!"

The title of Earl of Oxford by which Mr. Asquith was to become known after he was raised to the peerage was singularly appropriate, for he had passed at Oxford the best years of his life—one might almost say he had spent his entire life there. A brilliant scholar of Balliol, it was there he achieved his first successes as an orator no less than as a student. In the course of time he made himself a home by the side of the Thames, quite near Oxford, to which while in office he resorted almost always for the week-end. In their turn, his sons went to the University and they also shone there. He had seen his own portrait placed among those of the "fellows" who have done honor to Balliol, and his son's name at the head of those Balliol men who have died for their country.

It is recorded that Mr. Lloyd George, on visiting Oxford, exclaimed: "I am glad I did not come here before for I should never have been able to tear myself away."

He was right. You cannot tear yourself away from the atmosphere of Oxford, once it has taken hold of you. Lord Oxford has given us evidence of that.

The reason, no doubt, is that at Oxford you take lessons not in matters of intelligence merely but also in character. You do not leave it a scholar merely but also a gentleman. And this is not just a social distinction; it is above all a moral idea.

This eminent man, upon whom, in society, all eyes were fixed, was by nature shy and reserved. He had a horror of putting himself forward, and public honors made him blush. This orator, one of the greatest of his country and of his time, whose elevation of thought and perfection of diction subjugated the fellow-members of the House of Commons, was

STATESMEN OF THE WAR

taciturn in private life. He allowed his wife to do the talking. A woman of rich and combative personality, she enjoyed publicity. As for him, he listened, rarely joining in the conversation. Finally, this leader of men, who in the vicissitudes of a very long career must have come to be familiar with all the brutalities of political conflict, was a man of sensitive disposition whose eyes filled with tears when he was moved.

Mr. Asquith was a believer. Often of a Sunday afternoon he would leave his house, escaping from his friends, and go to the village church to read the Bible to the few parishioners present. His faith was without ostentation but it impregnated his whole life and his political creed, and in this also he was a true son of the British nation.

The distinctive mark of the true gentleman is a moral quality, the finest quality of all, loyalty. In this respect, Mr. Asquith, throughout his whole life and in his whole character, was a true gentleman. Probably it was this that prevented him from being a great statesman and above all a man of war, for politics necessarily involve intrigues and forms of cleverness which were repugnant to his nature. As for war, that also calls for a certain cynicism. One form of loyalty is frankness. Lord Oxford was often accused, in his attitude towards both his friends and his foes, of being brusque and even a bit rough-spoken. This is a characteristic one would not look for in a man who was in no way domineering. But he would have considered it incompatible with loyalty not to say with complete frankness what he thought.

This profound sense of loyalty which he carried in his heart cast a shadow over the closing years of his life. The way in which Mr. Lloyd George behaved in regard to him caused him more grief than anger. For this man, who owed almost everything to him, became in his own Cabinet, in conjunction with his political enemies, an element of disturbance and of intrigue and finally of dissolution. What Mr. Asquith was never able to forgive in Mr. Lloyd George was not his action in overthrowing him, for he did not care for power: it was his betrayal of confidence.

Speaking of one of Lord Oxford's last public speeches, the *Observer* said: "His judgments are as straight as a Roman road."

It was his judgment, many decades earlier, that had won him the tribute from one of his Oxford masters: "Asquith is all directness."

Therein lay the great force of his eloquence—it so made itself felt. And Mr. Asquith had so often had occasion to note the effect produced by these qualities in the course of his career that in order to influence public opinion he had no belief in anything but candid explanations of his policy. That was the form of his Liberalism.

Mr. Asquith was a Liberal of the great English tradition. He had made his *début* in politics by a passionate and triumphant defense of the Irish leader, Parnell, and he had begun his ministerial career with advanced—almost radical—social ideas. But he was too profoundly English to remain for long an extremist of any kind. The Boer War showed him the road to conversion and thenceforward his Liberalism was absolutely according to tradition.

The difference between the Whigs and the Tories has been thus explained. The Tories govern the British people through an oligarchy; the Whigs also govern through an oligarchy but as far as possible with the people's consent. Mr. Asquith favored the method which consisted in asking the opinion of the people, while showing them the path of truth. But this definition becomes less and less exact; Mr. Asquith was, in truth, one of the last authentic representatives of the Liberal oligarchy.

Mr. Asquith had been Prime Minister for more than five years when the European crisis came about in the spring of 1914. He enjoyed great authority not only with his party and the country but also with the King, whose principal collaborator he had been ever since his accession and who regarded him as his political mentor. Mr. Asquith, therefore, combined all the subjective conditions requisite to carry the people with him, should he think it necessary.

The objective conditions were less favorable. England, under the Asquith government, had traversed a period of ardent political conflicts. After Mr. Lloyd George's contentious fiscal measures in 1909 had come the question of the House of Lords, awaking strong passions, then the question of Ireland. The country was on the eve of giving home rule to Ireland, and no one knew whether it would not be necessary to employ force against those most loyal of British subjects, the Orangemen of Ulster. The shadow of civil war was outlined upon the horizon and it was under these conditions that the government had to make decisions of the greatest importance.

Mr. Asquith recognized to the full the political and moral necessity for Great Britain of not abandoning France, should France be involved in a war. From the first he was, in the inner circle of the Cabinet, among those who wished to give assurances to France. In view of the engagements already entered into, his loyalty could not have allowed him to be otherwise. But he committed the same fault as his foreign minister. He overestimated, on the one hand, the diplomatic means at his disposal, on the other, the force of pacifist opinion.

To some one who asked him whether he had foreseen the

War, Mr. Asquith replied at a later date: "Yes and no." That is the reply which all the statesmen of Europe ought in honesty to have made. For they all saw, from a combination of many signs, that the war was coming, while no one in his heart of hearts believed that it would really come. That is why the English statesmen prolonged, hoping against hope, their attempts at mediation, thus perhaps aggravating the crisis by not bringing Germany's responsibilities home to her.

Another phrase of Mr. Asquith's throws light upon his attitude at this juncture. A diplomat had asked him if he did not think that by intervening earlier England would have prevented the War. Asquith replied simply by citing the words of Mirabeau: "Without the consent of public opinion not even the greatest talent could triumph over circumstances." A weighty question and a weighty reply. The man on whom at such an hour had rested such a responsibility, the man, who, doing violence to his past record, to all his personal feelings, had launched his country in the greatest war in history, the man who had seen die as the result of his decision millions of young men, among them his own eldest son, the hope of his race, the son of his heart and brain, was constrained, being loyal and a Christian, to ask himself often: "Have I done right?"

His own conscience could comfort him, for he had obeyed it. But the question whether he had acted for the best, given all the circumstances, is a different one, and this question may be asked.

Mr. Asquith, as we have said, was a Liberal in temperament. It was not his way to impose his authority; he sought always to convince. Confronted by opposition on the part of members of his Cabinet he tried to secure unanimity by means of persuasion. This took time and he did not even succeed, for three of his colleagues left him.

As for public opinion, we shall never know whether it would have agreed to war sooner. Mr. Asquith did not believe it would, and he did not reckon that he could dispense with it. Opinions may differ on this point. But he alone had the responsibility and we can understand that he may well have feared to throw into so terrible a war a people whom he did not see in agreement with him.

Once war was declared, Mr. Asquith had the great merit of emphasizing its moral and almost mystic character. He did so with all the authority which came from his earlier hesitation. In November, 1914, long before any of the other Allied statesmen, Mr. Asquith took the lead in defining the war aims, from England's standpoint, in the terms which were to acquire so historic a significance: "England," he declared, "would not again sheathe her sword, which she had not drawn lightly, until Belgium should have had restored to her what she had sacrificed—and more; until France had been safeguarded, in sufficient measure, against all menace of aggression; until the rights of the small nations should have been placed upon an unshakeable foundation; and until the military domination of Prussia should have been destroyed completely and forever."

All Mr. Asquith's speeches of this period were penetrated by the same idealism, and it is declared that President Wilson knew them by heart and that he was largely inspired by them in the wording of his own messages.

Idealism, in a time of war, is an act; it was idealism in the long run that won victory. But idealism has to rest upon adequate material means. "Barbed wire," as a general has remarked, "is not influenced by moral ascendency."

ASQUITH

Did Mr. Asquith give his country, and quickly enough, the material means which it needed to win victory for the right? That is the question which will be asked by history.

Princess Bibesco, his generous and clear-sighted biographer, has given this answer to it:—"Towards the end of the year, 1916, everything was going as badly as possible for the Allies; this was inevitable, as it was not to be expected that the innocent would be as well armed as the guilty, for time was needed for the Right to become Might, and as he was accused by the Press and the Opposition of taking the war too patiently—he who knew that no British Prime Minister could take it otherwise—he fell from power. . . ."

There is truth in this defense, but the absolute truth is somewhat other than that, perhaps. Mr. Asquith assuredly did for the War all he could. But he had to contend against his own temperament, and in this he was not always successful. A Liberal, he believed that the country could be governed in times of war as in times of peace. He was repelled by the idea of conscription, which is so contrary to British traditions. He was repelled by many other measures of public safety for which there were no precedent in the past of the Whig Party.

It was above all in his relations with his ministers that Mr. Asquith showed himself too much of a Liberal. He was himself War Minister in August, 1914. He called in Lord Kitchener at once and placed him at the head of military operations. Perhaps in his own mind he thought that this would suffice. He hated to impose his will on his colleagues. Moreover, he had no expert knowledge in these matters, and he knew it; therefore, he allowed his ministers and his generals a free hand. Now there were differences of opinion among these people, and the various departments, instead of working together, often came to loggerheads. Lord Kitchener quarreled with Mr. Lloyd George; Mr. Winston Churchill took measures on his own initiative; the English generals did not hit it off with the French. And the Premier had not the dictatorial temperament which would have been needed to get them all into agreement or to impose the ideas of some of them upon the others.

Finally he was worn out. The death of his eldest son, in the Dardanelles, under conditions of superhuman heroism, had been a very painful blow for him. The burden of power in these circumstances was too much for him. His intellectual energy was affected and he often postponed decisions which were urgent. His will power was there still, but its action was delayed.

The effects of this tendency to apathy have assuredly been exaggerated. If Mr. Lloyd George was able later to intensify Great Britain's war effort, this was thanks in great degree to the munitions which had been ordered and the measures which had been set on foot by the Asquith ministry. At bottom, Asquith was the victim less of his faults and of the intrigues of his colleagues than of the accuracy of his own forecasts. He had envisaged a war of long duration. Lord Kitchener had said "three years." Seeing the hostilities prolonged, the impatient peoples blamed those who had warned them from the start and whom they suspected of unconsciously prolonging the war to prove that they were right.

This does not excuse either the venomous attacks of which the Liberal premier was made the object or the criticisms passed on him by his Conservative colleagues, who plotted to put Mr. Lloyd George in his place. But it must be admitted that at the close of 1916 Mr. Asquith's departure had become a national necessity. Public opinion demanded it. It was at this moment that, despite the censorship, a newspaper was able to print this headline: "Alisquith in Blunderland". The maintenance of Mr. Asquith in power would at this juncture have given the impression to the British people and to the Allies that England was not disposed to pursue the War with all her strength and that she did not believe in victory.

The last years of Mr. Asquith were darkened by these memories. Philosopher though he was, he could never forgive Mr. Lloyd George completely. What he blamed him for was not so much the betrayal of himself as the splitting up of the Liberal Party, and the irremediable damage to its future.

Mr. Asquith regarded himself as a trustee. He had received the Liberal Party, rich in a glorious tradition, from the hands of Gladstone, Lord Rosebery and Sir Henry Campbell Bannerman. His duty was to transmit the inheritance intact to his successors. Through the fault of Mr. Lloyd George, he was unable to do so, and he never found consolation over this.

The political fates were all against Mr. Asquith in his old age. Defeated in 1919 in the constituency which he had always represented in the House of Commons, he was defeated again, three years later, in that in which he had found refuge. But his personal lot would have been bearable if he had not seen his party decimated and forced to abandon power, first to the Labor Party, then to the Conservatives. All the attempts at reconciliation with Mr. Lloyd George had only transient effects because confidence was lacking on the one side and submission on the other.

The political career of Mr. Asquith ended on the day when he agreed to make what Princess Bibesco calls his "fall upstairs." He entered the House of Lords, as we have seen, as

Earl of Oxford. But in spite of this new dignity, it is the name of Asquith which he caused to be inscribed in history, as that of the man who did not hesitate in 1914 to put all the forces of the British Empire at the service of Belgium violated and of Justice outraged.

BRIAND

M. ARISTIDE BRIAND BELIES HIS REPUTATION. HE IS SAID to be lazy, ignorant, variable, sceptical. His enemies reproach him with it, certain of his friends glory in it. He himself seems sometimes to take a delight in conforming to this portrait. "You forget," he will say, when people try to hurry him, "that I am an indolent man."

And yet he is not.

Lazy! A man who has risen from the most modest social circumstances, first to the school of law, then to the fame of a great pleader, and finally to the greatest career that any statesman of our time could aspire to. Lazy! A man who has been fifteen times a minister and eight times President of the Council, and who has always proved not only adequate to his task but in a fair way to tower above it. Lazy! Who would believe it?

The truth is very different. We live in an age of paper. Our civilization rests on the written document, our statesmen spend their days in reading reports and dictating memoranda. A book counts as the height of achievement. M. Poincaré is a worker because he spends hours writing at his desk. M. Briand is lazy because, with his hands in his pockets and a cigarette in his mouth, he takes life for his study, observing and listening.

M. Briand is an oral worker. He does not read the reports that are sent to him. He sends for the writers to explain them to him. After a few minutes' conversation he has learned more than is in the report.

M. Briand has the true orator's temperament. Speech is life to him. He has a horror of the written word: in his opinion the letter kills. M. Briand was once a journalist and whatever he may say of it at Press banquets his memories of that time are not pleasant. His daily article was for him, who in another sphere improvizes so brilliantly, a real burden, almost a torture.

He has not written a single book. We do not believe that even his speeches have been collected and published. They would not lend themselves to publication. M. Poincaré writes his speeches and learns them by heart. The orator's art in that case is only one facet of the writer's talent. There is nothing like that about M. Briand. His speech is always impromptu: typed and re-read the form of it might easily appear faulty.

What is eloquence? A contact between a man and a crowd. A speech prepared in the quiet of the study, written and conned over, is not a speech. Eloquence is improvization, it is the soul of the hearers reflected in the words of the orator.

It may be remembered—at Geneva it always will be— what an admirable speech M. Briand made in reply to Herr Stresemann on the day when Germany was admitted to the League of Nations. On the previous day it was learned that Herr Stresemann, himself a powerful impromptu speaker, would read his speech in view of the great importance of the occasion. M. Briand's colleagues urged him to do the same. He hesitated for a moment, then suddenly he spoke, "No, certainly not. When two great peoples come together again a man must give himself."

And verily, on the following day, M. Briand gave himself. That day he showed all the warmth of his heart, all the generosity of his nature.

Many people believe that he speaks extempore to avoid the trouble of preparing his speeches. Not at all. M. Briand prepares his speeches carefully and in two different ways.

First of all he studies the *milieu*, establishes contact with it, tries to get to the heart of it. M. Briand entered the French Chamber in 1902 at the age of forty, preceded by a great reputation for oratory won in socialist conferences and in the Assize Courts. The members awaited his first speech eagerly. They had to wait for it three years! M. Briand required all that time to absorb the complex ever-changing *milieu* of French parliamentary life. Three years of strolling about the lobbies, of inconsequent talk, of idle dreaming; three years apparently wasted. But after that time he made his maiden speech without a false note; it was a triumph. Six months later he was a minister.

When he came to Geneva for the first time as the French delegate to the Assembly, the process was repeated but in the reverse way. He began too soon; he had not had time to give sufficient study to a *milieu* so new to him, at once diplomatic and parliamentary, where the only eloquence that carries any weight is sober, almost academic. It was Mr. Balfour who reached perfection in that *milieu*. At first M. Briand was a disappointment. He himself acknowledged it. He did not immediately speak again, but he did not give up hope. He studied his *milieu* and when he had occasion to speak again at the Assembly or in the Council he was magnificent.

When you see M. Briand with his cigarette in his mouth, strolling along the lobbies of the Assembly, giving here a word, there a smile and a handshake, you can be sure that he will speak the following day from the rostrum.

M. Briand has another method of preparation. He prac-
tises his periods on a limited audience. He tries them over in
a circle of friends. Often when you hear him you find in his
speech whole sentences from the conversation you had with
him the day before. M. Briand's private conversations are
like rough sketches of the great pictures which he perfects
in public.

One day during the War I was lunching along with M.
Briand at the house of his friend M. Joseph Reinach. There
were about twenty people there. M. Briand was seated opposite the master of the house. For about a quarter of an hour
we all chatted desultorily to one another. Then gradually
above the hubbub arose one voice, deep, warm, musical, flex-
ible. Soon it dominated the rest and we heard no other; we all
fell silent. M. Briand, who had just left the government, was
telling the story of his last ministry. It was world history in its
most tragic phase expounded by the actor most directly concerned in it. We all hung on his words. The following day
M. Briand made that speech again in the Chamber.

Nevertheless it happens sometimes that M. Briand really
does improvize and it is then that his style can be best com-
prehended. One day at Geneva he was invited to a Press
luncheon. Different speakers were down to speak, but his fellow guests wanted to hear him. A cheer arose and he had to
submit. He began with a few light pleasantries; you felt
that he had nothing to say, that he was casting about in his
mind for his next word. That lasted for a few minutes. Then,
suddenly, a chance image opened up a great vista before him.
His voice became deeper, more vibrant, and he rose to one
of his greatest speeches—this time really impromptu.

The quality which M. Briand possesses above all others—
and it is a truly statesmanlike quality—is a keen sense of

the distinction between what is essential and what is second-ary. Our politics are cumbered with worn-out passions, mean little cares and anxieties, obsolete problems, out-of-date prejudices and overrated difficulties. It is to such things, of first importance to the average man, that M. Briand applies the full force of his indolence. He is convinced that to gain time it is often necessary to waste it, that things must be left to evolve naturally. Hence his reputation for laziness. But no one has ever known him to neglect a really vital matter.

It is the same with his ignorance as with his idleness. M. Briand is ignorant of what is written, he knows everything that comes by hearing. Granted he is not a scholar in the usual meaning of the word. As regards general education his knowledge comes from the *lycée*, the university, and life. He has read little but he has heard much, and remembered nearly all of it. When he has to explain some difficult question in a speech, he sends for a competent man to explain the problem to him. He picks up things very easily, masters the most difficult subjects almost in fun, and then presents them as simply as possible. He faces technical questions by putting himself in the place of the audience he is to address.

M. Briand is not an ignoramus, he is an artist. His art is politics and the handling of men, and he is master of it. Above all, along with his almost intuitive quickness of understanding, he has a genius for synthesis. When M. Briand is having an intricate problem explained to him with too much confusing detail it is he who is able very soon to explain it lucidly.

You should see him on committees or at the Council of the League. He gazes up into the air, dozes, draws things on his paper. He never listens. His eternal cigarette is staining his finger tips already yellow from many others. Nothing seems to interest him. Then all at once when the discussion has been talked out into irrevocable confusion, M. Briand rises to speak, sums up what has been said, points out the contradictions, stresses the relevant facts, throws the light of his reason on it, and finds the solution.

At all events, one thing that this ignoramus does know is the human heart. His eloquence and his political success are due to his fine psychological sense. It has often been said that crowds are like women, mobile and variable. M. Briand said it himself one memorable day.

It was in 1910. He had just delivered the speech that determined his career. Up till then he had been socialist, even revolutionary; now he had just come from breaking the railway strike. He had cut himself adrift from his old friends and henceforward was to figure as the protector of the social order. In the chamber he was hotly challenged by the Socialists. "To defend law and order," he maintained, "I would go outside the law if necessary." It was a paraphrase of a saying of Napoleon III—a somewhat dangerous association to the French mind. His friends were anxious, but all he said to them as he came out was, "I felt the Chamber wanted to be kissed on the neck."

Only a man of great charm could carry that off. M. Briand can. One day I was saying that I was to lunch with him the next day when some one asked, "How many marchionesses will be there?" As a matter of fact there were three. Women adore M. Briand—and he makes no effort to attract them. In contrast to M. Poincaré, who is typically middle class, M. Briand might be said to be of the people. He still is. His way of life is simple, he adores nature, he is completely happy spending his vacation on his little property at Cocherel, with his peasants, his trees and his fish. For his ruling passion is angling. If one of his lady admirers were to come on him unawares she would be distinctly surprised at the costume in which she would find her hero.

It takes understanding to see what is to be seen; it takes intuition to see what is hidden; it takes imagination to see what is yet to come. M. Briand possesses all three qualities in the highest degree. Some one has said, "To govern is to foresee." M. Briand governs.

Sometimes his imagination runs away with him, hence comes his reputation for taking liberties with the truth. On that day when he had so brilliantly expounded the history of his government to his fellow guests some one said after he had gone, "Briand forgets that we happen to know some history." But are we to dismiss as a liar the poet, the orator, the artist who puts things as they might be, not as they are in fact? At any rate, one thing that no one denies is that M. Briand believes what he says. If he lies it is because he deceives himself.

Further, M. Briand is blamed not so much for his falsehoods as for his changeableness. There is some justification for this. He has changed a good deal during his life. He has changed as often as circumstances, if not oftener.

M. Briand began in politics as a revolutionary Socialist. He made a name for himself by preaching a general strike in the face of the more moderate heads of his party. Then he went over to the Moderates, defending his comrade Millerand, then a Minister, against the extremists. Then he became a minister himself with a very definite program, the separation of Church and State. which was really the policy of the radical party.

Then he mounted one more rung of the ladder and became President of the Council. In this capacity he broke the railway strike by mobilizing the railway men, and so did the opposite of what he had preached in his youth. Finally, strong in the credit that this decisive action had given him with the middle classes, he went all through the country preaching conciliation. That word signified both the end of his anti-clericalism and his rupture with the radical party, whose policy he himself had previously pursued.

M. Briand's enemies have made out from these changes that he is untrustworthy, an opportunist, and a sceptic. But the opposite inference may also be drawn; it gives proof of his statesmanlike qualities and the essential unity of his career.

M. Briand rose gradually to an ever greater conception of his duty as a statesman. Although he came from the most active radical opposition he felt the need of a positive policy. He saw that this policy could be founded neither on popular disorder (the railway strike) nor on spiritual strife (anti-clericalism). Finally, the idea of a national unity, which he tried to bring about during the War and sought to extend to all Europe after it, was the guiding thread through all his changes.

M. Briand is indeed an opportunist, if by that we mean that he takes circumstances into account and adapts himself to them. One day, speaking of M. Painlevé, who is well known as a great mathematician, he gave this admirable definition: "There are in the world mathematicians and politicians. The mathematician draws a line and follows it, even if it goes through a house. The politician sees the house and walks round it." Another time he said, "When the pot boils, you must either sit on it or take off the lid." M. Briand all his life has walked round houses and taken off lids.

Does that justify us in calling him a sceptic? If M. Briand

is a sceptic, he is one of a peculiar kind, for two or three times in his existence he has sacrificed his political career for his ideals. Once before the War, when, after being returned on an anti-clerical majority he promulgated the idea of conciliation and offended his supporters; a second time, during the War, over the Salonika expedition; a third time, after the War, on the subject of the Franco-German reconciliation.

M. Briand was in power from the middle of 1915 to the end of 1916. In 1915 the Germans were everywhere victorious and everywhere had the initiative; at the beginning of 1916 they were attacking Verdun; at the end of the year from the gates of Paris they withdrew forty kilometers to one of the fairest regions of France, which they had cultivated and sown. They were preparing other withdrawals and were making their offer of peace.

M. Clémenceau said later: "I am making war," that is to say, "I have no time for anything else." M. Briand belonged to a different school. "When you are making a war you must be busy in every other sphere." It was he who began propaganda at the front and in Germany. In 1916 more than forty riots were provoked by Allied agents in German towns. It was he who organized the Inter-Allied committees in London, which helped so greatly in revictualing Europe. It was he who laid the foundations for unity of command by the coöperation of the general staff during 1916 and before the offensive of 1917.

But M. Briand's great conception to which he dedicated all his powers was the Salonika expedition. During Viviani's ministry M. Briand had suggested reëstablishing communication with Russia through the Balkans. The defection of Bulgaria hindered the realization of this project. When M. Briand came into power he took the matter in hand. It is all the more credit to him that he had to force his idea on the whole world; nobody would hear of it at first. The French General Staff thought that the Salonika expedition was eccentric and wasteful. They maintained that the decisive action would take place in France; each man taken from the western front was a man lost. At each demand for reinforcements General Joffre groaned "as if his ribs were being torn out." The English wanted to attack the Turks from the Suez Canal and refused to divide their troops. The Italians and the Russians were opposed to it for dynastic reasons, namely, to humor the King of Greece, to whom Lord Kitchener had made certain promises. Finally, all the Allies were hostile to General Sarrail, who had been sent there because he was not persona grata in France. On the other hand, Sarrail, who was a politician, had many friends in the parliamentary committees, and it was felt that Briand never defended him strongly enough.

In spite of all these difficulties M. Briand did not give up his idea. He attended all the Inter-Allied councils, some of which were very stormy. Then the day came when it seemed as if he were to reap the fruit of his efforts. Rumania's entry into the War was his achievement and the whole world did him honor for it.

But alas, we know that the results of the Rumanian intervention were not what has been expected. The Russians did not come to the help of Rumania. The Italians and even the French were not in a position to undertake the necessary offensives to relieve them. The fault lay with the general staff, which had given false promises to M. Briand. But the moral responsibility rested on the President of the Council and he resigned—too soon.

A fortnight later the first Austrian peace proposals arrived in Paris. If they had come into the hands of M. Briand for

ARISTIDE BRIAND

whom they were intended, millions of lives might have been saved. M. Briand never doubted that there would be a final victory. As early as 1916 he said to his colleagues, "Germany is crushed; there is no longer any loyalty to the monarchy; it will fall to pieces some day." But he was alarmed at the heedless expenditure of his country's resources, which he knew were limited. The Russian Revolution made a profound impression on him. He was inclined to accept the overtures which Austria and Germany seemed desirous of making. "The soldier strikes the blows," he said. "The politician at his back seeks to turn them to account: the two functions are indispensable." In order to save countless lives he was ready to risk his popularity, go to Switzerland and confer with M. de Laucken and the German Chancellor. The government forbade it. The War was fought to a finish and it ended by a decisive victory on the very Salonika front which he had brought into being.

It is unfortunate that M. Briand was not present at the drawing up of the Treaty of Versailles. It was a great pity, for he would have been the very man for such a situation. His versatility, his imagination, his moderation and his charm would have made compromise possible on many points. He would have found a congenial companion in Mr. Lloyd George, for their temperaments would have brought them together.

M. Briand found himself called upon to assist in working out this peace which he had neither made nor approved. He tried to apply it in a different spirit from that in which it was conceived. Once victory was achieved M. Briand did not lose his head. He saw clearly that if his country was victorious she was also exhausted. Bolshevism caused him anxiety. Moral warfare with Germany could not be allowed to continue indefinitely after peace had been declared, and a solution had to be found for the difficulties which the peace had created and left unsolved. He saw above all that the most favorable moment for the resumption of relations with Germany was when France was in all the glory of her victory and Germany in the shame of her downfall.

It has often been said that M. Briand does not understand economics. Doubtless that is true. But when all the French economists deluded themselves into believing that Germany could pay the reparations, he was the only man to see that the sums demanded from her were "atmospheric"—the word is his. He saw that conflicts between nations cannot be settled on a strictly legal basis like a suit between private individuals. As early as 1921 he was striving to find an amicable solution to the problem of reparations and an arrangement with Germany.

Such an idea was not popular, but this so-called sceptic held on to what he believed to be the truth. It was that conviction which led once more to his defeat.

M. Poincaré replaced him and occupied the Ruhr. Such an experiment had to be made; any policy of reconciliation between France and Germany would have been doomed to all kinds of checks and vicissitudes if the way had not been cleared beforehand. Two years were to be lost before anything was gained. The mirage of the policy of force had to be dissolved. M. Briand himself said later in his inimitable ironic way: "The French people had been persuaded that somewhere there existed a golden fleece, and a Jason ready to go and find it. He went, and when he came back our peasants, who like things visible and tangible, asked to see the golden fleece. Then they realized that it was nothing but an old sheepskin."

Thus M. Poincaré paved the way for M. Briand: he created the conditions which permitted Locarno to succeed. But it was M. Briand who alone could bring the idea to fruition. I can see him still on the evening of the signing of the Treaty of Locarno, a prematurely bent man, standing on the boat that was taking us on an excursion. Behind him Lake Maggiore lay bathed in rosy light. M. Briand seemed to be supremely happy. He had just completed the greatest achievement of his life, the achievement with which his name will be linked for ever. No one would have dreamed of calling him a sceptic then.

Then came Thoiry and the tête-à-tête lunch with Herr Stresemann within sight of the majestic outline of Mont Blanc. There is a widespread impression that nothing resulted from that conversation, but it is not so. The arrangements which the two statesmen discussed there will come into being some day. But it will take time, the nations will have to be won over, and the United States led to certain sacrifices. M. Briand is ill and may never reap the fruit of what he has sown but he will have been the good laborer for the harvest.

Mention must be made here of the gratitude which Europe owes to these three men: M. Briand, Sir Austen Chamberlain and Herr Stresemann. Their common friendship has been a leading factor in international politics during the last few years. When one or other of them speaks of his colleagues the word "confidence" recurs again and again in the conversation. When M. Briand is speaking Sir Austen sits rapt in admiration. Thus they are all willing to help each other to sweep away the difficulties from their path and to minimize the effect of certain inevitable "incidents."

No one can measure the conflict, the confusion, the shocks, the crises from which the friendship of these men has saved

Europe. But the effects of it can be seen; Germany is readmitted into the harmony of nations, the League of Nations is strengthened, peace is assured and prosperity increases.

That is why in spite of his detractors M. Briand will not live in history as a sceptic. He may be a sceptic in little things but he has proved on more than one occasion that in vital matters he has faith. His lasting achievement was wrought by faith. He is one of the few statesmen who have fully understood the age we live in.

It has been said of M. Briand that, like Mazarin, he possessed the greatest quality of a statesman, luck. M. Briand is a lucky man, fortune smiles on him, difficulties melt away in his hands. But does not his luck come particularly from his talents? And are not his talents the three great qualities of his race: good sense, balance and moderation?

VIGOROUS CHARITY

HOOVER

GUSTAVE ADOR

HOOVER

IT IS NOT PRIMARILY AS A BENEFACTOR THAT WE IN EUROPE think of Mr. Hoover; it is as a man of business.

This descendant of a French colonist—his name is a corruption of the French Hubert—this son of a blacksmith in Iowa had already had a remarkable career when he arrived for the first time in London. At twenty-three he had been in charge of a mining enterprise in Western Australia; from there he had gone to China, where he took an active part in the defense of Tien-Tsin during the Boxer War and where, when the war was over, he salvaged a mining business which had gone to pieces. This exploit brought him before the notice of the company concerned in the business and they got him to return to London in 1902. This was his first contact with Europe.

From that moment on his activities were turned in another direction. Until this point he had been chiefly an engineer; henceforth he was to be chiefly and almost exclusively a business man, and to specialize in the reconstruction of companies in difficulties—thus foreshadowing his activities in the Great War, when it was possible to dub him "a specialist in catastrophes." In this way, in less than ten years, he reorganized and controlled in succession the mines of the Whitaker Wright group, the great copper and iron mines of the Urals, the lead mines of Burma, and the zinc and lead mines of New South Wales. When the War broke out, he occupied, as either managing director, chairman of directors, or manager, important functions in businesses which in the aggregate employed more than one hundred and twenty-five thousand workers.

A career of this kind may not seem anything out of the way to Americans. No doubt among their prominent business men one might find a great number with analogous records. But in Europe, where promotion goes by seniority, so rapid a progress, activities so diverse, so sudden an acquisition of great wealth, have on one a stupefying effect. Mr. Hoover's career down to the War was pursued almost entirely outside his own country, but only American conceptions and the possibilities they open to men of mark, made it practicable. Down to the opening of the War one sees no trace of idealism in this career. It is the career of a financier who conducts businesses and "makes good" in them. But this does not mean that the man is lacking in ideals. Mr. Hoover was very soon to prove this by placing his genius as an organizer at the service of the community.

In this new phase of his life, which lasted from 1914 to 1921, Mr. Hoover did not advertise his idealism and his sensibility any more than he had done in the previous phase. He acted simply as a business man, placing all the resources of his talent at the disposal of the aims he set himself. It was the aims that were disinterested and beneficent. Mr. Hoover's philanthropy has always had an unconscious air about it. Therein has lain its worth. Mr. Hoover has taken an interest in his task by reason of its difficulty and irrespective of its aims. He has staked his pride upon bringing things to success, not merely because the aims were generous but also because the task was hard.

It was the force of circumstances, it was almost a mere chance, that involved Mr. Hoover at the beginning of August,

1914, in the work to which he was to devote seven years of his life and which was to win him world-wide celebrity.

The War having broken out unexpectedly in the very middle of summer, a great number of Americans who were visiting Europe found themselves suddenly poor, it being impossible for them to cash their cheques at any bank. With their pockets full of cheques, they were penniless. It was necessary to come to their help, to rescue them and repatriate them. A committee was formed of which Mr. Hoover, a conspicuous member of the American community, was elected chairman. This committee came to the help of nearly twenty-five thousand Americans.

Meanwhile, a tragedy without precedent was being enacted in Belgium. The German invasion had brought the whole economic and social life of the country to a standstill, interrupted the harvest, interfered with the transport service, caused a general stoppage of industry accompanied by dreadful need. By the terms of the Hague Convention, it was the duty of the Germans to feed the population of the occupied territories. But they had many other things to preoccupy them and perhaps they were not troubling their minds about this. Winter approached, the need of the Belgians was increasing, and disquietude was being felt as to what would become of the poor of the country when the cold should set in.

In the foremost ranks of the personages who became absorbed in this problem was the United States Minister at Brussels, Mr. Brand Whitlock, who, impelled by benevolent feelings, had remained in the Belgian capital, expressly in order to come to the assistance of the inhabitants, and who acquitted himself of this task throughout nearly three years with admirable devotion, authority and tact. It was at the United States Legation that a meeting took place on October

16th, 1914, of Belgian, German and neutral notabilities, who decided on the one hand to appeal to America for financial help and on the other to ask the British government's permission to import cereals. Two Belgians of mark, M. Francqui and Baron Lambert, went to London for this purpose, furnished with letters of recommendation from Mr. Brand Whitlock. But when these gentlemen arrived in England they found that the work for which they came had already been taken in hand.

They had been preceded by another American, Mr. Millard Shaler, who before the War had been living in Brussels. From the very beginning of the occupation he had taken the initiative, with his friend Mr. Heinemann, in negotiations with the Germans; he had gone to The Hague to buy provisions but had not succeeded in getting them into Belgium. He had subsequently gone on to London on the same mission and he had discovered there that the provisioning of a country in time of war was a matter beyond the powers of individuals of good will. He had spoken about these things with Mr. Hoover, whom he knew personally, and with the United States Ambassador at London, Mr. Page. Mr. Hoover, whose work in Europe had seemed to be at an end, was on the point of returning to the United States. This was the decisive moment in his life. The legend—often more instructive than mere history—thus describes the scene: [1]

"The conversation which began between the two men (Mr. Page and Mr. Hoover) ended in the room of Sir Edward Grey. It was there that came into shape the idea of feeding an entire people throughout the lapse of an indefinite period. The British Admiralty raised objections. Would not provisions stocked in Belgium be utilized by the German army? 'No,'

[1] *Echo de Paris*, June 19th, 1928.

replied Mr. Page and Mr. Hoover, 'because our government will guarantee their destination.' 'But who will undertake the control of such an enterprise?' Mr. Page went on to remark. Then, suddenly, turning towards his compatriot, he added: 'It will be you!' Hoover made no reply. He said neither yes nor no. He looked at his watch and left the room, returning presently to continue the discussion: 'It just crossed my mind,' he explained, 'that the New York Stock Exchange will be closed in an hour's time. I made haste, therefore, to buy some millions of bushels of corn for the Belgians by cablegram.' "

Some days later Mr. Hoover cabled to Mr. Brand Whitlock that he had organized the Committee and that he would at once put in hand the necessary mechanism for the purchase and despatch of provisions.

When M. Francqui, who had known Mr. Hoover in China, returned to Brussels, he described him to Mr. Whitlock. He drew a bold impressionistic picture of him, full of infectious admiration. He ended with a sweeping gesture of his hand under his own chin: "A man with a jaw, you know!" Mr. Brand Whitlock himself was soon to see Mr. Hoover. He gives a vivid picture of the man in his book: the slim figure, the small hands and feet; the youthful clean-shaven face, not suggestive of a man of business—a sensitive face, marked by the look of fatigue which comes from overtaxing one's nervous force; and with dark eyes beneath the wide white brow, over which the black hair fell almost in disorder: a face that would have suggested rather an idealist, were it not for one predominant feature which told unmistakably of the man of will—the strong and massive jaw which caught one's attention immediately and which recalled M. Francqui's graphic gesture!

The work which Mr. Hoover now entered upon with a

light heart soon assumed formidable proportions. Mr. Brand Whitlock reminds us of its scope. It was a matter of finding ten million dollars a month; of buying provisions in the most distant markets of the world—in the Argentine, in Canada, in the United States; of finding means of transport upon dangerous seas; of distributing these provisions among seven millions of men in a country in which the mechanism of life had broken down, in which the ordinary means of communication no longer existed: and all this had to be achieved in the midst of armies engaged in war! In times of peace, as Mr. Whitlock remarks, the task of creating such an organization would have been difficult enough. In the chaos produced by the War, in an atmosphere charged with suspicions, jealousies, hatreds, envies, all the passions let loose upon the world, it seemed almost impossible.

Mr. Hoover triumphed over all the difficulties. Far from allowing himself to be stopped in his work, he never ceased to extend it. To Belgium, with its seven million inhabitants, he added Northern France and Luxembourg. He himself has given an impressive *résumé* of the outcome of his efforts. The work had organized, he says, a perfect machine for distributing the provisions with equality, so that the poor, maintained in a normal condition physically, were able to offer a moral resistance to the enemy; it had furnished a rallying point for the local authorities; its delegates, in their capacity as eye-witnesses, had put a bridle upon the German officials and had prevented many a brutality.

Admittedly, this enormous work was not the work of Mr. Hoover alone. "The Committee for Relief in Belgium" counted no fewer than one hundred and fifty members in Belgium itself, one hundred in London, Rotterdam and New York, while there were five thousand local committees in

America and elsewhere for the collection of funds. But Mr. Hoover was the life and soul of the whole work and it is thanks to his personal qualities that it was able to triumph over its obstacles.

There is a saying: to govern is to foresee. Mr. Hoover had a foreseeing mind. On the day when the first of his collaborators arrived in Brussels, some one asked him: "How long will the war last?"

"Mr. Hoover," came the reply, with a certain hesitation in the tones in which it was delivered, "Mr. Hoover is making his arrangements on the basis of three years."

Three years! That was Kitchener's estimate, too.

Mr. Hoover possessed also the talent, so rare among men of the highest order, of knowing how to find and recruit his helpers. To begin with, he placed his hand on forty young Americans at Oxford—Rhodes scholars; then he looked for the right people to manage his different services; and Mr. Brand Whitlock, who saw them close at hand, is never tired of praising the quality of his choice.

In this work Mr. Hoover exerted the great faculty which has made him an organizer of the highest order: a practical mind. Idealism and sensibility are, assuredly, not lacking in him. He has given numerous proofs of that. On the day when for the first time he inspected the distribution of soup in Brussels, his eyes were filled with tears and he had to turn aside to wipe them away. When he talked of the sufferings of the Belgians or of the inhabitants of northern France, it was always with profound sympathy and genuine understanding. Sunk in an armchair—so Mr. Brand Whitlock describes him— he would talk of their woes in his deep compassionate voice. But his mind would soon turn to practical means.

His great strength lay in knowing how far he could go

in his demands and how far in his resistance. When the Germans wanted to subject his delegates in Belgium to a humiliating control, "he gave them a prompt and resolute 'No'; rather than consent, he preferred to see the work ended." The Germans did not insist! Mr. Hoover had divined what others were presently to learn: "the only tone which they understood was that which they themselves employed."

On another occasion, the Germans having again threatened to restrict the privileges of the American agents, Mr. Hoover sent an open cablegram ordering them to stop work and close their accounts. The Germans did not want to see the work stopped and to be obliged themselves—they who were short of everything—to feed ten million Belgians and Frenchmen of the occupied territories; so they gave in. Which moved M. Francqui to make the remark: "Hoover is the best diplomat of us all!" And yet Hoover was then in America three thousand miles away (at a time when communications were slow and difficult), out of touch with the situation and with no clue to the essential element—the atmosphere of the moment.

The strength of Mr. Hoover and of his colleagues just then lay in their disinterestedness. America was giving ten million dollars a month without any apparent motive except generosity. That is what the Germans found it most difficult to understand. They were unceasingly on the lookout for *arrière-pensées*, for hidden motives. They were continually asking: "What do you Americans get out of all this? Where is your profit?"

One day, Mr. Hoover, angered by this constantly recurring inquiry, looked the high official who had asked it straight in the face, his eyes blazing, and replied: "As it is impossible for you Germans to understand that one may do a thing from humanitarian motives and quite unselfishly, I shall not try to explain it."

The Belgians are deeply conscious of how much Hoover did for them. Immediately after the War, the Brussels municipality prepared a ceremony in his honor to express their gratitude to him. The school children, "who owed him their lives," were to file past him and Mayor Max had prepared a speech in which he said: "America has saved Belgium twice. For the American armies would only have freed a vast cemetery if they had not been preceded by the magnificent piece of work with which Mr. Hoover's name will always be associated."

Unfortunately, Hoover was prevented from coming by pressing duties elsewhere and the ceremony did not take place.

This work into which he had put all his heart and in which he had employed all his talents had drawn upon Mr. Hoover the gaze not only of Europe but also of his own country. Thus, when America entered into the War, President Wilson, who had a liking for "experts," intimated to Mr. Hoover that he wanted to make him Food Controller of the United States.

The task in question was gigantic and unattractive. The United States, which produces in superabundance, is not accustomed to practice economy. It had become necessary to teach economy to this American people, to induce them to practice self-restraint, and that, not in a purely national interest, not for a purpose perceptible and immediate, but in the interest of foreign and distant nations, in the interest of that entity—mythical entity for many Americans—Europe. Mr. Hoover now employed new qualities, notably a capacity for propaganda and for advertisement, which he exercized for the good of the world, and for which the European nations should be profoundly grateful to him. For it was in a great measure thanks to him that they were able to get through the terrible crises of submarine warfare.

Switzerland, in particular, owes him a great debt of gratitude, for it was thanks to Hoover that she was then able to obtain food supplies under relatively satisfactory conditions. I remember, when I was in America with some colleagues from the Swiss press, a lunch given in our honor at which the food controller presided. Hoover is a silent man and we did not hear his voice very often during the meal. But afterwards he made a speech in the President's name and his own, on the philanthropic work carried out by Switzerland at that time and on the American government's wish to assist the Swiss people to the utmost of their ability. His speech gave evidence of a deep appreciation, of a knowledge of the facts and of experience in European affairs.

We must render to Cæsar the things that are Cæsar's. Mr. Hoover was powerfully assisted then in the provisioning of Europe by the Inter-Allied organizations of London, which foreshadowed as it were the actual League of Nations. But these organizations, which were charged with the transportation and distribution of raw materials and provisions, would have had nothing to transport and distribute if Mr. Hoover at the source had not succeeded in intensifying production and in restricting the consumption of his own people.

"It is not Mr. Lloyd George," some one said just then in London, "who has won the War. It is Sir Arthur Salter." [1]

May it not be said with greater truth that it was Mr. Hoover?

When the War was concluded, Mr. Hoover entered upon

---

[1] Now Director of the Economic Section of the League of Nations; then one of the officials of the Inter-Allied Shipping Executive.

a new phase. He had at first been called upon to feed Belgium and northern France, then the Allies and the neutrals. Now he was asked to feed the whole of Europe. The day the Germans appealed to President Wilson for an armistice, Hoover embarked from New York for Europe. The report was current that he was going to "feed the Germans." He denied vehemently this interpretation of his journey, for the questions which were about to be considered were of a general character. It was to be foreseen that at the moment when the frontiers were to be reopened, after four years of blockades and privations, profound disturbances must occur in the revictualing of the world. It was necessary to insure for the enemy countries the provisions which they needed; but it was necessary above all to protect the Allied and neutral countries against any improper competition. It was with this duty that Mr. Hoover was now charged; and in fulfilling successfully this new mission he rendered Europe a service which it would be difficult to exaggerate.

At this grave hour, a trifle might have sufficed to send certain countries over to Bolshevism. Mr. Hoover perceived this at once. He understood that if this rôle was not to show sentimentality towards the vanquished, elementary prudence demanded that he should save the victors from the contagion of revolution. For that, the surest means was to prevent famine in Germany and Austria. Mr. Hoover has often denied that he took any kind of anti-Bolshevik action—and it is true that his solicitude extended even to the Russians. But it is none the less true that, in provisioning the defeated countries, Mr. Hoover contributed powerfully towards the checking of the Bolshevist movements in Germany, Austria and Hungary. By feeding Europe he saved it from revolution.

It is said that Hoover has unpleasant memories of his

work in Europe and that he bears a grudge against the old world for all the misery he found there. Europe, at any rate, has a pleasant memory of the man who helped her to remedy that misery.

On returning to his own country in 1920, Mr. Hoover became quite soon Secretary of Commerce. That is not a post which offers to a man of silent temperament and with a dislike of personal advertisement many chances of covering himself with glory. However, there are men who always are bigger than their posts. Mr. Hoover found in this new position means of applying to the administration of his own country the experiences which he had amassed during the War.

His intimate knowledge of world economy served him in his contest with the British rubber monopoly; habits of rapid improvization enabled him to go effectually to the aid of the Mississippi sufferers. But it is above all the measures taken during the War to promote production in the United States and to prevent waste that have led Mr. Hoover to understand the importance for industry of as rational and economic a production as possible. That is perhaps, the greatest benefit that America has reaped from the War.

The work accomplished by Mr. Hoover in Europe has not merely served his fame. It has not merely opened to him a statesman's career. It has above all qualified him to be useful to his country.

GUSTAVE ADOR

THE NAME OF GUSTAVE ADOR CALLS TO MIND A TOWN RATHER than a man.

The destiny of Geneva is unusual and arresting. There are few cities that so clearly suggest the idea of a divine mission, for during the last three hundred years the part Geneva has played in the affairs of the world has been consistently more important than Geneva itself.

Geneva was a small place when John Calvin happened to visit it in the course of a journey, at the end of August, 1536. Although he was then only twenty-seven years of age, he was already famous for his writings, and the Genevese reformer Farel begged him to settle there and preach. This event alone was sufficient to transform the little town of merchants into one of those cities that have had the greatest influence upon the development of the human mind.

From that moment, Geneva not only became the center of the reform of the French language but also the headquarters of the entire Calvinistic reform movement, coming into touch with France, Italy, Germany, the Scandinavian countries, Hungary, Scotland, and later with the United States. For centuries this town was a sort of Christian Mecca towards which the eyes of the world were turned. It welcomed students of all nationalities and, in the midst of religious persecutions, offered shelter to countless unhappy exiles. When, after crossing the mountains surrounding Geneva, they caught a sudden glimpse of the cathedral towers outlined against the sky, many would burst into tears of joy and relief.

Centuries passed; the religious wars died down. Geneva became a little town again. Once more, at the will of fate or providence, it produced a man of genius, Jean-Jacques Rousseau, the apostle of democracy and of equality among men. No one had so great an influence upon the eighteenth century; he was a spiritual father of the American War of Independence and of the French Revolution.

In 1798 Geneva was annexed by France; her freedom regained in 1814, she gave herself to Switzerland. Her world importance seemed to end with her independence. Suddenly, in 1864, Geneva rose again by her own efforts to the level of world importance when Henry Dunant founded the International Red Cross.

Henry Dunant had been present at the battle of Solferino; he had witnessed the sufferings of the wounded and seen the lack of medical aid. Any other man would have gone home and have forgotten his emotion, no ordinary person would ever have thought of getting into touch with the governments of the world, any other than he would have been appalled by so superhuman a task. Not so Henry Dunant. Urged by the practical idealism that is the characteristic trait of the Swiss, accustomed as a Genevese to look upon the world as his playground and, as a republican, to regard kings as his equals, he did not shrink from his duty. He approached every king and every state, and this man, unaided and at that time unknown, succeeded by his own efforts in bringing about the Geneva Convention for the care of wounded soldiers, the most generous international act of the whole nineteenth century, which may be regarded as the corner stone of what was one day to be the League of Nations.

GUSTAVE ADOR

HERBERT CLARK HOOVER

GUSTAVE ADOR

Gustave Ador was the third president of the International Red Cross Committee, founded by Henry Dunant.

He came of a line of bankers, who knew how to make money in business but never forgot that their ancestors had fought and suffered for their faith and that spiritual riches are above material gain. The sons of bankers in Geneva are to be found all along the line, in the Church as pastors, at the University as professors, and in the State as leaders of men.

Gustave Ador held every public office in his town and in his country that was open to a man of his birth. He rose from rank to rank to the highest positions. His life was singularly happy; it flowed smoothly without encountering any serious difficulties or unsurmountable obstacles, almost without any troubles. But is not every great achievement a combination of talent and luck? Gustave Ador's ability lay in the fact that he was always ready for the good fortune that came his way and always equal to the tasks that were entrusted to him.

When he became president of the International Red Cross Committee in 1910, none could suppose that it would be called upon to fulfill a great destiny. Since it was founded it had had to intervene only in wars restricted to a few states, and there was nothing to foretell what it would be able to undertake in event of a general war.

The three factors necessary to enable the Red Cross to function to its fullest capacity during the War were Gustave Ador's personality, the atmosphere of Geneva, and Swiss neutrality.

Gustave Ador already had a great international reputation in 1914. He did not hesitate, at the beginning of the War, to exceed in the interests of humanity the strict limits of his authority and to go beyond the literal meaning of treaties. He did exactly as Henry Dunant had done. He, an ordinary citizen of a republican country, entered into negotiations with the governments of the world as their equal. He repeatedly denounced the violation of rights, the atrocities committed by the armies and the abuses to which civil populations were subject. He protested against the use of poison gas, the submarine blockade, the bombardment of hospitals, propaganda campaigns and reprisals, etc. He exerted his moral authority to the utmost and it grew as he used it.

But if the Red Cross had been content merely to protest, if its activity had been only negative and unproductive, the world would soon have become tired of it. Far from this, its great achievement was the Prisoners of War Agency, founded on August 27th, 1914, in the midst of universal confusion. Originally the one aim of the Red Cross was to help the wounded. But it soon became evident that in a long war the prisoners might be in still greater need. The Red Cross accordingly organized this agency in Geneva. Of modest beginnings, it grew as the need for it grew, employing as many as twelve hundred voluntary helpers, recruited from all classes of society. An average of thirty thousand letters were received daily, information was sent to countless prisoners' families, nearly two million parcels and eighteen million francs ($3,-600,000) in small sums were forwarded to prisoners to enable them to provide themselves with a little comfort.

In order to understand what this work was and to appreciate the moral and material support it gave to thousands of human beings, one must have seen the people from all parts of the world who flocked to Geneva, torn with anxiety, to find out if a son, a fiancé, or a father were still alive and to seek news of him. Once more Geneva became a refuge, the only place in the world where people of certain nationalities could meet without killing each other. The great white flag with the red cross flying over the Prisoners of War Agency became a symbol of peace, and the radiant personality of Gustave Ador its very incarnation.

The Prisoners of War Agency did still more. It used its influence with the governments to obtain better treatment of the prisoners; it sent delegates to the camps of the various nations and pointed out to the various governments where reform was most urgently needed. It brought about the mutual repatriation of medical staff, then of the severely wounded, the sick, and the disabled. It arranged that thousands of sick prisoners should be interned in Switzerland, and supervised the evacuation of the civil population in the north of France and Belgium. After the War it organized the repatriation of all the prisoners.

This résumé can give only a vague idea of the material difficulties encountered and of the high human endeavor demanded by such a work. For years the hopes of thousands of individuals were concentrated upon Geneva, the Agency, and upon Gustave Ador, as representing, in the midst of all the slaughter, the only humane impulse, the only disinterested desire for peace. Such an organization entailed endless journeys, continual negotiations, and much study on the part of the leaders.

Two circumstances were essential to the success of this undertaking: the unanimous coöperation of the Genevese, and Swiss neutrality. The fact that the members of the International Red Cross Committee were exclusively Genevese has sometimes been criticized. This was the secret of its success; if it had been of a truly international character, it would have been during the War the scene of intrigue, competition, and dispute, and would have been unable to impose its moral authority upon the belligerents. It was on account of its recognized impartiality that it was able to exert an even greater influence on the warring nations than the highest moral authority in the world at that time, the Papacy.

But this very political impartiality would have been inconceivable without the permanent neutrality of Switzerland. For the last hundred years the Swiss Confederation has not taken part in any war, has not had any serious dispute with any country, nor desired any increase of territory. Her government has always endeavored, even in times of peace, to avoid favoring one of her neighbors to the detriment of another, and by this policy she has now earned a greater political and moral credit than that of any other country.

When in 1917, in consequence of a mistake on the part of one of her officials. her neutrality was temporarily threatened, it was Gustave Ador to whom the Swiss people appealed to assume power and to restore the glory and the reputation of Swiss neutrality. From having been sheltered by Swiss neutrality the International Red Cross Committee became its guarantor.

Swiss neutrality is not a negative idea. It represents an international undertaking whereby certain great powers have pledged themselves to keep peace. Switzerland declared permanent neutrality not in her own interests but in those of Europe. President Wilson recognized this when he said that the United States has something to learn from every nation but that few can teach them so much as the Swiss.

Neutrality demands loyalty but does not exclude courage. In 1917 the Swiss became impatient of the silence of their government and greatly appreciated certain statements

made by Gustave Ador that recalled or were the forerunners of some of the most famous of President Wilson's
speeches:

"Every one in Switzerland hopes for peace, but we must
agree as to the nature of that peace. . . . In order to protect
Europe from as terrible a disaster as that which we have
witnessed for the past three years, in order that after this
horrible war there may be in the world more true solidarity
and a wider understanding of the aspirations of all peoples,
we must hope for a peace that shall not be a mere temporary
cessation of hostilities but a regenerating and lasting peace.
But no peace can be lasting unless it is based upon the eternal
principles of justice, of right and of liberty and upon respect for the freely expressed desires of the people. . . ."

Thus, after having been the embodiment of international
philanthropy, then of justice between nations, Gustave Ador
found himself, in 1919, the President of Switzerland at the
time when the Peace Conference decided to establish the
headquarters of the League of Nations in Geneva.

There were many reasons for this decision, but two of the
most important cannot be overlooked: the confidence felt
by all nations in Switzerland's political loyalty, and the great
international past of Geneva. Swiss neutrality and the International Red Cross have become the very foundations of the
League of Nations. For the Red Cross was the first great
work of international coöperation from which all the later international organizations have sprung, and which prepared the
moral and legal ground for the foundation of the League of
Nations. Swiss neutrality was the first collective attempt to
insure permanent peace in one particular part of the world.
Traces of these two ideas can be seen very clearly in the
League of Nations Covenant. And the man who better than

any other represents both these ideas may well be called the forerunner of the League of Nations.

It is an impressive thought that the influence of this man upon the fate of the world, of one who had always remained outside high international politics, who had had neither navies nor armies at his disposal, should by reason of his sheer spiritual power and intuition have been greater than that of the greatest.

AMERICAN INTERVENTION

PRESIDENT WILSON

COLONEL HOUSE

PRESIDENT WILSON

IT WAS THE PRIVILEGE AND THE GREAT MERIT OF AMERICAN democracy on each of the three occasions of national crisis which it has traversed to produce the man of outstanding gifts whom the nation needed: Washington, Lincoln, Wilson. It is not for us to say which of them will in the long run appear the greatest in the eyes of his fellow citizens. But it was Wilson, beyond a doubt, who exercised the most profound influence upon the history of the world.

There is an infallible sign by which we may recognize great men: namely, grave circumstances magnify their stature. The War submerged all our European statesmen—one may say, without exception; alone the personality of President Wilson was made to look infinitely more impressive by this formidable ordeal.

In the Presidential career of Woodrow Wilson we must note two phases. The first was what we may call the American phase—that tremendous parleying between the President and the people which lasted nearly three years and ended in the declaration of war on the 6th of April, 1917. The second phase, which we may call the European, was that during which the President of the United States exercised over our Continent a greater moral influence than ever before belonged to any one man.

To us Europeans it seems that President Wilson's career is to be explained primarily by the thoroughgoing knowledge he possessed of his own race. We are aware that Americans are not agreed upon the subject. Some of them accuse him of having been a party-man and an autocrat. Assuredly President Wilson was conscious of his powers and made full use of them. But he never was blind to their source; he realized that he could do everything with public opinion behind him, and nothing without it. His rule, absolute seemingly, and authoritative in its acts, was, in all the full meaning of the term, a rule of public opinion,—a democratic force.

Elected in 1912 by a kind of fluke, Wilson devoted the first four years of his presidency to internal reforms of a social character, destined to ensure him popularity. Then, on the solid basis thus constructed for his authority, he launched his country on the greatest adventure in all history.

Misunderstood and undervalued throughout three years, President Wilson conducted the foreign policy of the United States with a sense of vision, an energy and a logical consistency that deserved the admiration of posterity. A target for the passionate attack of his opponents and of all those who could not see into his intentions, he did not allow himself to be turned aside from the task he had mapped out for himself. Re-reading now the long series of his messages and notes to Germany on the submarine warfare, one can follow the harmonious and ascending curve of his line of thought. These documents, which seemed so utterly feeble and for which Europe had not sarcasms enough, were, on the contrary, masterpieces of moral dialectics and political tactics. They attained their dual object, which was to convince the American public of the necessity of entering the War and the German public of the injustice of their cause.

In America, as in Europe, the reproach has been brought against President Wilson that he delayed his intervention in the War too long: this is to misunderstand the conditions of his task. The American public felt for European entanglements an instinctive horror traceable to a dictum of Washington's. A premature decision, the meaning of which the people could not have grasped, would have met with sullen resistance or violent opposition. The country would have been divided and American intervention would therefore have been ineffective.

The president's great power lay in the fact that he had evolved with his people. At first he was opposed to the War, but by degrees and not without severe searching of conscience he came to see that it was necessary. This internal conflict was the source of the moral strength that inspired his people to follow him.

President Wilson rendered Europe a much greater service by taking his time and leading his people gradually to view the War, as he himself viewed it, as a crusade. It was only in this way that his intervention could have its moral and material effect.

Once in the War, President Wilson immediately took in hand its spiritual control, by reason less of the material resources at his command than of his political program, the wide range of his horizon, the clearness of his ideas, the loftiness of his thoughts.

The intervention of the United States did not merely modify the perspective of the War, ruining the hopes of Germany and making up for the defection of Russia. It changed the moral orientation of the conflict from top to bottom, bathed Europe in a flood of new idealism and gave new life to the cause of the Allies by identifying it for good and all with the cause of Liberty.

Germany had entered into the War in 1914 to upset for her own benefit the diplomatic and military equilibrium of

Europe; she wished to insure the peace of the world by methods of her own, to the exclusion of the liberty of others. That was the idea expressed by Von Bethman-Hollweg when he said, in a naïve phrase, that Germany was ready to place herself "at the head" of the League of Nations.

President Wilson saw clearly that this German conception of European hegemony was in its essence one of never-ending war. Europe has never borne with hegemony, neither under Philip II, nor under Louis XIV, nor under Napoleon. How could it have borne with hegemony under William II? All dominations provoke coalitions. In fighting to bar the road against German hegemony President Wilson fought to win for Europe a lasting peace. His war was an affirmation of the solidarity of mankind.

From this, people have drawn the conclusion that it was an entirely disinterested war from the American point of view. President Wilson would certainly have rejected a piece of praise which would have involved a grave accusation. For the first duty of a statesman, faithful to his oath, is to safeguard the interests of his own country.

But in this world of ours, human solidarity does not stop short at national frontiers. Isolation nowadays is an illusion and an impossibility. I remember once asking the American Senator James Reed this question: "Do you believe that isolation is possible for your country?"

"Of course," he replied, "we do not want to be isolated from the world trade."

Diplomacy is the guardian of commerce, and a country cannot isolate itself politically if it does not want to be isolated commercially. It was, in the first instance, the freedom of the sea, i. e., the safeguarding of American commerce, that drew President Wilson into the War. But maritime commerce is to be safeguarded not only on the sea. Commerce demands peace. Its interest is that peace should reign all the world over, and above all in Europe. The President, therefore, decided on one single war aim, at once selfish and altruistic: the establishment in Europe of a lasting peace.

But that, some one will say, was an idea common to all the belligerents. No one ever fights except for peace. Yes and no, for if all wanted peace, almost all pursued some other aim in the War—the recovery of Alsace-Lorraine, the restruction of the German navy, the winning back of the regions torn by Austria from Italy, etc. The United States alone entered into the struggle without any other objective than peace and with a clear view of the essential conditions.

"The United States," President Wilson declared, "will go to the Peace Conference resolved to ask nothing for themselves and to prevent any one else from getting anything." The League of Nations, in the view of the President, was not a more or less theoretical and personal conception. It was the logical and necessary consequence of his intervention, the actual realization of his war aim. It is strange to reflect that this man whom Europe so often accused of lack of comprehension, whom she so long misunderstood, first flattering him, then calumniating him, but never understanding him, was the only one who really divined Europe and her needs!

President Wilson had one precursor in history, Alexander I of Russia. Russia was scarcely less remote from western Europe in 1815, scarcely less foreign to its preoccupation than is the United States to-day. At the Congress of Vienna Alexander played the rôle which was later to be played by President Wilson—the rôle of the disinterested arbiter, faithful to principles, and of the protector to the small nations. His prestige was immense. Women fainted from emotion at the very sight of him. Unfortunately Alexander I did not remain faithful to his mission; he sought territorial advantages in which his authority at last was submerged.

It was quite otherwise with President Wilson. Confronted with men immersed in everyday affairs, absorbed in current events, their eyes riveted on small details, the President had the great advantage of being able to take large views. Standing far off enough to perceive the general in the particular, the permanent in the momentary, the essential in the subsidiary, disinterested enough to inspire confidence, powerful enough to be able to insist on his point of view, President Wilson possessed in addition the talent so rare among statesmen: he knew how to speak to the people.

The masses like to be talked to about the ideal. Our statesmen of the old world, inheritors of a civilization colored by scepticism, forget this all too often. American statesmen, whose frequent duty it is to converse with the masses, remember it. To President Wilson's mind, steeped in Puritan tradition and influence, there came quite naturally the words which, after prevailing on the United States to enter into the War, were to prove equally efficacious in bringing about peace in Europe.

In order to realize nowadays the effect which President Wilson's messages had in Europe, we have to remind ourselves of the state of exhaustion we then were in. Years of mourning, of anxieties, of privations, had ended by exhausting our energies and lacerating our nerves. It was at a moment when the end of the struggle could not be seen, on the morrow of the Russian Revolution and of the check to Germany's submarine warfare, that President Wilson brought to the Allies the strength to achieve victory and to the Central Powers the hope of being given justice.

The Fourteen Points, an outline of an ideal organization of the world, went to the heads of the peoples after their long fast. It was the Fourteen Points that overcame the resistance of the Bulgarians, the Austrians and the Germans, that took the force out of the offensive of 1918 and forced General Ludendorf to sue for peace.

Finally it was President Wilson who by refusing to treat with the old government drove Germany and her Allies into revolution. However great may have been the exhaustion of Germany it is probable that in 1918, without Wilson, Foch would not have been victorious. For in Germany it was not the army that first gave in, it was the mind of the public.

Every effort of the President from then onwards was to be concentrated on the peace negotiations.

In coming to Europe, President Wilson did a brave thing. His people did not view with favor a displacement in which they saw the violation if not of a written law at least of a tradition deserving of respect. They feared lest their President might, while away, lose contact with American affairs and preoccupations.

In Paris, the President was to run risks of another kind. His authority in respect to European questions did not come merely from the clarity of his views and the breadth of his conceptions and of his political intuition. It came also from his remoteness. The President had been able to proclaim what was right without regard for any one in Europe because he had seen things from without and in perspective, unembarrassed by personal considerations or selfish interests. He had been soaring aloft above the fray. Coming down now into the midst of things, President Wilson incurred the risk of losing some measure of his independence, of being entangled in the intrigues of antechambers and back-stairs, of finding political problems complicated by considerations of politeness and good manners. It is a source of strength for a negotiator to be able to say no on behalf of some one else. President Wilson risked being less strong than at Washington, less strong than his colleagues.

If the President, who was not blind to any of these perils, decided nevertheless to cross the ocean, he had peremptory reasons for doing so.

To begin with, he had not among his official following any man capable of representing him. It has often been made a matter for criticism that the President acted alone and did not take any one into his confidence; and that he was not able to surround himself with men of the highest order. That, doubtless, was his weak point. But it was the result of the very nature of his thought and of his task. Few of the men around him were really capable of seeing what he saw, of understanding what he understood; not one of them could *will* what he willed with the same force as he. Hence his isolation, of which as a matter of fact too much has been made. As for his American opponents, in taking them with him to Paris he would have compromised the unity, the cohesion and the authority of his delegation. President Wilson was on this occasion the victim of his own supremacy.

The President did not arrive in Europe with fixed ideas about the peace and a determination to insist upon them. He had only one idea and that was that he must keep the promise which was made to the world at the moment the United States entered into the War and for which millions of soldiers had died: that this war should be the last and that there should be a League of Nations.

The League of Nations was no invention of his, it did not issue forth, fully armed, from his brain. It is the outcome of

WOODROW WILSON

the whole economic and political evolution of the nineteenth century. The development of machinery and of means of communication has created needs for all countries, even for the richest, needs in respect to raw materials and markets which bind them together. The law of the world is no longer reciprocal independence but interdependence. The League of Nations had been in existence potentially *de facto* long before it came into existence *de jure*. Herein lies the guarantee of its power and its solidity. What it had previously lacked was a spirit forceful enough to deduce from these facts the truth which they embodied. President Wilson brought it this spirit.

The League of Nations was about to submit to the Peace Conference two problems, one a matter of procedure, the other fundamental.

The President perceived that if the pact were not incorporated in the Treaty of Peace, if the League were not born at once, at the moment when all the Allies needed each other's support, a new war would be required to produce it. Without the League of Nations, moreover, how were the questions involved in the peace to be settled—the question of the Sarre, of Danzig, of Uppr Silesia, of the German colonies, of Austria, etc., etc.? And what would be the good of settling them? Would not such settlements be made open to question again almost at once? Before constructing the edifice, they must see to the foundation.

M. Clémenceau and Mr. Lloyd George did not see the grandeur of the President's conception. When together, they made a joke of it. In their eyes the only thing that mattered was the definition of the frontier. It was necessary to get ahead quickly, they felt, and impose on Germany a preliminary peace, leaving all other questions for a second Congress, as had been done in 1814.

President Wilson opposed this procedure. He wanted to carry the Pact with him back to Washington in February. It was to please him that his colleagues agreed to set up, at the first meeting of the Peace Conference, the League of Nations Commission of which Mr. Wilson himself became president and whose activities he at once set in motion. In thus acting he rendered mankind a service for which he cannot be too highly praised. For he enabled the League of Nations to be constituted at the only moment possible.

As to the general problem of peace, President Wilson's ideas, still somewhat vague on his arrival in Europe, came gradually into shape in the course of the Conference, influenced by contact with Lord Robert Cecil and General Smuts. But there was one point upon which the President never changed: namely, that the League of Nations must substitute for the old régime of alliances and of the balance of power (the consequences of which had been periodical warfare), a new system of security. To this end it was necessary that the League should obtain a general and reciprocal undertaking from all the states which were members of it that they would come to the assistance of any country made a victim of an aggression. Over and above this, in order that the undertaking should be made effective, it was necessary that no state should in the future be strong enough to oppose victoriously the action of the League. Hence the determination of the President to oppose any form whatever of supremacy, whether on the Continent or on the seas.

On his arrival in Europe Mr. Wilson had no intention of entering into any political or diplomatic maneuverings in his dealings with the Allies. But he could not entirely forget that England was the only country which had dared to oppose his Fourteen Points on an essential question, the freedom of the seas. So he decided to place the British government in a dilemma: a limitation of armaments or a competition in armaments.

When the *George Washington* reached Brest, a French official delegation, which had come thither to welcome the President, went on board. President Wilson delivered a little speech to them in the course of which he more or less suggested that the French and he together should become the arbiters of the world. When a translation of what he said was shown to the French Minister of Foreign Affairs, M. Pichon, who understood no English, he raised his hands to Heaven exclaiming: "Oh, but it will never do to say that! What would the English think?" The delegation went back to the President who replied: "I don't hold by my actual words. Put into my mouth whatever you like."

The French did not know how to profit by this attitude of amiability. M. Clémenceau laughed at the League of Nations and he could never resist the temptation of poking fun at this "homme de Dieu," as he called the President. In one speech he spoke of the President's "noble candeur." The word "candeur" has not quite the same meaning as the English "candor" and President Wilson was vexed. Later M. Poincaré said to him: "When you have seen our battle fields you will understand. . . ." President Wilson thought it was intended to give him a lesson.

On top of all, Mr. Wilson, who saw in the liberty of the seas the safeguarding of peace and the independence of the nations, was astonished to hear M. Clémenceau declare to him that he would not suffer the naval supremacy of Great Britain, the basis of European security, to be touched.

The President began to feel morally isolated in Paris.

It was about this time that President Wilson went to England. He was admirably received there. He visited the sacred shrines of his race and was much moved. He was treated by the English with that noble simplicity which is peculiar to them. Mr. Lloyd George in his clever way gave the President all the comforting assurances he needed in respect to the freedom of the seas. The President formed the impression that it was easier to come to an understanding with men of the same race and the same tongue. If it may be said that the Treaty of Versailles was an Anglo-Saxon Treaty that is due in part to the President's visit to England.

In President Wilson's character there was a singular contradiction. He was a man of the study. He was often reproached for holding himself aloof. He never felt so fully in touch with his people as when alone. At Washington he saw nobody and played golf three hours a day. In Paris this man who had so solemnly condemned "secret diplomacy" shut himself up for months in a tête-à-tête with a few European ministers; he found them, indeed, too many, and these councils became smaller and smaller and more and more secret.

And yet the President loved to address himself to the people. He enjoyed educating the masses. He lived in the illusion that the masses are more pacific than the governments and he tried on several occasions to make direct appeals to them over the heads of their governments. Thus it was that in Rome he affected when speaking in public not to be addressing the government, with which he was at issue over a grave matter.

Italy before entering the War on the side of the Allies had concluded a treaty which had guaranteed her certain advantages whenever peace should be made. Now certain of these advantages were contrary to the principles of President Wilson, who, moreover, did not consider himself bound by the treaty in question which he had never signed.

Mr. Wilson showed himself generous towards Italy. He accorded her without discussion the Brenner frontier; he is declared not to have known at the time that he was thus giving to Italy, to her strategic advantage, a region inhabited by hundreds of thousands of Germans, and he is said to have been much disturbed when he learnt this afterwards. A day came, however, when he said to the Italians: "So far and no further!" On that day, Italian delegates quitted the Peace Conference.

The President had thought he would find more understanding of justice in the Italian people than in Signor Orlando or Baron Sonnino. "Matters await our attention," he said in Rome, "which are more difficult than the matters we have dealt with. For it is easy to talk about Right and Justice, but it is sometimes difficult to put them in practice, and this task will demand a purity of intention and a disinterestedness such as the world has never witnessed. . . ."

Perhaps the President enjoyed the illusion of having succeeded, for in Italy he had been made the object of ovations surpassing anything he had ever experienced elsewhere. But the meaning of these ovations was not what he believed: the Italians, far from being convinced by his words, were trying to win him over.

The relative failure of President Wilson in his relations with the peoples of Europe was due to several causes. First of all, he had underestimated the influence of the governments over the public opinion of their countries; secondly, it was impossible for him to make himself understood by peoples whose language he could not speak; finally, his ideas were often forestalled by the Socialists, and he became embroiled unwittingly and unintentionally in the strife of parties.

But his most serious fault consisted in not perceiving that in Europe only the small countries could be sincere partisans of his ideas, which were contrary to all the traditions of the great nations. Instead of leaning on the small countries he kept them out of the deliberations and thus deprived himself of valuable support.

Nor did the President insist on getting into touch with the representatives of the vanquished powers. He allowed himself to be closeted in Paris with M. Clémenceau. Professor Lammasch, who had been the last President of the Council of the Emperor Charles of Austria, asked the French authorities to give him a passport. He was willing to come to France "between two gendarmes" if only he might speak with the President for an hour. In vain! He did not get it.

Finally, the President, who hailed from a country to which the War had not come near, did not take in at first glance the seriousness of the ills it had wrought. He came to Europe not to talk about the War but to effect peace. He said as much in a remarkable phrase to M. Hymans, Belgian Minister of Foreign Affairs, who was seeking for his country the privilege of possessing the headquarters of the League of Nations. "The more you speak of the sufferings of your country," President Wilson said, "the more emphatically I shall declare that the League cannot have its headquarters there. For its task will be the reconciliation of the peoples, and the Germans will never, at Brussels, be able to look other nations in the face."

This feeling—a feeling fundamentally right—that his task was the making of peace and nothing else, prevented Mr. Wilson from paying his visit to the devastated region which the French persisted in expecting of him. This was regrettable. For his failure to do so hurt the feelings of France, alienated from him certain sympathies, and made it impossible for him to oppose with the requisite authority the excessive claims of the French delegates in the matter of reparations.

President Wilson stamped the Peace with his imprint: all that is best in it is due to him. "I know," he said, "that the Peace is not in complete accordance with the Fourteen Points but I never hoped that it could be more so." Unfortunately the peoples, for their part, did cherish that hope. In the eyes of the vanquished the Fourteen Points, having been accepted by the Allied governments and made the basis for Germany's capitulation, had the character of a mutual agreement and ought, it was felt, to be made the basis of the Peace. They were profoundly disappointed therefore when they found that in regard to many questions such was not the case. President Wilson did not even consent to hear their delegates. The vanquished, having put themselves in his hands, felt that they had been humbugged, tricked, duped. They have never forgiven President Wilson for what they considered a felony.

The President committed one other mistake and perhaps a still more serious one in its results: that was in imagining that the peoples were as generous and as clear-seeing as himself—his own people in particular. In reality, he was in advance of his time. This it was that made him a man isolated and apart.

He discovered the fact when he returned to his own country. Already in order to show regard for American susceptibilities President Wilson had been obliged to introduce into the Pact of the League of Nations some provisions such as the Monroe Doctrine reservation that were not very compatible with his general principles.

On his return home, he found his work cut out for him: he found he had to face the fact that his own people, in whose name he had been speaking, on whom he had been counting, were no longer behind him.

It was at this juncture that the full measure of the man was to be taken. Weary and worn by his labors, he did not hesitate a moment as to what was his duty. He undertook to explain to the people direct, over the heads of their representatives, and regardless of parties, what he had done, what the Treaty was, what the League of Nations amounted to. The world has known few finer speeches, better suited to their audience, more reasonable, more convincing, more elevated in tone, than those delivered by President Wilson in the course of his famous tour through the United States. If illness had not struck him down, if he had been able to keep on and continue kindling public opinion as he had done so often, the face of history would have been changed.

"We are assisting," he exclaimed once at a sitting of the Supreme Council, "at a race between Peace and Anarchy. Let us so act that Peace shall be the winner!" In this race Peace was obstructed suddenly at the beginning of the winter of 1920 by the most unforeseen of obstacles. The President had been struck down in the midst of the fight. And the direct consequences were the rejection of the Treaty of Versailles by the Senate of the United States, the weakening of the League of Nations, the prolongation of the existing state of political and social insecurity throughout.

President Wilson is dead but his work survives him. The influence he wielded over the history of the world has been deeper and more beneficent than that of any of his contemporaries. Most of the faults charged against him were faults which he could not help—and almost everything the Peace contains that is good and lasting and really constructive was his work.

The day President Wilson arrived in Europe for the first time, in December, 1918, at the height of his prestige, he said to one of his intimates with an intuition of genius: "I am on the road to my calvary." Alas, it was but too true. But if to-day his name is uttered with veneration by millions of men, if his tomb has become a place of pilgrimage, and if the League of Nations exists—it is because President Wilson died for an idea!

COLONEL HOUSE

> "Mr. House is my second self. He is
> myself, independent of me. His thoughts
> and mine are one."
>
> —*Woodrow Wilson*

WE HAVE NOW TO TELL THE STORY OF A GREAT FRIEND-
ship.

What makes the personality of Colonel House so fascinating and mysterious is that it is composed of contradictory
attributes. This modest man is a proud man; this disinterested man has a thirst for power; this taciturn man is open
and loyal; this quiet-looking man is a man of passion; this
man of peace is a man of adventurous bent. You will find all
these characteristics in his memoirs and they are all necessary
to explain one of the most singular careers of our time. For,
if the rôle of *Éminence grise* is no rare one in history, if we
have frequently seen men almost unknown to the general
public exercising almost absolute power in the name of a
sovereign, this phenomenon takes on a really extraordinary
aspect when it is transplanted into the modern democracy
which is fondest of the full light of day.

Colonel House is a man of adventurous bent; there was
the making of a great military leader in this little man who
was called in Paris during the Peace Conference "The White
Mouse." From the days of his childhood spent in the confines
of Mexico, in regions that were not yet entirely civilized, during and after the War of Secession, he has retained in his mind
an inexhaustible collection of tales of brigands and of law-

234

less affrays. At the height of his career he once let fall the remark that fighting between nations was horrible but that it was wholesome and legitimate between individuals. He has retained a peculiar affection for those thrilling boyhood tales of his and enjoys telling them.

A certain taste for paradox is to be noted in his telling of these tales. Colonel House has a fondness for concealing his real personality. He likes to be quite different from what people expect him to be. When he visited Geneva for the last time, the Secretary-General of the League of Nations had all the most important members of the secretariat to meet him. Some kind of political discourse, some words of advice and encouragement, were looked for from the man who, to such a great degree, was responsible for the existence of the League, the man who had been President Wilson's inspirer and who was trustee of his thoughts. From the commencement of the reception to the end Colonel House would talk of nothing but his adventurous youth in that American Corsica which Texas then was!

Prevented by weak health from giving full vent to his combative tastes, House, when he reached man's estate, turned them to account in political life. There is no field of activity so reminiscent of guerilla warfare. Edward House's poor physique did not allow him to enter into active politics with all their attendant wear and tear in the shape of electoral campaigning and all the responsibilities attached to public office. It was behind the scenes that he satisfied his tastes, and it was behind the scenes that he was to spend the whole of his career.

For nearly two decades he was the friend and inspirer of successive Governors of Texas and in particular of Governor Culbertson, who gave him the title of Colonel. House has

often made fun of this title which caused him to be taken in
Germany for a military officer of note, but he has always
found enjoyment in it; and herein we have one more reminder
of his boyish propensities.

But whatever interests he may have found in the political
life of Texas, the time came when it grew to be monotonous;
this field seemed to him too narrow and he took it into his
head to have a say in the selection of the candidate who was
to be "run" in 1912 for the Presidency of the United States.
House divined that the electoral situation would be more
favorable for the Democratic Party than it had been for
twenty years and he resolved to take a hand in this adventure.

Without any sort of mandate he set out to find the providential man. He got into touch with all the possible can-
didates and was not pleased with any of them. Thus it happened that he was led, theoretically at first and without ever
having set eyes on him, to espouse the cause of Governor
Woodrow Wilson, of New Jersey.

When these two men, already united by their political
outlook without knowing each other personally, met at last
for the first time in November, 1911, the effect was magnetic:
they found that they were in agreement in all their ideas, and
a friendship at once sprang up between them which was
soon to prove of historical importance.

One episode at this juncture illustrates well Colonel
House's horror of any kind of public action. The Democratic
Convention of 1912 at Baltimore was of a very feverish
kind; it was only at the 46th ballot that Wilson was chosen
as candidate. Colonel House attached enormous importance to
this choice. He had been working for it for months. Nevertheless, on the very day the Convention opened he started
from New York for Europe, leaving to others the business

of completing in public the work for which he had laid all the plans in secret.

Wilson, however, did not misunderstand him. It was to House he owed his success and it was to House he gave his gratitude. It was moreover House—an old political hand, which Wilson was not—who organized the electoral campaign and who conducted Wilson to triumph. On the morrow of the vote, he was free to ask anything of the new President, who owed everything to him: he might have become a member of the administration or Ambassador—no post would have been too high for him. Then it was that the depth of his disinterestedness and wisdom was to be seen—a disinterestedness which was to give him an ever-increasing influence over Wilson right to the end of his Presidency.

This influence rested at once upon moral qualities and upon intellectual qualities.

Colonel House's disinterestedness was absolute and President Wilson knew it. House showed himself not merely disinterested in his refusal of all public offices and distinctions, but also in his readiness to undertake disagreeable tasks and to accept all duties in which his services were really necessary. That is the history of his different missions to Europe, which he often entered upon though it went against the grain to do so.

Disinterestedness is not so rare a virtue as it is generally believed to be. But Colonel House displayed in his relations with the President a much more exceptional virtue, that of discretion. He was always ready to give advice. The word "ready" should be understood in all its significance. He had always studied in advance all the questions in regard to which the President might wish to consult him. He knew all the people concerned, all the facts, all the antecedent circumstances, all the wheels within wheels. He was the President's eye and saw everything. He spared Wilson countless hours of wearisome study and the hazards of decisions which a man has to make without feeling that he has mastered the whole subject. For President Wilson, House was an admirable preparer of the ground.

But when the President did not question him, he held his tongue. He never proffered his advice or took the initiative in any steps. His little office in Thirty-third Street in New York was connected by special wire with the President's private room in the White House. He could telephone at any moment and secretly. But he never rang up. The day the *Lusitania* was sunk some of his friends rushed in to see him, urging him to make the President do this or that. "I shall not move in the matter," said House. "If the President has need of my advice, he will ask for it; if he doesn't want it, I shan't give it."

One must have extraordinary self-control to be able to hold aloof when there are at stake questions of such importance and ideas by which one sets great store. Unselfish in his private capacity, House was by no means indifferent and detached in regard to the joys and sorrows of this world. He knew how to put extraordinary passion into his work. "The life I lead," he used to say, "beats all novels in respect to interest and excitement." "This problem," he said once to Wilson, "is fascinating and of enormous importance. I would like to see it settled to the eternal glory of your Presidency and of our American civilization." This man, working enthusiastically for the good of the public, ambitious for his friend and for his country, was always able to maintain silence when the President did not seek his advice.

From an intellectual standpoint, Colonel House possessed

both information and judgment. It was his judgment which Wilson began by appreciating and above all his understanding of men. House was of great use to him in the composition of his administration, no easy task as the Democratic party had not been in power for twenty years. Above all, House protected him from hundreds of applications. He saw people on the President's behalf; he took upon himself the ungrateful task of saying no. Ambitious on behalf of this Democratic President, alike from party spirit and from a feeling of personal friendship, House wanted to see Wilson achieving great things. How would this have been possible for Wilson had he been absorbed all day in minor matters? House took these minor matters in hand. "He has the opportunity," he wrote on November 4th, 1912, "to become the greatest President we have ever had and I want him to make good. He can do it if the office-seekers give him leisure, and I am going to try and help him get it."

Such a plan, however generous in its motive, is apt to be not unattended by dangers. It was to have certain unpleasant consequences for Wilson side by side with its great advantages.

President Wilson's isolation has often been deplored. That isolation was due, at least in part, to the vigilance of House, who allowed only interesting people and useful affairs to reach him. Now, however skillfully such a process of selection may be carried out, it is bound to diminish somewhat a statesman's contact with the world and to rarefy the atmosphere in which he lives.

Secondly, the individuality of the Colonel and the part which he played created difficulties for the President within his administration. That was fatal. President Wilson had, if not two policies, at least two diplomatic systems. One portion of public affairs went through the Department of State and the Ambassadors. But the President had a profound distaste for the diplomats, and everything that interested him personally, everything that had a political bearing, was dealt with by Colonel House and by himself. Despite all the good will of individuals it was inevitable that certain clashes should result. Two Secretaries of State in succession, Bryan and Lansing, came into conflict with the President from causes not solely connected with the presence of Colonel House but due in large measure to him. During the Peace Conference the relations between House and Lansing had gradually become very bad and were the cause of innumerable difficulties among the members of the American delegation. Each had his partisans. Lansing's said: "House is a Rasputin; he has bewitched the President." Those of House said: "Lansing is the President's evil genius. The Colonel is busy all the time making good his mistakes."

Unfortunate conditions, it will be agreed, for working in unison for the peace of the world!

The rôle of Colonel House was to undergo substantial changes in the course of the years. At first, as we have seen, he was occupied chiefly in relieving the President of wearisome tasks, settling personal matters for him and piloting him in party politics. But the Colonel House who for reasons of health spent several weeks every year in Europe turned out to have many more ideas about international politics than the President himself. Quite naturally, therefore, he began to advise and pilot Wilson in this province also. It was in the spring of 1914 that he was charged with his first semi-official mission to Europe. In London he saw some English statesmen, in Berlin the Emperor William. His idea would seem to have been to bring about a rapprochement between Germany and England; that mission was fruitless, but it put him into touch with the people with whom he would have to deal when the War was on.

The President—very American in this—was more interested in men than in abstract ideas, and House, on his return from Europe, notes in his Diary: "The personalities of the heads of governments interest him particularly and in the course of our conversation he told me that my knowledge of these men and of their standing in Europe would without doubt be very useful to him."

It has been said that Colonel House foresaw the World War. All careful observers of European politics at that moment felt the storm coming. But all cherished the hope that a miracle would occur at the last moment—all believed that the catastrophe was almost impossible. There is nothing to show that House's mind worked in any way differently.

That mission of his and the relations which it enabled him to establish enhanced House's credit with the President and made him the inspirer of the American war policy. During the War he paid several more visits to Europe to study the possibilities of American intervention for the restoration of peace. These visits, if they bore no immediate fruit, were not in vain. They enabled the President to intimate clearly to the Allied statesmen the real aims of his policy. It was in the course of these visits and these conversations that the fundamental ideas were formed upon which House was to base the American war policy, after having first based upon them the American peace policy.

Thus it is that we saw evolve and take definite shape gradually in his correspondence the three ideas which he was to defend stubbornly later: the freedom of the seas, the League of Nations, the exclusion of the Hohenzollerns.

STATESMEN OF THE WAR

The freedom of the seas is a traditional item of American policy. President Wilson, who was an historian and who held by the heritages of the past, took a special interest in this idea: "Madison and I," he said once to House, "are the only Princeton men that have become Presidents. The circumstances of 1812 and now run parallel. I sincerely hope they will not go further."

In the spring of 1915 Colonel House experienced the surprise of finding the English favorable to the freedom of the seas; the Germans, who were suffering from the blockade, were enthusiastic. This idea seemed to him suitable, therefore, as a first possible basis for peace negotiations.

On the other hand, it is in a letter from Sir Edward Grey to Colonel House, dated April 24, 1915, that we first find the expression "League of Nations."

As to the notion that it would be impossible to make peace with William II, it germinated in the Colonel's mind in the course of his second visit to Berlin. On January 27, 1916, Ambassador Gerard told House that the Emperor had said to him: "I and my cousins George and Nicholas will make peace when the time comes." The Emperor had uttered many other follies, and House notes: "I am wondering how long any part of the world will continue to be ruled by such masters."

The only point on which House and Wilson were not entirely agreed in the course of these years was in regard to military preparedness. House quickly realized in the course of his missions that the President's advice respecting peace would be better listened to if the United States had at their disposal an armed force capable of weighing in the balance. He had felt revive in him, as it were unconsciously, the memories of the military ambitions of his youth. This man, for whom political life was probably only a make-shift, felt within him now the soul of a Napoleon. "The Americans," he would say, "would probably have changed the course of history if, at the beginning of the war, they had armed to the teeth, ready to intervene at the opportune moment. That, I believe, was our great mistake, for Germany and the Allies would have given attention to our threat of intervention and, well prepared to fight, we could have imposed almost any conditions of peace we pleased."

The President gave a cold reception to these ideas. He did not view in the same way the rôle which was to be incumbent upon his country. According to him, the United States ought to give the world an example of peaceful idealism—an ideal which was scarcely compatible with military preparations.[1]

Events were to force President Wilson to accept Colonel House's view. In the course of the years these two men, always in agreement as to the measures to be taken, ceased sometimes to be so as to the goal to be aimed at. The President still wished, if it were possible, to avoid the gravest decisions. "The President," wrote Colonel House on April 2nd, 1916, one year before the United States entered the war, "allows himself to be so dominated by his tendency towards inaction that he hesitates to make a move. But if only he would do so, I have full confidence that he will pursue his course in a way that will do him honor."

Colonel House's rôle would seem to be attenuated a little during the War when military preparations were all that mattered. He did not, however, remain inactive. He did a thing which was in entire keeping with his character—he prepared for peace. While the other countries, entirely absorbed in the War, scarcely gave a thought to what should follow,

[1] See "The Intimate Papers of Colonel House."

Colonel House collected round him a staff of workers of the highest order to study all the questions which might arise at the declaration of peace and to prepare all the necessary documents for the President and his associates. This staff was later to form part of "the American Commission to negotiate Peace."

But if all these men worked under the orders of Colonel House, the Colonel himself did not allow his mind to be absorbed in their labors. When Germany asked for an armistice, he embarked almost immediately to come and represent President Wilson at the Inter-Allied Council. This was the first official post which he occupied and almost the only one.

In Paris and at Versailles, Colonel House worked, as was his wont, modestly, silently, efficiently. He had at last behind him that formidable armed force of which he had dreamed and which gave weight to his words.

President Wilson had quite made up his mind not to treat with the Kaiser; Colonel House encouraged him in regard to this. It may be asked whether they were not mistaken. As it was desired to impose upon Germany a pitiless peace, it would have been more logical to treat with those who were responsible for the War. However that may be, House reckoned that in the armistice one single clause sufficed—the dethronement of the Kaiser. For the rest, the military situation and the word of the United States should be enough for the Allies. The latter were of a different opinion. They wished to avail themselves of the armistice to secure safeguards. The dynastic question, on the contrary, did not seem to them to have a military aspect. Colonel House did not persist. "Do as you like, we will sign everything," he said to them. "All we are interested in is the peace." The Allies took him at his word; they went to work with a will and made the armistice as

Edward M. House

severe as they could. On leaving the Council room, Colonel House rubbed his hands together. "They haven't noticed," he said with a laugh, "that they have dethroned the Kaiser." The Colonel's rôle at the Peace Conference is blended with that of the President and it is difficult to distinguish between them, for they were agreed on all essentials. House wished the President to come to Europe. He approved of the President's policy in regard to Italy and never ceased to inspire him in all that regarded the League of Nations. For him, as for the President, the League of Nations had to be a purely moral force. The League, he contended, bore its sanction in itself; the unanimous public opinion of the world was a sufficient force to win respect for it. What was necessary was that all the nations of the world should learn to think aright.

Perhaps the Colonel's most important function during the Peace Conference was giving interviews in the President's place, as he used to do in Washington to the innumerable persons who wanted to see him. As is known, the neutral countries were not allowed to be represented at the Conference. This was due to a decision which Colonel House himself had urged upon President Wilson at the time when the United States, still neutral, was offering her services towards the ending of the War. "It will be a matter of course," he had said, "that only the belligerents shall take part in the Peace Conference."

He did not change his opinion at this point. But among the neutral countries were some which had important communications to make and useful advice to give, especially as regards the elaboration of the League of Nations Pact. It was Colonel House who served as intermediary between them and the President; in practice, the neutrals were as well situated as many of the belligerent states which were unable, although members of the Conference, to make their voices heard by the Council of Four.

Colonel House relieved the President also of certain decisions which, although very important in themselves, did not call for the personal intervention of the head of the state. Thus it was that he came to occupy himself with the selection of the city which was to be the headquarters of the League.

The choice of a neutral country and in particular of Switzerland—the only country which was suitable from its geographical situation—was easy. But there was long hesitation as between Geneva and Lausanne. Like all persons of delicate health, Colonel House attached great importance to climate, all the more that he contemplated having to stay frequently himself in the town selected. He had been assured that the climate of Lausanne was the better and this argument had impressed him. One day, however, seeing a native of Geneva enter his room, he exclaimed: "I have come to a decision at last. We shall go to Geneva!" On being questioned as to his reasons for this sudden change, he replied: "The waiter who brings me my chocolate is a Vaudois. I asked him: 'Which is the better town to live in, Geneva or Lausanne?' He answered: 'Geneva. Lausanne is too hot in summer.'"

Colonel House proceeded to constitute the sub-committee which was to present a report calculated to ensure unanimity in favor of Geneva. After the sitting at which the matter was settled, a Swiss delegate thanked him for his intervention and said to him that he would one day have a monument erected in his honor on the shore of the Lake of Geneva. He replied that it was not worth while and that Paderewski had already promised him one in Warsaw! "But," he went on, "I think I might ask for one to the memory of my waiter at the hotel. He certainly deserves one."

Relations between the President and the Colonel were slightly strained when Wilson returned to the United States from Paris in February, 1919. He thought that during his absence, Colonel House had allowed himself to be carried away by his instinct for conciliation and that he had yielded too much to the European statesmen. The breach widened when upon his return to the United States he had to make a determined struggle in favor of the League of Nations Covenant.

House, with his politician's instinct, was disposed to make certain concessions, to agree to certain restrictions. The President, who was not on good terms with the Senate, preferred to force its hand by leaning upon the people and thus to enter upon a frontal attack along the whole line. It is impossible to say which of the two was wiser, for who can tell what would have happened had Wilson not been struck down in the course of the campaign?

Since then, Colonel House has retired into the background —that background out of which he has never in the whole course of his career sought to emerge. He has closed the prodigious parenthesis in his life which was opened by the election of Woodrow Wilson as President of the United States. But this does not signify that he has lost interest in the fate of the work.

One day, after having hesitated for long, Colonel House came to Geneva. He wished to pass unnoticed as he has always wished to pass unnoticed everywhere. He visited the secretariat; he read the words on the commemorative *plaque* which does honor to the memory of President Wilson. He did not disguise his opinion that the work done by the League was not what he had hoped. He had wanted to build up a vast international city—and he found an old hotel marked by dissensions amongst its occupants. But, however disappointed he may have been, Colonel House has too much political and philosophical wisdom not to realize that where there is a seed at work there is life and hope. Death alone is immutable and irreparable.

PEACE ON THE WAY

COUNT CZERNIN

COUNT CZERNIN

FOR CHARLES OF HAPSBURG TO BECOME EMPEROR OF
Austria and King of Hungary, the suicide of the Archduke
Rudolph, the assassination of Francis-Ferdinand and the premature death of his own father had to take place. This explains why the young sovereign was not prepared for the
overwhelming burden that was unexpectedly laid upon him.
He was at that time a tall young man, attractive, intelligent,
idealistic, and warm-hearted, but superficial, somewhat illog-
ical, and profoundly influenced by four women: the Empress,
his mother, his grandmother and his mother-in-law. He had
perhaps a certain force of character, but the difficulties he
encountered in the form of circumstances and persons were
beyond his strength. His chief difficulty was that he could
not find among his advisers the new type of statesman that
a new policy demanded.

Having no technical knowledge and knowing nothing
of the majority of the questions with which he had to deal,
he was unable to gauge the importance of the obstacles in
his path or to uphold his own opinion against those of his
advisers or his wife, who was much more intelligent and self-
willed than he. His reign, short and tragic as it was, is the
history of his vacillations. At a time when a man with an
iron will, fully determined to overcome every obstacle, was
needed for the throne of Austria-Hungary, Fate placed upon
it an inexperienced, inconsistent youth.

Charles I saw clearly where his duty lay. His grandfather,

by having reigned too long, had brought untold misfortunes upon the peoples of Austria-Hungary. It was necessary, therefore, in the first place, completely to reverse his policy; abroad to endeavor to stop the War at the lowest possible cost to his country while at the same time being ready to make any sacrifice that might be necessary, and at home to reëstablish constitutional institutions so that they might at least function in their present form until he should feel sufficiently powerful to transform them.

The constitution of the monarchy under Francis-Joseph was based upon the hegemony of the Germans and the Magyars, who were in the minority when compared with the nationalists of other races. It no longer harmonized with the actual political and social situation, and for this reason could not function. "The greatest thing that my government has done," said Count Stürghk, one day during the War, as he was passing the House of Parliament in Vienna, "is to have turned that building into a hospital!"

The Emperor Charles also profited by the lesson to be learned from Austrian history, though not in the same way as his great-uncle. He saw that the country could not be ruled under traditional forms of government and that illegal methods led to revolution. He made a great effort to grasp the political possibilities and at the same time decided to summon Parliament and to transform the country.

The reëstablishment of constitutional freedom entailed the loss of German and Magyar support; it meant seeking to unite the nationalities of the other races and depending upon them for support. This was why the young emperor surrounded himself with Slavs: Clau-Martinez as President of the Council in Austria, Prince Lobkowitz as Marshal at court, Count Polzer as head of the civil cabinet, and, in particular, Count Ottokar Czernin as Minister of Foreign Affairs.

Count Czernin was a Czech, of that race of denationalized noblemen whose only patriotism consists in dynastic loyalty to their sovereign. It is remarkable that, among so many statesmen of Germanic race, the two who showed the greatest insight during the War should have been Slavs, Lichnowsky in Germany and Czernin in Austria.

The latter had had an almost romantic friendship with the Archduke Francis-Ferdinand. For fifteen years these two men had not passed a single day without meeting or writing to each other. Count Czernin made the following severe criticism of his friend: "No one could hate or love better than he, but he hates considerably more often than he loves." But he also said that Francis-Ferdinand could not tolerate flatterers or liars and it is a fact that Count Czernin prided himself upon being truthful. "It is obvious, M. Radeff," he remarked one day to the Bulgarian Minister, "that neither you nor I are professional diplomats. In diplomacy one must tell the truth occasionally and be able to lie. You never speak the truth and I never lie."

Count Czernin was regarded as the man of the coming reign. When at the Archduke's request, his name was submitted to Francis-Joseph for nomination as member of the Herrenhaus, the aged emperor replied, "Is that the man who will be Minister for Foreign Affairs at my death? Yes, let us appoint him so that he may learn something."

Upon the death of Francis-Ferdinand every one thought that Count Czernin's political life was over, for the relations between the archduke heir and his nephew were not such as would incline the latter to keep his uncle's advisers. He did so, however, and he carried out Francis-Ferdinand's intentions by summoning Count Czernin to the Ballplatz. This was not solely because he had not had time to choose his own advisers but particularly as evidence that he intended to adhere to a certain policy.

What policy was this? It was federalism, something resembling the American Constitution with a monarchy at the head. Francis-Ferdinand had intended at his accession to refuse to take the oath of the Austrian and the Hungarian Constitutions, declaring that these texts were contradictory and that he could not take the oath of both. This refusal would have caused both constitutions to be revised from a federal standpoint. Francis-Ferdinand had been fully aware that the existing system hampered the cultural development of the majority of the populations in the monarchy, all those who were neither German nor Magyar, and forced them to place all their hopes in the destruction of the state. The only way to recapture their loyalty and patriotism was to provide them with the means of developing freely within Austria-Hungary.

Had it been applied in time, this policy might have averted the Great War. When the Emperor Charles came to the throne it could still have facilitated the conclusion of peace with the Allies, for at that moment the various nationalities would doubtless have been satisfied with a reliable form of federalism and the Allies would not have continued fighting merely to offer them more. The appointment of Czernin is a proof of the Emperor Charles' political foresight.

But such a policy was beset with countless difficulties and was fiercely resented both within the monarchy and abroad. The essential condition for its success would have been that Czernin could count upon unfailing energy and unshaken faithfulness on the part of the Emperor. This unfortunately was not the case and therein lies the reason why the policy failed.

The Emperor Charles desired peace upon sentimental rather than upon political grounds. Weary of a war for which he was in no way responsible, the young ruler was, under his wife's influence, considerably more in sympathy with France and Italy than with Germany. He had the impression that he was supporting the wrong cause and had already given up all hope of victory when he came to the throne. Above all he realized, vaguely perhaps, that the only way to avoid revolution was to put an end to the peoples' sufferings as soon as possible.

What the Emperor Charles, on the other hand, did not see sufficiently clearly was that whereas the different peoples wanted peace their leaders were not all equally willing to accept the conditions of peace. It thus came about that this emperor, entirely devoted to his people and striving to re-establish peace, was unpopular with the only two sections of the monarchy that counted, politically speaking, the Germans and the Magyars.

Marie-Antoinette, Queen of France, died in days gone by, of having been surnamed the Austrian. In Vienna, immediately after the battle of Piave, it was almost openly said, "Die Welsche hat uns verraten!" "The Italian woman has betrayed us!" One day in the suburbs, there were cries of "Pfui Parma!" "Down with Parma!" as the Emperor went by. The people of the capital had never forgiven Charles for the act of mercy that marked his accession. Charles had realized that it was impossible to pursue a policy in favor of the nationalities while keeping their leaders in prison. He pardoned Kramarcz, Klofac and other Czech notables. The people saw in this action only a pardon granted to Czech soldiers, who at the beginning of the War had by deserting been the cause of the disaster of Rava-Ruska. The Emperor was, in their eyes, one who rewarded traitors.

In Hungary, the Emperor was criticized for his preference for the Croats. The hate formerly inspired by the Archduke Francis-Ferdinand was transferred to his minister if not to him. This caused Count Czernin, then Minister in Bucharest, to remark, "Here I am abused because I represent Hungary and in Budapest because I betray her!"

The Emperor Charles' policy was understood no better in the enemy countries. In a coalition mutual trust is the foundation of success. Whereas Austria was a less important enemy to France and England, she was Russia's and particularly Italy's chief enemy. Any move towards a separate peace could arouse the worst suspicions in Rome and Petrograd and threaten the unity of the coalition, its essential quality for victory. There was absolute loyalty among the Allies but a lack of communication. When Emperor Charles' letter proposing peace was received in Paris no one knew that the King of England had received a similar letter and that the English government was entirely ignorant of the letter addressed to Poincaré. In Paris the Austrian offer was refused because it did not mention the English colonies and in London because it was silent with regard to Alsace-Lorraine. Dire consequences of keeping a secret too well!

In the second place, the Emperor Charles did not define his offers sufficiently clearly. If he had made radical reforms at home, had proclaimed federalism, had given proofs of good faith without negotiating, without asking for promises, without demanding compensating concessions, he would have made an impression upon the public opinion of the world. He would have removed one of the Allies' reasons for fighting; he would have inclined their thoughts toward peace. But faced with conditional offers for the future the Allies had grounds for wondering whether the Emperor really intended to fulfill his offers and more especially whether he would be strong enough to do so.

As soon as the United States came into the War the peoples' right of self-determination became one of the Allies' main objects of the War. This principle was enthusiastically taken up by the Slav populations of the monarchy. Czech and Polish legions were organized on the Allied fronts. The official representatives of these peoples in the Allied countries, the Paderewskis, the Masaryks, the Bénès, had more and more influence upon public opinion. Some time earlier they might perhaps have regarded federalism as a wonderful gift, but now their hopes and ambitions went further and they were no longer disposed to be content with federalism.

The Emperor Charles' offer came too late. His autograph letter brought by Prince Sixte of Bourbon reached Paris on March 31st, 1917. It was intended for Briand, who had left office on March 20th. It fell into the hands of Ribot, whose one idea was to warn Italy. This he did at the Conference of Saint-Jean de Maurienne and wrecked the whole affair. Peace was lost by a fortnight.

Things became worse when Clémenceau was made President of the Council. He believed only in military victory, in victory at the front. He was incapable of making a distinction between one German and another. In his eyes enemies were enemies. Moreover, Clémenceau had, before the War, been intimately connected with Austria through his family and was afraid that he might be suspected of not having completely severed these connections. When he heard that in a speech Czernin had referred to the peace negotiations as having been started by the Allies, he replied with his customary bluntness, "He lies!" and published the Emperor Charles' autographed letter.

The effect of this outburst was to deliver the Emperor, bound hand and foot, into the hands of his formidable ally.

Germany constituted the delicate point in Austria's peace policy. If she were to inform the German government of her intentions there was the danger that Germany would break off the negotiations or attempt to use them to her own advantage, thus arousing suspicion in the minds of the enemies who were to be won over. If Austria were not to inform Germany, if she were to seek a separate peace, which would have been an act of pure treachery towards her late ally, there was the danger that she might be found out and that Germany might treat her as an enemy.

Both lines of action could be defended from the political point of view, but it was essential to choose between them and not to employ both methods at the same time. This neither the Emperor Charles nor Count Czernin understood and their lack of comprehension was their ruin.

Count Czernin had frequently said that Austria-Hungary could not betray Germany. On all the fronts German and Austrian armies were inextricably mixed and, since Austria had often needed Germany's help, the command was everywhere in the hands of German officers. Financially Germany could ruin Austria at any moment, for her exchange depended wholly upon the Reichsbank. A separate peace would not have been peace for Austria, it would have meant a fresh war among allied regiments on the entire front.

Austria could not negotiate without Germany's knowledge; but she could force her enemy's hand and oblige her to make peace. It was with this idea that Count Czernin made his famous speech in Budapest on October 3rd, 1917, in which he upheld President Wilson's principles with enthusiasm. He then went to Germany, showed himself to the people, ingratiated himself with them in order to obtain a personal triumph, so that he might then turn to the German government, and to the Staff Headquarters, saying, "Look! your people are with me. They want peace."

Could such tactics succeed? This question must always remain unanswered, for Czernin did not have time to carry out his design. He could do nothing hurriedly and each move had to be kept secret. Great impatience was felt in court circles, where Count Czernin had many enemies. It was rumored that he had been bought by Germany, that he was pro-German, that he was working against all attempts to obtain peace, still worse, that he was betraying the Emperor by revealing his secret negotiations to the Germans.

Urged by his wife and his advisers, Emperor Charles finally decided to intervene personally. In place of Count Czernin's diplomatic tactics he relied upon the weight of his own personal influence, and tried its effect in all directions. He sent his former tutor, Professor Lammasch, to Switzerland to interview a real or supposed friend of President Wilson. He sent Count Revetera to confer with Baron Armand. He commissioned the Pope to act as intermediary between him and the Allies. To crown all he summoned to Vienna his brother-in-law, Prince Sixte of Bourbon-Parma, an officer in the Belgian army, in order to give him a letter intended for Poincaré together with verbal instructions.

I shall not easily forget the account Prince Sixte once gave me of this expedition. An imperial car met him at the Swiss frontier. He arrived at Schönbrunn in the middle of the night and was let into the palace by a hidden door so that he might escape all prying eyes. In a dimly lit room he found his sister, the Empress Zita, and his brother-in-law. They talked together for a long time, now of personal now of political matters, exchanging news of friends and sighing sadly from time to time. The position was serious. Political unrest at home, wild pacifism on the part of the Socialists, daring revolt of the Czechs, lack of understanding on the part of the Hungarians, Polish rising against Germany, terrible situation as regards food supplies, economic ruin and ever increasing supremacy of Germany.

These two young rulers of thirty felt that they might at any moment be overwhelmed by revolution. Sadly in the lamplight they poured out their troubles to the beloved brother. Their future and that of their children and the dynasty depended upon the success of Prince Sixte's mission.

The prince left for Paris, carrying with him the precious and indiscreet letter in which the Emperor of Austria-Hungary offered Alsace-Lorraine to France. He saw Poincaré but his mission failed.

They had forgotten in Vienna that France was a republic. Theidea that the personality of Prince Sixte of Bourbon and the personal good will of the Emperor of Austria could make the slightest impression upon France showed complete ignorance of the actual state of affairs. In Paris, where all public men are jealous of each other and keep mutual watch upon one another, no one dared take the responsibility of continuing the conversation. They were suspicious, they scented a trap, they thought that Germany might be behind the proposal. They dared not spread the idea of peace among the public for fear of appearing cowardly in the eyes of Italy or of offending England, and so forth.

Nothing came of the affair, the only consequence being

that when Clémenceau made it public, the Emperor Charles was seriously compromised in the eyes of Germany and was obliged to give her pledges.

William II and Charles I had never been upon good terms with each other. The German Emperor had nothing but scorn for this presumptuous young man. It was he who prevented him, upon his succession, from taking the title of Charles VIII, which would have made him the successor of the emperors of the Holy Roman Empire. Charles chafed under his ally's patronizing manner, but being so much weaker he could only submit.

A Pole once told the Emperor Charles that he should free himself from the Germans, his only enemies after the defeat of the Russians and Italians. The Emperor borrowed his notebook and wrote "Ich möchte schon, aber wie?" "I would an if I could."

This was why in 1917, Charles summoned Professor Lammasch and suggested that he should take office. Lammasch begged to be allowed to consider the matter, for, as he said, he could do nothing against Germany's all-powerful influence. The Emperor insisted. The whole world would have seen in his nomination a promise of freedom for the peoples in the empire and peace for its enemies. In the meanwhile the Emperor left for the German headquarters and upon his return informed Lammasch that he had reconsidered the matter. . . .

Germany's hold tightened when it became known that the Emperor Charles had attempted to conclude a separate peace and had failed. Austria-Hungary had no further hope of freeing herself from German supremacy. Charles had to give his word that he would make no other attempt; he had to send Austrian regiments to the French front, accept Germany's cooperation in Italy. After the victory of Caporetto he sent word to Paris that his intentions remained unchanged and that if he went to the front, it was against his will and only to please his enemies. The trap was closing.

It was in these circumstances that Czernin represented his country, first at Brest-Litowsk then in Budapest. He, the man who wanted a conciliatory peace, a peace without annexations or indemnities, was obliged at Brest to put his signature to a peace that was a violent outrage of all his principles, a peace by which Russia lost fifty-three millions of inhabitants and 1,135,111 square kilometers of territory while Germany gained an area as large as Austria-Hungary—a peace that was the work of General Hoffmann and General Ludendorf. How, after that, could he attempt to convince the Allies of his good faith?

Things became still worse at Bucharest. The German and Austrian conceptions of peace with Rumania were entirely opposed, for the two countries' interests were different. Austria wanted to conclude a conciliatory peace that would permit of friendliness later. It was Czernin who sent an emissary to King Ferdinand at Jassy promising him that he should keep his throne if he would sign the peace. Only one thing was of importance to Austria, it was to have a friendly Rumania on her frontiers.

Germany wished to prevent this at all costs. For her, Rumania was one stage on the way to the East, a country to be exploited economically on account of her corn and petrol wells. Germany wanted to subjugate Rumania and to attach her to herself. This she did, and it was in order to have a free hand in Rumania that she pretended to favor the Emperor Charles' aspirations to the Polish throne, a bill without any backing.

Germany was supported by Hungary, who was afraid that too friendly relations with Rumania might be dangerous to the territorial integrity of the Crown of St. Stephen. More than that, she demanded a "rectification of the frontiers" between the two countries. This rectification was restricted, it is true, but nevertheless constituted a fresh attack upon the principles upon which Count Czernin's policy was based.

Rumania had been conquered by Marshal Mackensen, was occupied by the German armies, and Hungary was in agreement with Germany. How could Count Czernin have resisted the force of such circumstances? Nevertheless he was blamed in Vienna for his failure. The Emperor's advisers and particularly those of the Empress, among whom were several of his personal enemies, seized the opportunity of doing him an ill turn. The old accusations were repeated: Czernin was pro-German, Czernin was a traitor. Charles I, who had never particularly cared for his minister, yielded to this pressure. It was during the conference at Bucharest that Count Czernin heard that he was to be dismissed.

He then returned to Vienna and a violent scene took place between him and the Emperor. Each accused the other of having lied, and it was immediately after this interview, that, in revenge, Count Czernin committed the most represensible action of his whole career. He, who had known about all the Emperor Charles' peace negotiations and who had with his own hand added a marginal note to the letter to Poincaré, publicly exposed his sovereign and provided Clémenceau with the opportunity of an easy triumph.

Count Czernin's retirement did no more to prevent the defeat of his country, revolution, and dismemberment than his presence. He was crushed by the disaster he had so fiercely striven to avert. He lost his emperor and, with him, his loyalty. He lost his country and his worldly possessions, which were in Czecho-Slovakia. He even lost the good opinion of his fellowmen, who never forgave him for not having been able to save the dynasty.

It is said that one of the rites of certain ancient religions required that a man should be immured when laying the foundations of a new city. Count Czernin was the sacrificial victim entombed in the City of To-morrow.

THE LIBERATION OF PEOPLES

PRESIDENT MASARYK AND DR. BÉNÈS

PILSUDSKI AND PADEREWSKI

PRESIDENT MASARYK AND DR. BÉNÈS

IS THERE ANY WORK OF MAN TO BE COMPARED, IN RESPECT to its difficulties and its magnitude, with that which consists in the creating of a nation? If we say that this has been the task successfully fulfilled by President Masaryk and Dr. Bénès, we do not mean to insinuate that their work has been artificial and without historic basis. The nation which they have brought into being had a previous existence, down to 1526. But in those days it had neither the same name nor the same frontiers. Its continuity had been broken since then by nearly four centuries of servitude. Its national consciousness has experienced a long eclipse. In the year before the War no one dreamt of the resurrection of the Bohemia of old or of the creation of a new state with an unknown name.

It is no service to a statesman to attribute to him a kind of prescience which could not possibly have been his. When Dr. Bénès, at Dijon before the War, expounded his thesis, *"Le problème autrichien et la question tchèque,"* he had no thought of a separatist solution of the problem and of the constitution of a national state. Even during the War, both Dr. Masaryk and Dr. Bénès believed at certain junctures that they could come to terms with Austria. Circumstances and the obstinacy of the Austrian government in some sort constrained them to take in hand a task which at first they had not contemplated.

But once the necessity of a radical solution appeared, Masaryk and Bénès had no hesitation about devoting themselves

STATESMEN OF THE WAR
entirely to this work. Isolated from a people which could do
nothing to help them, they took on themselves terrible responsibilities—and it is only right, now that they have succeeded,
to give them the credit and glory of their achievements.

What has characterized the action of President Masaryk
has been at once his moral elevation and his acute feeling for
the practical. This very rare combination in him of idealism
and realism has given to his personality a power and authority
seldom met with in the same degree.

President Masaryk is a self-made man. He comes of a
very humble stock and began life as apprentice to a lock-
maker. It was through unremitting industry that, by giving
lessons himself, he managed to pay the cost of his philosophical studies. Appointed at first a *privat-docent* at the University of Vienna, he was called in 1882 as Professor to the Czech
University at Prague, the ancient mediæval Charles University which the Austrian government had revived.

Almost immediately, he acquired a unique position there.
The Bohemians, so long deprived of a national center of higher
education, had some difficulty in getting together a professional corps of a high standing of culture. Most of the professors were of a provincial type. Masaryk, on the contrary,
showed himself at once to be a man of outstanding gifts; he
fought unceasingly against all tendencies to put up with the
second-class and the mediocre and against all forms of narrowness of mind. He opposed everything calculated to isolate
Czech culture from Western culture. He was, in a word,
against all the movements—Provincialism, Nationalism, Pan-
slavism—then in favor with the students.

His unpopularity was at times extreme. For months together it prevented him from delivering his lectures. It reached
268

its maximum on the occasion of the so-called "Königinhof manuscripts." What was in question was a cycle of songs and legends, akin to the Nibelungen Lied, the existence of which proved that the literary culture of the Czech people was more ancient than that of the Germans. Theories were built up on this basis, national pride was excited, it looked as though the whole country would identify itself with the case for the genuineness of these manuscripts. Masaryk, standing quite alone, declared that they were false and that he could prove it.

A Protestant, firm in his creed, President Masaryk maintained that it was not permissible to sacrifice truth and moral right to the supposed interests of the nation. When, in this case, he felt he must take up his stand in opposition to the general feeling of his compatriots, he did so without hesitation, just as he did again in the case of a young Jew accused wrongly of a ritual crime. And this characteristic of his imparted great force to all his interventions when these were on behalf of his own people as, for instance, in the Friedjung case, when he denounced the fraudulent charges brought against the Croats by the Austrian government.

The moral considerations which President Masaryk brought into politics were of a nature to enhance his authority and his reputation but not his popularity. The masses like to be flattered. When Masaryk founded a party, to which he characteristically gave the name "The Realist Party," he was followed by some intellectuals, but the mass of the people held aloof from him. He was able to get into Parliament thanks to his personal prestige, but he never succeeded in getting any other deputy elected.

Masaryk was then a federalist and a sincere one. He believed in the possibility of changing Austria from within, by democratic means. He was a radical and fought against militarism and clericalism, not to destroy the State but to save it. That is what distinguished him from his adversary, M. Kramarcz, who also preached federalism but with the idea of destroying the monarchy.

When war broke out, Masaryk, whose age, sixty-four years, excluded him from military service, went to Switzerland and Italy to learn what was going on and to make himself acquainted with European tendencies in general. He was about to return home in December, 1914, when one of his former pupils, Edward Bénès, with whom he had not previously had occasion to establish any close relationship, learned that on his return he (Masaryk) would be arrested. Young Bénès went at once to Zürich to warn him. Masaryk remained in Switzerland and Bénès kept coming and going between Prague and Geneva throughout the year 1915, acting as intermediary between Masaryk and his friends. In September, 1915, these comings and goings had awakened the suspicions of the Austrian police, who decided to arrest Bénès. But there were Czechs in all the government offices. Bénès, warned half an hour before his intended arrest, managed once again to cross the German frontier, on foot, and, after passing through Bavaria, to penetrate into Switzerland.

It was now in Geneva that the meeting took place between Masaryk, Bénès and Stefanik in the course of which was decided the formation of the National Czecho-Slovak Committee; this hyphenated name appeared then officially for the first time. It was decided that Bénès should install himself in Paris, to organize a Czecho-Slovak corps among the prisoners of war in alliance with the French and Italian armies, and that Masaryk should go to London. When the Russian Revolution broke out, he left England for Russia, where he organized a corps of Czecho-Slovak volunteers on the eastern front. Finally, driven from Russia by the Bolshevist Revolution, he went to America.

It was a country which he knew well, for he had married an American. Now he contrived to get into personal touch with Colonel House and President Wilson and he induced them to give recognition to the Czecho-Slovak National Committee. This prepared the way for the recognition of the future state which was officially founded at Geneva, a week before the fall of the Hapsburg monarchy.

It would be difficult to exaggerate the difficulty of the work achieved in the course of the War by the Czecho-Slovak National Committee—that is to say, by the Masaryk-Bénès-Stefanik triumvirate—or to exaggerate its importance.

The governments were then distrustful. It was necessary for Austrian subjects to make themselves acceptable first of all before being allowed to come to the Allied countries. In 1915 the French military authorities wanted to put Dr. Bénès into a concentration camp. He had to force them to recognize the existence of a Czech nation and to satisfy them that the Czechs did not really cherish the feeling of loyalty to the Hapsburg dynasty which they were obliged publicly to profess. It was necessary to make this clear to both the governments and the public opinion of the Allied countries and to convince them that the three men, isolated, without mandates, without personal authority, ought to be recognized as the government of a country which did not yet exist and that they should be treated with on a basis of equality as an ally.

All this would, doubtless, have been impracticable if the Czecho-Slovak National Committee had not been in a position to render the Allies certain services of great value. We are not now speaking of the Czecho-Slovak army, which Bénès organized upon several fronts among the prisoners of war belonging to his nation at the risk of provoking terrible reprisals in Austria. The chief purpose of the army was to demonstrate the existence of the Czech people, to make this people tangible in the eyes of those who had never heard of it before. The army could not in itself play a very great rôle in the War.

Far more important, for the conduct of operations, was the mutiny of a Czech regiment at the very beginning of the War at Rava-Ruska; it enabled the Russians to pierce the Austrian front and forced the Germans to run to the support of their allies—a circumstance that had very momentous political consequences.

But it was in another field that the Czecho-Slovak National Committee was able to give its most valuable aid to the Allies. Thanks to it, owing to the presence of Czechs in all the Austro-Hungarian governments, the headquarters staffs of the Allies were kept constantly informed regarding everything that happened in the Dual Monarchy, even the most secret things. The Emperor and Marshal Conrad never held a conversation but the substance of it was known in Paris by the end of a week. It was the Czechs who revealed all the German intrigues in the United States; the governess to Count Bernstorff's children was a Czech and knew everything that went on in his household. On the other hand, all the declarations of the Czech deputies in the Austrian parliament had been submitted in advance to the Allied governments. Some days later they would appear in the Austrian papers. It was the Allies who at the last moment prevented the revolution in Bohemia. In August, 1918, Bénès said: "I can't hold them back any longer."

"You must continue to hold them back a while," he was told in Paris.

"Well, it won't be possible after November!"

Thomas Garrigue Masaryk

Edward Bénès

All this underground work might easily have called forth mistrust. Its strength lay in the confidence which Masaryk and Bénès had been able to inspire. Thus it was that all their actions in this decisive period of history, their influence and their authority, were the outcome of their high moral character. Their reward was to be able to get Czecho-Slovakia recognized at the Peace Conference—although it did not exist and although it remained a part of Austria right to the end—as an Allied state. In October the Czech soldiers were still fighting in the ranks of the Austrian Army; in November the Czech delegates had their places at the Conference table among the victors. We do not believe that any other man of our generation has achieved a more remarkable *tour de force.*

It was a just recompense for Dr. Masaryk that he should have been unanimously elected President of the new republic. And it was quite natural that his entry into the Hradsin, into that old palace at Prague which comprises and symbolizes the entire history of the Czech people, should have been a triumph. But the work was not yet finished. This country had as yet no frontiers. What remained to be done was not the easiest thing—and it was done by Edward Bénès in person at the Peace Conference.

Rarely have two men complemented each other so admirably as President Masaryk and Dr. Bénès; and rarely have two men been more necessary the one to the other. Without Masaryk's prestige, Bénès, who was a man of little account when he quitted his country and who exerted there no personal authority, would have been able to do nothing. But without Bénès and his knowledge of Europe and his political instincts and skill, Masaryk would have been paralyzed and impotent.

Dr. Bénès, like President Masaryk, is of modest origin. His parents were peasants and he was the youngest of a large family. It was thanks to the savings of brothers much older than himself that he was able to pursue his studies and become a professor of sociology and political economy in a school of commerce. Such was his status when he left Prague clandestinely in the autumn of 1915. He was to return thither as Minister of Foreign Affairs and one of the most notable men in Europe.

In this extraordinary success the rôle played by chance was very slight indeed; almost everything was due to talent. This little man, who looks so unimportant, who speaks foreign languages with difficulty, whose pronunciation is uneven and whose vowel sounds are indistinct, has not impressed people through any physical quality or outward grace. He has done so by the lucidity of his mind, the breadth of his horizon, his keen appreciation of contingencies and possibilities, the honesty of his spoken word, the veracity of his statements. In other words, he impressed Europe by the same intellectual and moral qualities which explain the authority of President Masaryk—faith in their ideal combined with a sense of realities.

If diplomacy were merely a matter of bargaining, as it is so often conceived to be, Dr. Bénès would not have been able to play any rôle at the Peace Conference, for he had nothing to offer any one—he had no assets to exploit. But he realized that bargaining of the *do ut des* order is often corrected by the intervention of spiritual forces. These forces played in favor of Czecho-Slovakia and Dr. Bénès made every possible use of them. The right of peoples to self-determination, the Fourteen Points of President Wilson, and the League of Nations—these were his arms and his dogmas. Through them alone had he any standing; by reason of them he felt in a strong position.

I remember hearing Dr. Bénès expound his views at the beginning of the Conference. We were in that little office of his in the Rue Bonaparte in Paris which for three years was the seat of government of a nation not yet in being. "We shall be uncompromising," he said to me, "on all that constitutes for us vital necessities and only on them. We shall view matters consistently from the standpoint of general interest."

Such was the secret of his influence at the Conference. He was able to make people feel that he was viewing matters from the standpoint of general interest. On occasion he had the wisdom to sacrifice the personal interest of his country to a more collective interest. His objectivity in debate enabled him to recognize the force of his opponents' arguments—sometimes even to supply them.

This was no mere matter of attitude or tactics. It was the outcome of his conviction that Czecho-Slovakia could not exist and survive except in a pacified and prosperous Europe. In concerning himself with the interests of all, he had the conviction that he was working in the true interest of his country. This power of distinguishing the permanent from the ephemeral, and this innate feeling for international solidarity, won for him from the very first day a place apart among the statesmen of Europe, many of whom had grown old under the influence of superannuated formulas. His power lay in his freshness of mind and, if one may say so, in his inexperience.

Dr. Bénès had not much to contend with in Paris. Once the principle of the Czecho-Slovak state was accepted—and it had been accepted in advance—no one thought of refusing it the extent of territory to which it was entitled. Dr. Bénès' talent lay in the way in which he convinced his hearers from the outset that he was asking for no more. And he succeeded so well that every one vied with him in zeal on behalf of his demands and that eventually he was given more than he claimed. He was even given Ruthenia into the bargain, solely because no one knew what else to do with it!

It was not in Paris that he encountered his difficulties— it was among his compatriots. For even in his delegation he had Nationalists, such as Kramarcz, who kept asking too much and whose following at home was stronger than his. Their demands threatened to compromise the position which he took up, and in which lay his strength. "I am startled," Dr. Bénès said at the time to one of his friends, "I am startled at the way in which they give me everything I ask. It is too much. I can't decline to pass on my countrymen's claims and I am never refused anything. I ask myself how far this can go!"

This objectivity of mind, this feeling for the general interest and for the solidarity of the nations, has continued since then to inspire the policy of Dr. Bénès and has not ceased to enhance his authority.

One day he was explaining to me why in a treaty of disarmament it was necessary to take account of the industrial capacity of states. "If one did not do so," he said, "a country like mine, endowed with great industrial capacity, would be in too favorable a situation compared with an agricultural country like Hungary." On another occasion, some one had drawn attention to the fact that the Czecho-Slovakian member of a technical committee of the League of Nations was pursuing an ardently Protectionist policy and placing difficulties in the way of a settlement. "That is intolerable!" Bénès exclaimed. "Show him up! Make him ashamed of himself. Our industrialists must learn to think like Europeans."

The example set by Dr. Bénès is beneficent in a high degree, for it proves that one succeeds better in the world and even in politics by good faith and disinterestedness than by duplicity and Machiavellianism.

We must, however, agree as to the meaning of the word "disinterestedness." Dr. Bénès is not disinterested in respect to his country. An ardent patriot, he has only one thought and one duty: to serve Czecho-Slovakia. It is on this basis only that he can command the necessary authority to conduct a European policy. If he were preoccupied *only* with the general interest, he would not be long in succumbing at home. Even the services which he has rendered to his people and his unquestioned patriotism would not suffice to protect him from attacks if he did not always allow himself to be guided first and foremost by the interest of his country.

But he is convinced that on the essential point, the maintenance of peace, this interest coincides with that of the whole world. Dr. Bénès said to me once: "A state is not built up in a day. My country, in order to achieve its economic and moral unity, has need of twenty years of peace." Dr. Bénès has no other aim in life than that of ensuring Czecho-Slovakia the twenty years of peace which she needs.

It is this that makes him the most European statesman in Europe. While most of his colleagues pursue the policy of peace only with reservations, and within certain limits, he alone does so with his whole heart and without an *arrière-pensée*. But he adopts different and appropriate methods, according to circumstances. Immediately after the rejection of the Treaty of Versailles by the American Senate, not knowing what would now happen to the League of Nations, he concluded the Little Entente, which is an alliance of the old type. When he perceived that the League of Nations was functioning and acquiring strength, he took part in its labors and came to acquire in it an authority without parallel. He was one of the authors of the Geneva protocol. At Locarno, he played the rôle of mediator between Poland and Germany. Convinced that Czecho-Slovakia has the same interests that France has, to maintain the treaties of peace which created her, he is equally convinced that she must keep up good relations with her neighbor, Germany, across whose territory pass all the lines of communication which connect her with the sea. He has, therefore, made himself an active equal in the work of Franco-German rapprochement and of European pacification. In relation to Austria he has pursued a changing policy but one always of an amicable kind, while calculated to strengthen Czecho-Slovakia's independence.

In all circumstances, he has been willing to work for the fairest and the most international solutions. Wherever there has been question of the conciliation of conflicting interests, of settling disputes, of soothing suspicions, of overcoming antagonisms, you will find Dr. Bénès busy. But he is no Utopian and does not lose sight of the political realities of the moment.

That is what makes his conversation so interesting. Dr. Bénès is not what one would call a brilliant talker, for he is only a mediocre linguist, and his utterance, very difficult to follow in public, is not agreeable even on intimate terms. It is an individual trait in the man—and a thing remarkable in our times—that he should have been able to achieve such a career without being in the least an orator.

But if Dr. Bénès does not captivate his hearers by the charm of his speech, he keeps their interest by the clearness and cogency of his reasoning. He possesses that rarest of qualities, common sense. His thought always, in all circumstances, rings true. And as he combines a great freedom of expression with abundant knowledge, and as he assumes in his listeners the same good faith as his own, his conversation is extraordinarily instructive.

It might be supposed that with all these qualities of heart and mind, Dr. Bénès must have a standing without equal in his own country. That is so in a sense. He has been Minister of Foreign Affairs for ten years and no one has sought to interrupt his activities. For every one realizes at Prague that his retirement would be for Czecho-Slovakia the equivalent of a defeat.

But his authority is much greater outside the frontiers of his country than inside. Dr. Bénès is not a party man and consequently has not many faithful supporters in Parliament. Besides, it was inevitable in a land which has never before had self-government and which has always been animated by a spirit of opposition that political passions should be more bitter, more negative and at the same time pettier than elsewhere. The breadth of view which characterizes Dr. Bénès, far from standing him in good stead in this *milieu*, could not but tell against him. So also with his regard for morality, and the energy he has shown in denouncing certain scandals, holding aloof from certain cliques, and refusing the appeals of certain place-hunters. It is easy to make enemies in a new country in which all the official posts have to be filled and in which every one feels qualified for anything.

The only period—a brief enough period—during which he was Premier brought him more attacks than successes. His main strength in his own country lies in his being the friend of President Masaryk.

But this friendship has its reverse side. The President has a prestige and an authority which place him above attacks. The people see in him the Liberator, and he has won their gratitude.

They see in him the indispensable man, who insures the unity of the state and the continuity of his policy. They recognize, moreover, in the great veteran of seventy-eight a personality of high moral distinction, whose rectitude of conscience enforces respect.

No one in Czecho-Slovakia would stand up openly as an-opponent of the President. But Dr. Masaryk remains a man of combative spirit; he is still as uncompromising in respect to what he regards as the truth as he was in his younger days. If his person inspires the respect of all, his policies are not unanimously approved.

President Masaryk's most recent act—an act by which he has given his measure as a statesman—has been to include representatives of the German minority in the government. This act within the field of home politics was in keeping with the policy of rapprochement and good relations which Dr. Bénès has pursued in the field of international politics. The purpose in both cases is to destroy irredentism and separatism. For Czecho-Slovakia is not a homogeneous state from a racial standpoint, any more than Austria-Hungary was, and if she were to commit the same faults as the Hapsburgs, her fate one day or another would be the same.

Dr. Masaryk and Dr. Bénès realize this, but the Czech Nationalists have not realized it. On this occasion, as in many others, Dr. Bénès has served as a buckler for his master, the President of the Republic. It is against him that the opponents of the Presidential policy direct their attacks. And while the President renders Dr. Bénès the service of covering him with his authority, Dr. Bénès in return covers the President with his body!

Among all the states newly created or enlarged by the War, Czecho-Slovakia alone has had the privilege of possessing two statesmen really worthy of the name. It is to this privilege, that is to say, to these men, that she owes her present prosperity and the unique place which she occupies in the world.

PILSUDSKI AND PADEREWSKI

THE RECONSTRUCTION OF POLAND WAS NOT THE WORK OF one man but rather the achievement of a nation. It was brought about, in the first place, by the people themselves, by their unshaken faith in their country, their sufferings and their resistance to their oppressors.

When the War broke out in 1914, the Poles at once realized that they must seize this opportunity of achieving independence or give up all hope of it. If Poland was not now restored, could it be expected that another such catastrophe would ever bring her freedom? If however a war between Russia and Germany were to meet Poland's two great demands for independence and unity, both adversaries must suffer defeat. It is difficult to believe in the miraculous, and the miracle that took place seemed an impossibility.

Unexpected vistas had suddenly opened before her and opinions varied. Some people attached the greater importance to national unity, that could come only through the victory of Russia; others thought that the main problem was to insure the existence of an independent Poland and that the reconstitution of her unity would be the work of the future. Some counted upon a Russian victory and believed the manifestos of the Grand Duke Nicolas and Russia's promises, confirmed by the Western powers. Others accepted Austria's word; she had always treated them well and Poles had considerable influence in her government.

Far from harming the country, this diversity of opinion

was to her advantage. The belligerents vied with each other, in words if not in deeds, to prevent the Polish people from coming under the influence of their enemies.

But circumstances alone cannot prevail; man must interpret them. In her hour of need, Poland was able to produce three men, of different origin, training, and temperament, but of equal patriotism, all three of whom played an important part in her renaissance: a soldier, Pilsudski; an artist, Paderewski; a politician, Dmowski.

There is a slight exaggeration in referring to Marshal Pilsudski as a soldier, for in the beginning he was only incidentally a soldier.

By profession Pilsudski is a revolutionary. During his youth he prepared the revolution and at a riper age he carried it out. While still at school, he and some friends founded a secret center for national studies. As a medical student he took part in some demonstrations organized by his friends and was expelled from the University. He was then sentenced to five years exile in Siberia for being concerned in a plot against the life of the Tsar. In 1892 he set up a clandestine printing press and from 1894 on published a paper. He married but the Russian police were continually on his heels, and the married couple were unable to live together. He was ultimately arrested and on May 13th, 1901, managed to escape from prison in Warsaw.

He went to live in London and then in Cracow. But he often crossed the frontier under false names and in various disguises and kept in close contact with the Polish Socialist party in Russia. In spite of his noble origin, Pilsudski was always convinced that the working classes alone were sufficiently fired by revolutionary zeal to rise one day against the

STATESMEN OF THE WAR

oppressor. There had never been for Pilsudski before the War any enemy but Russia, or any weapon but armed revolution.

His people did not understand him. They had paid too dearly in the disastrous experiences of 1830 and 1867; there had been too much bloodshed; they would not face a repetition. How look to arms to free the country in a Europe of apparently fixed frontiers and against the three most powerful empires on the continent?

Pilsudski held fast to his idea. During the Russo-Japanese War, he organized the riots in Warsaw to hinder recruiting. He then went to Japan and proposed that she should arm the Polish people and attack Russia on her western frontiers. At Tokio, he came into conflict with Roman Dmowski, who from that moment became his most bitter enemy. Dmowski, skilled as he was in diplomatic methods, did not believe in revolution, and, in view of these two contrary opinions, the Japanese government hesitated and the idea was dropped.

After this failure, Pilsudski returned to Europe and it was only then, at the age of forty-one, that he discovered his military gifts. His great achievement was to foresee the War and to prepare for it. In 1908 he founded an organization, in Austria, whose aim was to attract young Poles from Russia and give them military training. In 1910, these organizations were made public and received support in Austro-Hungarian military circles. In 1912, Pilsudski founded a war treasury to cover the expenses of a national army, should occasion arise.

The War broke out too soon for Pilsudski. His organizations were still in the initial stages; enthusiasm was great but there was a lack of money, arms, munitions and of a list of officers. He had to negotiate with the leaders of the Austro-Hungarian army, who were mistrustful. The Poles in

Russia were unfavorable, trusting rather in a Russian victory.

Pilsudski, with his indomitable will, overcame all these obstacles, organized two Polish legions and fought as a colonel on the side of Austria-Hungary. He took part in numerous battles; although he had, till then, never had the right to an official uniform, he proved himself to be a brilliant soldier, and in 1916 covered the Austro-Hungarian retreat before the victorious offensive of General Broussilof.

Suddenly at this decisive moment, in his own life and that of the Polish nation, the strength of will and political genius of the leader of the legions became apparent. The Germans had taken Warsaw, the Russian army was in retreat, and any other man would have thought that this was the moment to make terms with the conqueror. To Pilsudski these events suggested the contrary; since Russia was no longer to be feared, Germany must be opposed. Then for the first time there dawned for the Polish nation the possibility that her great hope, the simultaneous defeat of the three empires, might be realized.

Pilsudski had succeeded, as time went on, in transforming the Polish legions into a first class military weapon but had no hesitation in breaking this weapon in his hand. Germany had proclaimed Polish independence and had constituted a Polish government. She required only in return that she might raise troops in Poland and that the Polish army should take an oath declaring brotherhood in arms with the German and Austrian armies. Pilsudski and five thousand legionaries with him, refused to take this oath. He was arrested and imprisoned in Magdeburg.

He had now proven his patriotism and his courage. Should Germany be beaten, he would automatically become the leader of the country, the only man capable of controlling its many parties and divisions.

So it was. The revolution in Germany threw open the doors of the Magdeburg prison. Pilsudski returned immediately to Warsaw, where on November 10th, 1918, the Regency Council, set up by the Germans, placed the power in his hands.

Thus Pilsudski found himself master and sovereign of a restored Poland, more than that, dictator, and still more, the idol of his people. But there was nothing to support him, neither government, staff, money nor army. The people were starving, the country was in a state of devastation, overrun by the Germans, who were retreating in disorder, in fear of the Bolshevists, perhaps in greater fear of the prisoners of war who were set free, destitute, on the frontier. Pilsudski now took a bold line of action. He was everywhere. He forced the Germans to evacuate Warsaw, by leading them to believe that he had an army. He organized one almost from nothing, created a government, and, in January, 1919, instituted universal suffrage and summoned the electors—this in a country that was despoiled of everything and that had not been free for one hundred and thirty years. The state came into being.

But notwithstanding his authority and prestige, Pilsudski would have been unable to carry out this gigantic task alone. One essential condition was lacking, credit with the Allies who in Paris were to settle the frontiers of restored Poland.

At this moment he had the good fortune to meet a man, Paderewski, with a world-wide reputation, who was on intimate terms with several of the leading European and American statesmen. In spite of widely divergent opinions and methods, Pilsudski understood him and made him President of the Council and Polish representative in Paris.

PILSUDSKI AND PADEREWSKI

Paderewski was not destined for politics: Providence had intended him to be an artist and a poet.

In common with Pilsudski and Dmowski, Paderewski was one of the 1860 generation. He was born at the time of the last great Polish rising, had grown up in the memory of that tragedy, his whole youth colored by its consequences.

He was brought up in the country by his mother, who had musical tastes, and his genius soon showed itself. Misfortune developed his gifts; his mother's death and the imprisonment of his father, who had taken part in the great revolt of 1863, left him to his artistic pursuits. At the age of five he began to show evidence of astonishing gifts and, entering the Warsaw conservatory when very young, amazed his teachers by his ability.

Most artists believe in themselves; one day, at the age of seventeen, without telling any one, he left Warsaw with a friend to give concerts in Russia. He had many disappointments and few successes and returned, at the end of a year, a wiser man. He then resumed his studies and completed them in Vienna, where in 1887 he had his first great success, at the age of twenty-seven. In one night, Paderewski became a European celebrity. He went to America where he achieved untold success. He traveled all over the world and was fêted everywhere. He had only to win the appreciation of his own countrymen, but he hesitated a long time. He made the attempt in 1899 and was received by his native town with wild ovations.

From that moment he reëstablished close relations with his people. His opera, "Manrou," given at Lwow in 1901, is of a particularly national character and his symphony in A minor, first given in Boston in 1908, was regarded as the

287

musical expression of the Polish spirit at the time of the 1905 revolt.

Until then Paderewski had taken no part in politics. An ardent patriot, in common with every one of his nation, he had nevertheless not been involved in any manifestation. Circumstances and not his own tastes made him a kind of national hero.

A subdued country, such as Poland then was, and, moreover, divided among several powers, naturally turns to what will unite and glorify it and give evidence of its vitality and civilization. Paderewski did all this, and thus had the whole of Poland at his feet. Already in his lifetime he became the symbol of national greatness.

In 1910, upon the occasion of the fifth centenary of the Battle of Grunwald, in which the Poles were victorious over the Knights of the Teutonic Order, Paderewski offered the town of Cracow a monument of Ladislas Jagellon; he then made his first and last political speech before the War.

1914 found Paderewski in Switzerland, where together with the great author, Henry Sienkiewiecz, he founded the "Polish War Victims Committee." In 1916 he was present at the meeting of the Polish National Committee and his political career dates from this moment.

The Polish National Committee had been founded at Warsaw by Roman Dmowski immediately after war was declared. "When attacked by two robbers," said Dmowski, "one deals with the more dangerous first." To him this meant Germany, and he believed that Russia would restore the unity of Poland.

He soon found that his confidence was misplaced. The Russian government had no serious intention of keeping the generous promises made by the Grand Duke Nicholas. Dmow-

IGNACE JAN PADEREWSKI

MARSHAL PILSUDSKI

ski and his friends decided to approach the Western powers behind the back of the Russian government. Thus in 1916, the National Committee created diplomatic posts in the various countries and asked Paderewski to represent Poland in the United States.

Paderewski had great influence in the United States, on account of his reputation, his genius and his charm. He gave a triumphal series of concerts in aid of Polish war work, and his negotiations with the President and Colonel House in Washington were decisive. The Colonel and Paderewski understood each other so well that the latter once wrote to House saying, "It has always been the ambition of my life to find the one man my country needs. My ambition has been realized."

Poland demanded three things: recognition of the international importance of the Polish question, independence and unity. Russia was only explicit with regard to the third, she was absolutely negative with regard to the first and vague concerning the second. In order to avoid offending the Russian government, her allies were obliged, until the Revolution, to maintain a noncommittal attitude to the Polish question. In their reply to President Wilson, at the beginning of 1917, they still appeared to regard the matter as a purely Russian question. Paderewski succeeded in convincing the President that this was not the case, and President Wilson's declaration of January 23rd, 1917, was the first international act to give complete satisfaction to the Polish people. It aroused sympathy in the whole of Poland, and the entry of the United States into the War was celebrated in Warsaw, under the eyes of the Germans, as a national fête.

After the intervention of the United States and the Russian Revolution, the Allies felt themselves freer with regard to

Poland. Dmowski then obtained a promise from Balfour that the Allies would not settle any question concerning Poland in the absence of her representatives. On March 3rd, 1918, in the fourth year of the War and long after President Wilson's famous message, the Allies declared "that a united and free Poland with access to the sea is essential to the lasting peace of Europe."

Immediately the Armistice was declared, Paderewski returned. He landed at Danzig and went straight to Posen. He was received in triumph. The town rose at his bidding, together with all German Poland. From there he went to Warsaw, where he arrived during the last days of 1918, in the double glory of artist and deliverer. On January 16th, 1919, the head of the state, Pilsudski, put him into power, as being the one man who could gain the sympathy and confidence of the Allies for restored Poland.

It was fortunate for Poland that besides Dmowski, who was fiercely passionate, Paderewski should have been present at the Peace Conference; with his charm and moderation he was able to exert a soothing influence and remove many difficulties.

Dmowski had rendered great service to Poland during the War. At a time when the Allies might have been inclined to confuse Poland with the central empires, he made himself responsible for her attitude. At home, he prevented any unanimity for an understanding with Germany. Abroad, as an unofficial ambassador, he successfully demonstrated the absence of any such unanimity. While certain Polish troops were fighting in the Austrian ranks, Dmowski, in the face of countless difficulties, organized a Polish army on the western front. It is impossible to overestimate the service he thus rendered his country. It is no exaggeration to say that he saved her; for had the Allies been able to believe, even wrongly, that Poland identified herself with the Austro-Germans, there would have been, after the victory, no traditions, reasons or principles strong enough to save her from oblivion and ruin.

But Dmowski, the patriot, was also a party leader, and this caused him to make serious mistakes with regard to his country's interests. He thought that in order to maintain his position in the party, he must return to Warsaw with "his hands full." This explains his line of action at the Peace Conference, where he continually urged Poland's maximum claims. His fundamental mistake lay in paying insufficient attention to principles, justice, the people's right of determination, caution and the future. That was all nonsense! His idea was European equilibrium; since Russia had disappeared, Poland should take her place as France's ally in order to counterbalance Germany.

If she was to play such a part, Poland must be strong, that is to say, great. He thought in terms of soldiers. It was useless to explain to him that size and strength are no synonymous but frequently contradictory, and that as Poland increased in size her strength would diminish, for she would then find herself surrounded by enemies and troubled by racial differences and irredentism. Dmowski was never able to understand this point of view and did not hesitate to burden his country with the terrible weight of a five-fold, Russian, Ukrainian, Lithuanian, German and Czech, irredentism.

His ideas pleased France, for they suited her purpose at the moment. But they offended England; Dmowski and Lloyd George disliked each other, and the latter's sudden change of front, in the spring of 1919, which cost Poland Danzig and part of Upper Silesia, was doubtless not unconnected with a letter written by Dmowski concerning the English Prime Minister, the contents of which were public knowledge at the Conference.

Paderewski's chief task at the Conference, in virtue of his great authority and his friendship with Wilson, Clémenceau, Lloyd George, Poincaré, and Venezelos, was to smooth out these differences. More moderate in his claims than Dmowski, more amenable in his negotiations, and more influential in Warsaw, he facilitated the work of the Conference and profoundly influenced the final reconstitution of his country's frontiers.

Hardly reconstituted, Poland was faced with Bolshevism. Moscow realized that Poland formed the keystone of new Europe and an out-post for the West. Therefore the Bolshevists attacked the new state before she had had time to consolidate. Pilsudski, perhaps rashly, followed them into their own country. But armies are lost in Russian plains, as is well known since the time of Napoleon. The Bolshevists resumed the offensive and appeared outside Warsaw. Upon the point of taking the town, they suddenly withdrew. Who performed this second miracle of the Marne, on the Vistula? The French, who were on a military mission there, thought that it was they, but the Poles thought that it was the head of the state, the man they had named "The Marshal"; and this fresh victory further increased his popularity, prestige and authority.

Pilsudski came of a line of princes but his life had been that of a revolutionary; in the organization of the state he showed himself to be both shrewd and calculating. He can be cold, even icy, and there are classic examples of his pride, but he can be charming when he chooses and can use his charm to advantage. He is a true leader by reason of the fascination he exerts over all those who come into touch with him.

A soldier is rarely a politician, but Pilsudski is perhaps a greater politician than soldier. His views on the frontier question were more moderate and reasonable than those of the majority of his compatriots, and had they prevailed in Paris, eastern Europe would have been assured of a well-founded and lasting peace.

After his triumph, Pilsudski could have made of Poland what he chose; she was at his feet. He quietly retired. For four years he left the country to itself, a prey to parliamentarism and fierce party warfare.

But in May, 1926, with his customary energy, he suddenly returned. Supported by the army who adored him, he again took power. It might be supposed that, this time at least, he would play the part of dictator. On the contrary, he refused all offers of office and took his place—in fact the first —in the ranks.

What an enigmatic figure the man presents!—a socialist and a militarist, democratic and imperious, continually seeking power and refusing to exercise it, governing against his will, a man whose actions can never be foretold and who has already been justified by history on two or three occasions contrary to the best reasoned forecasts.

THE SUPREME EFFORT

LLOYD GEORGE

CLÉMENCEAU

LLOYD GEORGE

IN NO COUNTRY BUT ENGLAND WOULD MR. LLOYD GEORGE
have been any phenomenon at all. The extraordinary thing
is that, with all his qualities and all his faults, he should have
succeeded in winning over the very nation which was least
calculated to appreciate either.

One of the doctrines which the Englishman holds most
tenaciously is that character counts for more than brains. So
much is this an article of the nation's faith that it instinctively looks with suspicion upon any man who is too clever.
Clever men, apparently, can never be entirely honest, and the
Englishman prefers men he can trust to those whom he can
merely admire.

Nevertheless, once or twice in a hundred years, the English
fall under the spell of an adventurer. When that happens they
cast to the wind their caution and their prejudices, and hand
over their destinies to men whose origin, outlook, and character would at any other time count against them.

In the nineteenth century there was Disraeli, the young
Jew who, after a chequered career, finished up as a Conservative statesman and became the confidential adviser of Queen
Victoria. It is easy to find among their many points of difference a certain resemblance between Disraeli—that "in-
credible creature," to use the words of Mr. Asquith—and
Lloyd George. By origin both were strangers to the true
British tradition: they both established their power by their
eloquence; and the means by which each of them at once dis-

quieted and beguiled his contemporaries were exactly the same.

An Englishman once said: "If you were to ask me who is the greatest living Englishman, I should have to admit that it is probably a Scotchman who was born in Ireland."

This paradox applies in a sense to Mr. Lloyd George who, although born in Manchester, is pure Welsh. He was brought up in Wales by an uncle who combined village cobbling with Baptist preaching. His mother tongue is not English but Welsh: his religion is not that of the established Church but of a nonconformist denomination—the Disciples of Christ. At bottom he is a stranger to the deep-rooted traditions of England, and this explains his revolutionary attitude to them in his youth.

Mr. Lloyd George has advanced to fame by several stages, and each stage has been a conflict with established authority. First of all he acquired a certain local notoriety by defending the small tenants against the great landowners; then he had the whole of Wales at his feet when he preached the disestablishment of the Church of England, and put his perfervid eloquence at the service of a cause which was near the hearts of all his co-religionists. His next step was to leave his little country for England and there, in Birmingham, the stronghold of Joe Chamberlain, to denounce the Boer War. Finally, he made a really national reputation by his Radical Budget in 1909, by his new taxation and his campaign against the landlords.

Mr. Lloyd George is a small town man, almost a village man, and the wrongs of the agricultural laborer have always made a stronger appeal to him than those of the industrial worker. His campaigns against the great landed proprietors were the most sincere of his whole career, and it was the same enemy that he was attacking in his denunciation of the House of Lords.

He made his name, therefore, by the radicalism of his religious, pacifist, and social policy.

When the War broke out, there was nothing in Mr. Lloyd George's past to indicate that he was destined to play a predominant rôle. It was even a matter of conjecture which side his temperament would lead him to take. Would his mysticism and his inherent pacifism get the upper hand? Apparently he was subjected to some heart searching towards the end of July, 1914, for, after having first of all advocated immediate intervention on the side of France, he was soon as Chancellor of the Exchequer hard pressed by the great City financiers.

It was his influence over the Cabinet that delayed the supreme decision for a day or two. He was on the point of resigning with his colleagues Lord Morley and John Burns, and it was only after the German invasion of Belgium and the patriotic exhortations of Mr. Asquith that he succeeded eventually in overcoming his moral and financial scruples.

But once the Rubicon was crossed the one-time pacifist showed that he had in him all the essential qualities of a great war minister and, in particular, vision and driving force.

A nation that goes to war must be prepared for innovations. It must create, improvize, face unexpected situations, calculate what the enemy will do. A stiff test for the English this, for in general they are not blessed with over-much imagination, and the foundation of their politics is respect for tradition, that is, for what has been done and demonstrated already.

Mr. Lloyd George is a Welshman, that is to say, a Celt, and a man of imagination. He has never had any respect for tradition, still less for routine. His marvelously adaptable mind enables him to cope with any new situation; he is never nonplussed by a sudden turn of events.

In time of war imagination is useless without decision, and decisiveness is a quality that Mr. Lloyd George possesses in a considerable and often alarming degree.

There is no question on which he cannot give a definite decision in ten minutes.

Indecision is often the result of a philosophical training. The habit of weighing the pros and cons of everything, the type of mind that tries to see the good in the bad, the advantages in the disadvantages—these are apt to paralyze the will. Mr. Lloyd George is completely devoid of any such training and even, if report can be believed, of any intellectual training at all, and that is what enables him to find an immediate solution for the most difficult problems, without having an inkling of their theoretical difficulty.

It was these qualities and these defects which at the beginning of the War made Mr. Lloyd George an excellent Minister of Munitions and later a great War Minister—after a German mine had delivered him from his rival for popular favor, Lord Kitchener. His work in these highly technical departments earned the respect and admiration of all who knew it.

But what could he do alone against ten men? The other departments had not been brought within his ambit. They continued their daily round as though there were no war. There was no driving force, for Mr. Asquith was too scrupulous and too gentlemanly to be equal to all the tasks that war entails.

Mr. Lloyd George had no use for such inopportune scruples, for he saw that they might well bring disaster on the country. Many a time he threatened to resign in order to carry some point that seemed to him of pressing importance. He never did in fact resign, but the day came in December, 1916, when he put his threat into execution. But it was Mr. Asquith who resigned, and Mr. Lloyd George succeeded him.

Such an act was unparalleled either in personal or national relations. Never before had any British government been overthrown or formed in such a fashion. Never before had one man opposed his will to that of Parliament and the King. It was a veritable revolution.

Mr. Lloyd George owed everything to Mr. Asquith. It was he who had taken the little Welsh politician and made him Chancellor of the Exchequer. It was he who had forced this troublesome agitator on his colleagues and handed over to him the financial destinies of Britain. It was he who in 1909 allowed him to bring in an almost revolutionary Budget and supported him in his crusade against the noble Lords. In 1914 he saved him from the scandal of the Marconi affair, and it was he who made him Minister of Munitions and had put him in the way of acquiring the prestige that he was now employing against his chief.

In a country where fair play is the sign of moral nobility and the hall-mark of a gentleman, such disloyalty is a blot on any man's reputation, and even at the height of his power Mr. Lloyd George never completely wiped it out.

Yet how could he have acted otherwise? Was he to put his personal scruples above the national good? In the life of every politician there are times when he has to face his conscience. To condemn or to absolve Mr. Lloyd George we must penetrate into his innermost heart and see whether the betrayal of his chief caused him pain or merely satisfied his personal ambitions. God alone can judge.

This much is certain, that the advent to power of Mr.

Lloyd George marked a turning point in the history of the War and the British Constitution.

The name that was often given to Mr. Lloyd George at the height of his power was "Prime Minister of Europe." Of all the men who wielded an influence over the destinies of the world during the War he was surely the most attractive, the most individual, the most self-willed, the most daring.

In four months he had brought about a two-fold revolution in Britain. His régime, based on the extraordinary powers given him by the Defense of the Realm Act, was in fact that of an absolute dictator. He changed the venerable foundations of British parliamentary life by concentrating all the executive power in the hands of a few and by making the Cabinet in point of fact a mere council of officials. He threw overboard the doctrine of collective ministerial responsibility, for he had eighty-three ministers and confined responsibility to the members of the War Cabinet. Finally he struck a heavy blow at the constitution by bringing about those far-reaching reforms without going to the country.

Mr. Lloyd George went even further. Not only did he change the political basis of the government; he even made changes in the country itself. He invited the Dominion Premiers to collaborate with the British Cabinet and turned Great Britain into a federal state for the purposes of defense. Every change within the empire which has taken place since—the settlement of the Irish question, the development of the Egyptian problem, the constitutional evolution of India, the independence of the Dominions as regards foreign policy—all these were latent in his reforms of 1917, which were themselves the logical outcome of the participation of all the British peoples in the War.

Mr. Lloyd George's advent to power made no less an impression in the realm of military operations. The great merit of the British Prime Minister was that he knew when to dispense with the advice of his military advisers. Indeed he had already formed a bad opinion of them. From the very creation of the new army in 1915 its generals had two obsessions, firstly, to take no orders from the French, and, secondly, to win an immediate victory. They all wanted to be Wellingtons, to conquer on the fields of Flanders, and to be beholden to nobody—a laudable ambition if the English generals had had the necessary means of attaining it. Unfortunately they had not. The English military chiefs were opposed to the Salonika front, opposed to the Italian front, opposed to all that was outside their own little war. In that respect they were no different from all the other military chiefs, and the only thing that made for possible agreement and that unity of command which was essential to victory was the imperious intervention of statesmen like Clémenceau and Lloyd George.

The favorable results of the 1916 campaign that culminated in the German retreat robbed this rivalry of its bitterness, for victorious generals are safe from criticism. But the year 1917 had less fortunate results, and opinion in Britain deeply resented the failures at Cambrai and in Flanders. The story goes that when Field-Marshal Sir Douglas Haig said to Mr. Lloyd George, "To-morrow I shall take Passchendaele," the Prime Minister retorted sharply, "You take one village and we lose Serbia. You take another and we lose Rumania. I've had enough of your villages!"

This unspoken rivalry and these defeats coincided with the advent to power in France of M. Clémenceau, who had set his heart on unity of command. Just as Lloyd George had been the only English statesman to comprehend the usefulness of the Salonika expedition and accordingly to give in to

STATESMEN OF THE WAR

M. Briand on this point, so he gradually came to share M. Clémenceau's views on the need for unity of command. It could not be brought about in a day. There was powerful opposition to be overcome in London, but Mr. Lloyd George, when entreated first at Rapallo and then at Versailles to sacrifice some small portion of the autonomy of the British command, took it upon himself to consent. Thus, little by little, he paved the way for the Doullens decision after the great disaster of the spring of 1918 to empower General Foch to "coördinate" the work of the Allied armies.

This decision, to which Marshal Haig himself agreed under pressure of circumstances, marked at once the most tragic hour of the War and the culminating achievement of Mr. Lloyd George's career. For from that moment the tide of war had turned and victory smiled on the Allied armies. Six months later Germany collapsed.

It must be said in justice to Mr. Lloyd George that he had been a great war minister, energetic, intelligent, capable of initiative and decision, forceful and farseeing. But, after bestowing upon him this well-merited praise, we must add that these same qualities were not manifest in his peace policy or at least they were neutralized by defects that had not been brought to light during the War.

His great mistake after the victory was that he was too clever. He was out to consolidate his success immediately. Just a few days after the Armistice he advised the King to dissolve the House of Commons (which had long outlived its constitutional duration) and embarked upon the election campaign which was to crown his triumph.

But it was only an ephemeral and specious victory. Mr. Lloyd George succeeded in crushing his opponents and preventing the reëlection of his former chief, Mr. Asquith. But it

David Lloyd George

was a success which marked a serious defeat, for the majority which had been returned was almost exclusively composed of his former adversaries, and the Liberal Party was decimated. From that moment he found himself in the peculiar position of being the Radical head of a parliamentary majority that was Conservative. The mandate given him by the country was one of reaction at home and uncompromising enmity to Germany. The former pacifist and enemy of the Church of England, the landed proprietors and the Lords, was now head of all that was most feudal, conservative, and nationalist.

Mr. Lloyd George, however, in his heart of hearts had not changed and he found himself involuntarily, perhaps even unconsciously, being put in a false position in regard to Europe, his own country, and his Parliamentary majority. It was then that his gravest defect disclosed itself, his lack of sincerity and loyalty, and his unreliability.

Mr. Lloyd George has the reputation of being a brave man. Certainly he does not lack physical courage. He has faced howling hostile mobs even to the extent of provoking his adversaries. But, contrary to the prevalent impression, physical and moral courage are two quite distinct qualities. Mr. Lloyd George possesses the one but not the other. In his youth it needed no moral courage to preach against the landlords and the Church of England, for that was what his Baptist friends and his Welsh electors desired, but later in his career, when he did need moral courage, he was found wanting. That is why he had been called a mere demagogue. His life is a tale of one change of front after another.

He has thrown over in succession all the ideas and all the causes which he had previously held most dear. During the War he postponed the carrying out of the Welsh disestablishment for which he had struggled so long, he suspended the

Land Tax which had been his political platform, and in the end he brought in Protection, which had always previously roused his bitter opposition. As regards Ireland too, he had pursued conflicting policies—he would be for Home Rule, then for federalism, then throw over both, employ both force and generosity in turn. He has made promises to everybody and kept them to none, failed both his adversaries and his friends, every party and every country.

There are many inconsistent people in this world, but there are very few who are so inconsistent as to forget what they have said and then attack and denounce it as absurd and indefensible. Mr. Lloyd George has often been guilty of this and it is doubtless that fact which gives rise to the opinion of those who know him that he lies as easily as he breathes. No doubt that view is too severe. He does not lie, he generally believes what he says, but he quickly forgets what he *has* said and quite easily believes the opposite. He is sincere by fits and starts. That is the most astounding trait in the character of this man whose Baptist upbringing might have been expected to save him from it.

This lack of principle which Mr. Lloyd George counts as a weapon in his armor proved to be a weakness at the Peace Conference. If he had played his part well he should have dominated the Conference, for he had the advantage over his colleagues of being disinterested. He had been clever enough to obtain in advance all England's war aims—the seizing of the German colonies and the German fleet; he therefore came to the Conference in the favorable position of being able to give everything and ask for nothing.

France expected much from the Peace, Italy even more, and England nothing. Besides, unlike President Wilson, Mr. Lloyd George was committed to no preconceived solution. He was in an ideal position to be the arbiter of his colleagues and the means of making justice triumphant.

He had also the advantage over the other delegates of certain natural gifts. He was younger than M. Clémenceau, more adaptable than President Wilson, and he possessed an extraordinary nimble mind, great ingenuity, an inexhaustible fund of formulæ and extraordinary intuition.

Mr. J. M. Keynes has said of Mr. Lloyd George that he had an "unerring, almost medium-like sensibility to every one immediately around him." He describes him at the Peace Conference "watching the company with six or seven senses not available to ordinary men, judging character, motive and subconscious impulse, perceiving what each was thinking and even what each was going to say next and compounding with telepathic instinct the argument or appeal best suited to the vanity, weakness or self-interest of his immediate auditor . . . " In that respect Mr. Lloyd George is very like M. Briand, to whom he has often been compared. Both of them detest reading and are only receptive to the spoken word. Both have a very highly developed psychological sense and a boundless flair for political opportunism.

How came it then that with gifts so rare and so fitting to the occasion Mr. Lloyd George did not exert at the Peace Conference the decisive influence which might have been expected? There were three explanations: his ignorance, his lack of principle, and his election promises.

First, his ignorance. There was a saying which went the rounds of Paris about the British delegation: "Mr. Balfour knows but does not care. Mr. Bonar Law cares but does not know. Mr. Lloyd George neither knows nor cares." And there was another: "Mr. Lloyd George is capable of more than he knows, but unfortunately he knows nothing." That is the one point in which he has respected the old British traditions! A century ago at the Congress of Vienna, Lord Castlereagh asked where Leipzig—the place where the decisive battle in the Napoleonic Wars had been fought the year before—was to be found. In the same way at the Peace Conference, Mr. Lloyd George with a yawn leaned over to M. Bratiano and said: "You were speaking about Transylvania—Show me it on the map." The map was spread out on the floor of President Wilson's study, where the Supreme Council was meeting, and Mr. Lloyd George was soon down on all fours searching for Transylvania with his finger.

What Mr. Lloyd George lacked, throughout his long career, was not the opportunity of learning but the ability to make use of it. His general education was not such that he could retain what he heard and still less what he read. So it was that he arrived at a fairly advanced age utterly ignorant not only of geography but also of many other things that he should have known.

More serious still than absence of knowledge is absence of principles. Mr. Lloyd George is reputed to have said at the Peace Conference: "What am I to do between a man who thinks he is Jesus Christ and another who thinks he is Napoleon?" There was an implied confession in this pleasantry. Between two men with principles, Mr. Lloyd George had none. He believed that the greatest Peace in history could be fashioned with little instruments. He believed that by creating dissension among his colleagues he could achieve his ends. He tried first of all to come to an understanding with President Wilson over the head of M. Clémenceau. At the end of a meeting, when M. Clémenceau was tired, he would bring forward all the proposals he had set his heart on and get them passed. Then when President Wilson was away he tried to reconsider their joint work in secret with his French colleague and confront the President on his return with a *fait accompli.* The natural outcome of these methods was that every one grew tired of him.

This opportunism was the more serious because of his election promises. During his election campaign, carried away by his own demagogic fervor and his love for oratorical slogans, he had promised England two things—that the Kaiser should be hanged and that Germany would pay the whole cost of the war. The first of these was absurd. The second was not only equally absurd, but contrary to the pledge given to Germany at the Armistice. Lloyd George was therefore forced to argue that the Allies were not bound by these pledges. "I am making war not peace," he had said of his speech of January 5th, 1918, regarding the Allies' conditions of peace. He strayed from the straight path of loyalty to the vanquished and espoused the cause of those who hoped to exploit victory.

So it came about that during the first part of the Peace Conference his constant anxiety was to draw President Wilson from his stand on principles by offering him a formula which respected them in appearance but violated them in fact.

Yet even that did not really satisfy him. He had too keen a sense of realities and of political opportunism not to see the dangers of a peace which humiliated Germany without weakening her.

Further, Mr. Lloyd George, with one eye to his parliamentary majority, had the other on the evolution of his country. He was conscious of growing discontent, and foresaw the time when another election would bring in a Labor majority in the House of Commons. Would he then be able to remain in power? Finally, events in Russia and Germany caused him increasing anxiety. The fear of Bolshevism was at that time the determining motive behind his actions.

During the Conference, Mr. Lloyd George had looked at the chapters of the Peace Treaty separately one by one. When he saw them in their entirety, however, the result appalled him. He had a sudden revulsion of feeling, and in twenty-four hours began to preach with his usual fervor the opposite of the policy he had previously advocated. The result was that the French, the Tories, President Wilson and the Liberals all felt they had been betrayed. He had at last succeeded in making simultaneous enemies of everybody.

He came home from the Peace Conference with a reputation not enhanced but diminished. He might have saved his prestige by immediate resignation but he had acquired a taste for power and therefore wished to continue the Coalition. That was his mistake. What is good in war is not necessarily good in peace. A coalition is repugnant to the political sense of the English because it prevents the normal functioning of its parliamentary system.

Repudiated by his own party, Mr. Lloyd George slipped into a growing dependence on the Conservatives, who formed the greater part of his majority and whose confidence he had not yet won. He was between two stools.

He made many mistakes then, both in home and foreign policy. The greatest of these was the ill-fated Asia Minor expedition in which he engaged the Greeks without exerting himself to help them. The defeat of the Greek army was a serious blow to the prestige of England, and the Dominions in particular never forgot it.

But, as often happens, Mr. Lloyd George owed his fall less to his mistakes than to efforts which were in themselves praiseworthy. At Genoa he attempted to hasten the economic

LLOYD GEORGE

reconstruction of Europe, but failed. The Conservatives reproached him above all with his liberal policy toward Egypt on the one hand and Ireland on the other. At bottom Mr. Lloyd George is profoundly anti-Catholic and has never approved of Irish demands. First and foremost a Welshman, he was a supporter not of Home Rule but of a federation of the British empire. In any case he was not long in seeing that the policy of repression into which his Tory supporters had involved him could come to no good end. It is impossible to destroy national feeling by force. In Egypt, as in Ireland, he saw that the only wise policy for the empire was generosity. His final error was to carry out a liberal policy on a reactionary majority.

His attitude since his fall has not been such as would find him friends. He has attacked the Peace Treaty which was his work and has denounced his own policy when it has been carried out by his successors. But in politics a man can never be said to be finished, and there is nothing to show that Mr. Lloyd George will not return to power one day.

Recently he was talking on the staircase of Buckingham Palace with Lord Birkenhead and Mr. Winston Churchill. The Prime Minister, Mr. Baldwin, happened to pass and as he saw them he turned to his companion and remarked, not without bitterness: "There go the heads of the next Coalition."

CLÉMENCEAU

THE FUNDAMENTAL CHARACTERISTIC OF M. CLÉMENCEAU
is pessimism. He has contempt of mankind ingrained in his
heart. His career has consisted in fighting against everything
around him, because everything has seemed to him all wrong.
His philosophy—for M. Clémenceau is a thinker and a
philosopher—is one of deep discouragement. His essential
atheism is a form of pessimism. His wit and his witticisms—
those hard, caustic, terrible epigrams of his which never make
you laugh but which make you rather want to weep—are inspired also by the idea that at bottom men are profoundly bad.

M. Clémenceau knows all this and boasts of it. Ask him
why he does not write his memories and he will answer you:
"Because I should demolish too many people!" He refuses to
attend a sitting of the French Academy of which he is a member, because, he says: "I should be too hard!"

The people have instinctively likened him to a beast of
prey—"the Tiger." He tears to pieces and devours. This nickname in some sort became classic when it was cited in connection with the honorary degree of Doctor conferred upon M.
Clémenceau by the University of Oxford; the former President of the French Council was alluded to on this occasion
as "tigrem gallicum." The phrase will stamp him permanently
as a man in whose eyes the world is uniformly wicked.

The career of M. Clémenceau, which has extended over
sixty years, has been consecrated to criticism, to negation and

to destruction, down to the evening of his days. This has been
made a matter of reproach to him, perhaps unjustly. It is not
absolutely M. Clémenceau's fault if in the course of forty
years of political life no President of the Republic wished to
intrust him with power, or if no President of the Council
dared to take him into his cabinet. When he *was* permitted
to give the measure of his abilities, the experiment proved a
success. But it is an historic fact that M. Clémenceau during
the greater part of his life was a man of the Opposition and
only that.

M. Clémenceau scorned all the ministers who succeeded
each other in office. He regarded them all as incapable and
attributed the worst intentions to all of them. He did not even
spare his own ministerial colleagues. Not to speak of M.
Pichon, whom he treated always as a faithful dog—to which
one is attached but to which one does not spare the whip—
he terrorized his other associates. At the Peace Conference, he
allowed his ministers and his "experts" to speak but not
seldom he threw them over roughly without even troubling to
save their face.

At bottom, M. Clémenceau has believed, throughout his
entire career, in only one person—himself. This it is that explains the remark, naïve even in a man arrived at the very
summit of fame, which he made on the evening of his defeat
in the election of the President of the Republic in 1920: "So
much the better for my family, so much the worse for my
country!"

At the moment of the outbreak of the War, which he had
foreseen as he has foreseen everything at all sad and unpleasant in this base world, M. Clémenceau was seventy-three years
old and was living almost in retirement. Immediately, his
fighting temperament asserted itself. At first he anticipated a

catastrophe. The statesmen, like the generals, seemed to him incapable of winning victory. Before every Allied offensive, he predicted failure; before every German offensive, success. At the moment of the Salonika expedition, he declared publicly that it was an abominable act of madness which would end in disaster: he almost wished for a disaster in order to secure a change of government. At the moment of Verdun, he said: "Verdun may fall, provided Chantilly [1] falls with it!" He had his own cabinet ready to step upon the stage. At bottom, M. Clémenceau's attitude towards the army of M. Briand and General Joffre was the same as that of the Republicans of 1870 towards the army of Napoleon III.

He was constrained to accept the evidence. Verdun did not fall. But he was impatient. Things were not going quickly enough. Why could they not win victory at once?

M. Clémenceau continued to believe in the weakness of the ministers, the stupidity of the generals, the muddles and intrigues of every one. He began again to harass the government, he got himself elected president of the two most important commissions in the senate, the army commission and the commission of foreign affairs. He became a power in the state, the guardian of the secrets of national defense. Meanwhile he continued to be a journalist of the Opposition. Every morning he attacked the government in his paper and every evening in the senate.

In 1917, rumors of treason began to spread. M. Clémenceau's opportunity had come. He alone had always been sure of treason, he alone seemed to have the right temperament for its suppression.

M. Clémenceau's pessimism, it is noteworthy, has this peculiarity: it does not encourage him to remain inactive. "We

[1] The Headquarters Staff of the French Army.

must act!" he wrote once. "Action is the principle, action is the means, action is the end!" His life has been nothing but one long fight, one unceasing battle.

He made his *début* under the Second Empire by organizing some students' outbreaks in the streets of Paris. Under the Commune, in 1871, he became Mayor of Montmartre, but he was unable to prevent two generals from being murdered by insurgents. When order was reëstablished, he entered the National Assembly and soon became the leader of the most active section of the Extreme Left. It was in this capacity that he fought against all the governments which in succession held office during the next twenty years. In 1879, he turned out M. de Marcère; in 1881, the Ferry Ministry; in 1882, first that of Gambetta, then that of Freycinet; in 1885 he forced M. Ferry to resign in connection with an incident in Tong King, then M. Brisson; in December, 1886, he placed M. de Freycinet in a minority again; in 1887 he demolished M. Goblet. And so on to the end!

To the reproach that he had upset ten ministries M. Clémenceau's reply was: "You are mistaken. I have upset only one. It was always the same!"

He was not altogether wrong. France, under the Third Republic, has been ruled continually by a small number of men in a variety of combinations. But, none the less, M. Clémenceau was an element of disturbance and instability at a period when the Republic was in great need of consolidation.

Just as M. Clémenceau could see in all these successive ministries nothing but their incapacity, their feebleness, their lack of character, and their duplicity, so he has never wished to believe that politics could be an honest game. If he has been mixed in three great scandals of the Republic, Boulangism, the Panama Affair and the *Affaire Dreyfus*, now on one side, now on the other, that is because it was natural to him to assume venality and duplicity in others.

At the beginning a friend and partisan of General Boulanger, he demolished him brutally when the general seemed to want to free himself from him. Hardly out of that affair, in which he lost some feathers, M. Clémenceau found himself involved up to the neck, by his intimate relations with the Jewish financier Cornelius Herz, in the *Affaire Panama*. His political career seemed ruined in 1893 when his electors turned him out of his seat. But in France a politician is never dead until he is buried. The Dreyfus Affair, in which M. Clémenceau took, with violence and with talent, the part of right and innocence against the majority, against the people of position, and against the constituted authorities, won for him soon a triumphant return into the world of public affairs.

Old age approached. Although M. Clémenceau's temperament had been softened in no way, the fifteen years which followed were relatively calm. In 1906 he made an effort to emerge from mere negation and he succeeded in governing for a few years. His government was one of combat in the domains of politics, of social administration, and of religion, alike. After three years of contests, strikes and agitations, France wanted rest and it was M. Briand who gave it to her.

We must admit with regard to this pessimist and man of negation that on one point his system of thought has been neither negative nor pessimistic. No one has ever believed more than he in France; no one has been more constantly inspired by one single feeling—patriotism.

M. Clémenceau has remained all his life long the man he was in youth. He has maintained into advanced old age his youthful temperament. Now M. Clémenceau belongs to the generation of 1870, the generation which experienced defeat and which longed for revenge.

At the moment of the declaration of war in 1870, M. Clémenceau was in the United States, where he had gone to seek a refuge from the rigors of the Imperial régime. He returned in hot haste, just soon enough to witness the fall of Napoleon III. Unfortunately the change of régime was not enough, as the Republicans had hoped, to save France. Despite the prospect of irremediable ruin, Clémenceau was for resistance at all costs, for war to the bitter end; and it was this that made him one with the Commune. At the Assembly of Bordeaux he was of those who wished not to acquiesce in the cession of Alsace-Lorraine. Since then his whole life has been directed towards restoring his country's loss.

To political opponents who have accused him of lack of patriotism, M. Clémenceau has replied that he has ever had his eyes directed towards the Rhine. That is the truth. He has been inimical to all colonial adventures. He opposed the acquisition of Tunisia and that of Tong King; of Syria, he has remarked: "It is a land of *curés*—I don't give a curse for them!" He believed, with Bismarck, that if France acquired colonies, she would let herself be distracted from the Rhine.

He was, moreover, faithful in this respect to his English sympathies.

M. Clémenceau's foreign policy has been absolutely consistent throughout his career. It was directed, out of hate for Germany, on the side of England. M. Clémenceau, who had learned English in America, was in a position to maintain a personal relationship with British circles. At the period when the English friendship and the Russian alliance seemed for France incompatible, he never hesitated. He was the man for

England—perhaps because it was not at that time the official policy of France.

This long fidelity stood M. Clémenceau in good stead in London and he benefited by it all through the War: it facilitated for him the settlement of certain questions, such as that of the unity of command. The English never suspected M. Clémenceau of ill-will. He himself liked to say that it was in this domain that he was in a position to render most service to his country. But towards the end of the War, these bonds became relaxed, and Mr. Lloyd George, who had no great liking for M. Clémenceau, ceased to feel in personal contact with him. M. Clémenceau's authority over the English evaporated at the very moment when it would have been most necessary for France. At the Peace Conference almost no trace of it was left.

A patriotism which was accentuated by adversity and by suspicion, the conviction that every man is capable of betraying his country for his own benefit, finally an active and combative disposition—such were the mingled qualities and defects which at the end of the eighteenth century produced the great men of the French Revolution—the Dantons, the Marats, the Robespierres. M. Clémenceau is of that race. A critic who is in no way unfriendly to him has been able to remark that M. Clémenceau's way of thinking belongs to "the philosophy of the demolishers of the eighteenth century." His atheism and his hatred of aristocrats connect him closely with the Jacobins, and it was not by mere chance that his hour arrived when the French nation found itself once again in the condition of mind of his great Revolutionary forerunners.

Under the exciting effects of the War, France experienced once again a revival of what used to be called ideology. She had the conviction that she was fighting for the Right, for Justice, and for Liberty, written in large letters; the immortal principles of 1789, which had been thought of as a little out of date, came back into high esteem. Revolutionary declamations were once again indulged in against tyrants—against those of Germany and Austria, naturally. During those winters, all the *revues* produced in Paris had their Revolutionary couplets. Revolutionary phraseology resumed its sway over the masses. Besides, this sudden war for which nothing was ready, neither the men, nor the armaments, nor the munitions, nor the money, recalled the campaigns of former days. Was not the fatherland once again in danger? Was not a rising *en masse* necessary to save her? "The crowd," wrote the State *des Débats* on July 14th, 1915, "which pressed in upon the progress of the coffin of Rouget de l'Isle [1] was on the same footing as that which acclaimed the volunteers of 1792. It was in unison with the thrilling figures of the Arc de Triomphe."

There are no revolutions without suspects. That is what, with his sure instinct, M. Clémenceau alone discovered. From the very beginning, he accustomed the people, by dint of pitiless criticism of all the authorities and of all their actions, to absorbing every morning a dose of poison. He continued to be at this juncture the man he had always been, the systematic decrier. Throughout three years he criticized everything that was done in France; his attacks were directed as much against positive undertakings as against omissions, and in regard to many things it could be asked whether, as a journalist, he possessed the sense of responsibility necessary to the president of the most important commissions of the Senate. There are useful and fruitful kinds of criticism, but it is difficult to

[1] The author of the Marseillaise.

reckon up what M. Clémenceau achieved in the course of those years and what he prevented.

M. Clémenceau has the gambler's temperament. He was a partisan of the offensive with all its risks and without troubling himself as to the means available. It was a blessing for France that he came to power at the moment when, thanks to the American intervention, the offensive had become possible. At an earlier date, it would have resulted in catastrophes.

"We ought to make an immediate offensive!" M. Clémenceau declared in 1915.

"And if it fails?"

"I am still capable of blowing myself up!"

He had no other conception of defeat!

If politics consisted of a distribution of prizes it might be asked whether M. Clémenceau deserved the honor of being called upon to save a situation which he had had a part in creating. But politics consist of the effort to bring about a result and an hour came when he seemed the indispensable man. M. Poincaré required generosity and self-abnegation to call to power the man who had lavished on him insults and attacks. But M. Poincaré understood that victory was perhaps to be won only at that price and he did not hesitate.

M. Clémenceau possesses qualities rare in the French Chamber. He has temperament, will, character. In a *milieu* in which the appetite for responsibilities is exceptional, he has a passion for them. He has been a man capable of every audacity—not of mere audacities of speech. France was tired of being gov rned by weak men, tired of seeing essential solutions postpon d; she felt ill at ease, confronted with the scepticism of s.atesmen who were too intelligent to make up

GEORGES CLEMENCEAU

their minds and who could see the pro's and con's of every point of view.

It was to this *malaise* that M. Clémenceau owed his fortune. The country felt a craving for authority. It trusted to the man who had denounced the scandals to put an end to them and to the man who blamed the government for the slowness of the war to speed it up. The people who are apt to gauge the courage of a journalist by the vigor of his language were grateful to him for daring to say what many thought. He was pushed into power by the faults of his predecessors and of his adversaries.

"My formula," he declared, on taking office, "is the same in everything. Home politics? I make war. Foreign politics? I make war. I make war all the time. . . . And I shall continue until the last quarter of an hour, for it is we who shall have the last quarter of an hour!"

Until then, the war governments had maintained *l'union sacrée*. This phrase awoke no echo in M. Clémenceau, who is all conflict. He cannot govern in conjunction with everybody. He must absolutely be acting against somebody. He now proceeded to govern against the defeatists and the suspects, against all those who were not prepared to go on to the very end; he even tried to govern against the Socialists, but he soon gave up his attempt when he perceived that it endangered the production of war munitions. For if M. Clémenceau is a strong-willed and obstinate man he is not blind to the teaching of hard facts.

His first business now was to impart sanity to public opinion. The offensives of 1917 had been welcomed in France with excessive hopes and had been followed by profound disappointment. The politicians blamed the generals; the generals threw the blame on the politicians. It was then that the vague but dangerous crime of "defeatism" came into existence. It was necessary to make some victims, to reassure the crowd. There were moments when it looked as though the scaffold might once again be raised up on the Place de la Concorde. M. Clémenceau had said, a few days before he became Premier: "I have made mistakes in my life, but I want to end it well. I shall govern and if blood must be shed—very well, shed it shall be!"

He knew how to prove himself the man who is not afraid to punish and who is not to be held back by old relationships. He did not hesitate over the arresting of Malvy and Caillaux; but he knew also how to nip scandals in the bud and by means of certain sensational steps he did away with the mistrust which was beginning to spread and to threaten the nation's will to victory.

On the front, he gave the same free hand to the generals, who until then had too often been prevented by parliamentary interference from repressing breaches of discipline. "I shall support you in every case," he told them.

In a word, he pursued a policy of "public safety," as was done in the days of the Great Revolution.

M. Clémenceau was never a soldier. But as often happens with civilians he had the military spirit. He made acquaintance with the army late in life and lost his heart to it. It responded to his liking for authority, to his feeling for order, to his own personal bravery and audacity and delight in danger. He never felt so well as among the troops. When he went to the front for the first time, he returned enchanted, declaring it had been the greatest day in his whole life. As he was soon to die, he said, he was sorry he had not met his death "over there!"

During his ministry, accordingly, his visits to the front became more and more frequent. His cane under his arm, his hat at a devil-may-care angle, he went right into the trenches and talked with the *poilus* in the kind of language to which they were used. One day standing on the parapet of a trench, he shook his fist at the enemy and cried out: "Cochons! salauds! on vous aura à la fin!" (Swine! we'll get you in the end!)

The physical courage of the old man, his good humor, his dash, and the touch of the Paris gamin about him—this mingling of lovable traits, so unlike the stiff formality of the head of the state, M. Poincaré—won him an immense popularity among the soldiers of the line. Clémenceau belonged to that type of man (feminine alone in this) for whom other men are willing to be killed.

M. Clémenceau has been criticized regarding those visits to the front, on the ground that they were useless and unnecessary and often detrimental to the administration of the state. These criticisms have something in them. M. Tardieu has told us that when he wanted to discuss the affairs of his office with the Premier he was obliged to accompany him to the front. But when they got there he could not talk because M. Clémenceau, whose heart is softer than his skin, had tears constantly in his eyes.

There is another trait in M. Clémenceau which is characteristic of soldiers. He may sometimes be brutal but he is never mean. He has never hated anything in the world so much as Germany. Yet one day on leaving the Peace Conference, he was overcome with compassion for Germany's fate and said to the officer who was with him: "This German government! It is sad to have brought a great country to such a pass! For, after all, there was something big about Germany!"

M. Clémenceau needed those visits. They were not made

out of a mere desire to win popularity. They were a tonic which kept up his courage. The rear, with its difficulties, its conflicts, its disputes, disgusted him, and he was obliged to go to the front as often as he could to overcome his innate pessimism. This atheist, noting the approach of old age, was haunted by the idea of death. He often said: "Je veux mourir en beauté." (I want to die beautifully.)

He felt at ease moving about among men who were dying as he would have liked to die himself.

But if M. Clémenceau loved the army, the soldiers, the military life, and the unostentatious bravery of the people engaged in the War, this does not mean that he was weak in his dealings with the generals. He never brooked a second government by the side of the civil power and under no ministry were the generals restricted so definitely to their military tasks. Rather it was Clémenceau who sometimes trespassed upon their provinces and it was possible for some one to say just then that the question of the unity of command was a struggle between "two commanders-in-chief; one of them was called Clémenceau and the other Lloyd George!" During the Peace Conference, Marshal Foch was not immune from the hot temper of the French Premier and certain discussions that took place between them were to become famous.

Rough at home with those who opposed his authority or who did not coöperate in the War with all their might, M. Clémenceau was equally rough with the enemies of France. This remark is attributed to him regarding the Germans and the Austrians, and the rumors as to efforts for a separate peace: "Let them go smash together or alone—I don't care which, so long as they go smash!"

M. Clémenceau wished to make no distinction between the different enemies; he had no wish to understand the hidden currents that ran through the central empires or to utilize them. He set out from the matter-of-fact standpoint that the different enemies were working by different means for the benefit of their own countries and that it would be the act of a simple-minded dupe to help them.

But distrust is akin to *naïveté:* both are characterized by absence of judgment. While M. Clémenceau was combating defeatism in his own country and was alive to its danger he shut his eyes to the defeatism of the enemy and thus deprived himself of a means of hastening on the victory.

Clémenceau came out of the War wearing the halo of the victor. This was only right in a sense, for if France had been vanquished he would have borne the weight of heaviest responsibility. It was only right also because he contributed to the victory by the energy of his domestic policy, the effecting of the unity of command, the solid support he gave to General Foch, the single-minded character which he gave to French policy, the will to victory which he implanted in the people, and the discouragement which spread therefrom among the foe.

But one would be wanting in the historic sense if one did not see that M. Clémenceau benefited while in power from the work of his forerunners whom he criticized so violently. The War was won in a large measure by M. Clémenceau. But it was won also by the Salonika expedition to which he was always opposed, by the intervention of America before he came to power, and by the Wilsonian idealism for which he had no comprehension whatever.

M. Clémenceau often allowed it to be understood that as soon as the War was over he would regard his rôle in life as terminated. But the armistice followed the War, and the Peace Conference followed the armistice in a natural sequence of events. M. Clémenceau allowed himself to be convinced that he must be the first delegate of his country at the Conference and must place at the disposal of France the authority he had won in Inter-Allied Councils.

"The victory," said M. Tardieu, the Premier's right-hand man at the beginning of the Conference, "will remain with those who have the best stomachs. That will be M. Clémenceau, Mr. Lloyd George and myself. The others, from fear of difficulties, will involve us in crises."

There was some truth in this sally. Despite his great age —he was now 78—and his fatigue and the criminal attempt that was made on his life in the middle of the Conference, M. Clémenceau displayed during the long and arduous sittings patience, gayety, and an admirable energy. Seated near the mantelpiece, opposite President Wilson, his hands always in grey gloves, he intervened rarely in the discussions; he kept himself for the big questions and those which directly concerned France. His age did not allow him to devote attention to details; he took general views only, but they were clear views. A daily observer of those discussions was able to say of M. Clémenceau that he surpassed all his colleagues. He sometimes went to sleep, especially towards the evening. But no case was known in which his vigilance proved at fault regarding any great interest of France.

There are people who in order to overwhelm M. Clémenceau make him responsible for everything that was done then. Nothing could be more unjust. The peace was a work of compromise, in which may be found the mark of a number of wills. No one will was predominant.

Nor is it any more the truth that M. Clémenceau stood up against President Wilson as the out and out champion of a peace of violence. That is altogether too simplified a picture of what happened. If it be true that at the start M. Clémenceau addressed some sarcasms to President Wilson, whose character was impenetrable to him, he was none the less affected in the course of the sittings by the loyalty, the good faith and the breadth of view of the President of the United States. Towards the close of the Conference M. Clémenceau was openly reproached in Paris with having become completely Wilsonian!

In point of fact M. Clémenceau was more moderate in his claims than the majority of his collaborators. It was Marshal Foch, supported by M. Poincaré, who demanded the left bank of the Rhine; M. Clémenceau contemplated only a temporary occupation, guaranteed by the Treaty, and he had lively discussions on this point with both the Marshal and the President of the Republic. In the same way, it was not M. Clémenceau, it was M. Klotz, the Minister of Finance, who fixed the total reparations due by Germany at an absurd figure. M. Clémenceau had a scorn for jurists and experts and for his collaborators in general, whom he often treated as though they were valets. Beyond counting were the slights to which he subjected the Minister for Foreign Affairs, whose only virtue in his eyes was his fidelity in good times and in bad!

What prevented M. Clémenceau from being a negotiator of the first order and from exercising a beneficent influence on the peace was the fact that he did not believe in the future which he was constructing. This was the final manifestation of his pessimism, and the worst.

We have all heard the famous remark with which M. Clémenceau interrupted some one who was talking about the League of Nations: "Do you really believe in the League of Nations?" Nor had he any belief in a durable peace, in the ending of wars, in disarmament. In his heart, M. Clémenceau, the radical republican, has never believed in progress. The human heart seems to him bad, irremediably and hopelessly bad. He does not even believe in evolution, although he professes to do so; if he did believe in it, he would have no difficulty in admitting, what he has never admitted, that, facts having changed, political institutions ought to change with them. M. Clémenceau has not believed in Europe. He saw in the peace only an interest purely French, and it was the narrowness of this conception that prevented him from being a really worthy partner of President Wilson, whose ideas, at once realistic and generous, he could never understand. What M. Clémenceau needed, if he was to help towards a durable peace, was to believe in it—even to conceive of such a thing as possible.

A man no longer changes his outlook at the age of seventy-eight. The philosophical work which he has written in retirement, *Au soir de la pensée*, merely reproduced doctrines which were in favor when he was young. M. Clémenceau is a man of 1848 and of 1870; he has remained so always.

On the evening of November 11th, 1918, M. Clémenceau, replying to some one who had praised his intelligence, said: "No, no! I am not an intelligent man! If I were, or even if I had any ambition, do you know what I should do? I should die to-night. In this way I should be sure of a fine funeral. Whereas if I wait until even the day after to-morrow . . ."

But human nature is full of inconsistencies!

M. Clémenceau had acquired a taste for power, and after the ratification of the Treaty of Peace, he conceived the singular idea of becoming President of the Republic. Singular in this man who had passed the greater portion of his life and expended treasures of wit in discrediting the position of President.

On every occasion when he had been able to exercise any influence in a presidential election, it had been in favor of the tamest, most harmless, most colorless candidate—of a Sadi Carnot, a Loubet, a Fallières, a Pams. And now, suddenly, he had a craving for this bauble!

M. Clémenceau, who had foreseen the storm, did not feel its approach. Misled by flatterers, he did not realize that the French Chamber had fallen away from him. More docile than the American Senate, the French Chamber had ratified the peace treaty; but it was not less dissatisfied with it, and it was only waiting for the first opportunity to make this clear to the man responsible for it.

A dictator should never demand a plebiscite unless he is sure of a majority. M. Clémenceau was defeated by the man least apt to be compared with him, M. Deschanel. It is said that such ingratitude drew tears from the Tiger.

Over what did he weep? Over the power lost or over the move bungled? If it was nothing more than that he will find ample compensation for it in the esteem of posterity.

M. Clémenceau, despite his mistakes and his weakness, is one of those personalities who strike the imagination of the crowd. He will live in the spirit of the people by the side of Bayard, Joan of Arc and Du Guesclin. His death, only, awaits his immortalization in bronze.